I

The Boy Problem

The Boy Problem

Educating Boys in Urban America, 1870–1970

JULIA GRANT

Johns Hopkins University Press
Baltimore

© 2014 Johns Hopkins University Press
All rights reserved. Published 2014
Printed in the United States of America on acid-free paper

2   4   6   8   9   7   5   3   1

The Johns Hopkins University Press
2715 North Charles Street
Baltimore, Maryland 21218-4363
www.press.jhu.edu

Library of Congress Cataloging-in-Publication Data

Grant, Julia, 1953–
The boy problem : educating boys in urban America, 1870–1970 / Julia Grant.
pages cm
Includes bibliographical references and index.
ISBN-13: 978-1-4214-1259-7 (hardcover : alk. paper)
ISBN-13: 978-1-4214-1260-3 (electronic)
ISBN-10: 1-4214-1259-4 (hardcover : alk. paper)
ISBN-10: 1-4214-1260-8 (electronic)   1. Boys—Education—United States.
2. City children—Education—United States. 3. Urban schools—United States.
4. Academic achievement—United States. I. Title.
LC1397.G73 2014
371.8211—dc23   2013021122

A catalog record for this book is available from the British Library.

*Special discounts are available for bulk purchases of this book. For more information,
please contact Special Sales at 410-516-6936 or specialsales@press.jhu.edu.*

Johns Hopkins University Press uses environmentally friendly book materials,
including recycled text paper that is composed of at least 30 percent post-consumer
waste, whenever possible.

To Bill Senior and Bill Junior,
who were both once boys

CONTENTS

Introduction

For decades, scholars and pundits have been calling on the American public to act on behalf of boys. Christina Hoff-Sommers issued one of the first such clarion calls in her provocatively titled book *The War on Boys*, when she charged that boys were the *real* "second sex" and blamed feminists for redirecting attention from the problems boys faced in school to issues of equality in girls' schooling.[1] Posing the issue as a zero-sum game where girls' academic gains were made at the expense of boys, feminism was the apparent culprit for whatever educational disadvantages that boys were encountering. But, as I hope this book will show, the most significant issues that boys encounter in school are not artifacts of feminism but rather a consequence of inadequate and punitive schools, poverty, race, ethnicity, and cultures of masculinity that emerge as an antidote to oppressive social structures.[2] Rather than a contemporary "war on boys," as Hoff-Summers termed it, we are dealing with a phenomenon that was present from the genesis of compulsory education.

Recently, scholars have begun making more weighty and complex claims about the threats to the well-being of boys of color, especially African American boys—who have been classified as "at risk," "imperiled," "in trouble," and "bad," even described as an "endangered species" in many contemporary writings. Although this language is hyperbolic, it speaks to some real disparities in the academic achievements and social success of boys of color, even in contrast to their disadvantaged female counterparts. The relative weakness of boys of color in school has surfaced in an era of accountability, when education has come to be seen as "the civil rights issue of our time."[3] We are also finally coming to grips with what Michelle Alexander has termed the "new Jim Crow": the deplorable overrepresentation of young black males in prison. Studies of what has been termed the "school-to-prison pipeline" demonstrate how such contemporary disciplinary practices as suspension and expulsion are leading many young men down the path to prison.[4]

We are in the midst of what might be called a "moral panic" about the fate of boys, especially African American and Latino boys. Usually, the term *moral panic* suggests an overinflated moral indignation in response to highly drama-tized events that portray a particular group of people as a threat to the social order.[5] In this case, the cause of this indignation has not been centered on events but on alarming statistics about the fate of boys of color in our public schools and prisons. What the moral panic masks is that all youth of color, including boys, have actually been making some progress in terms of dropout rates, high school completion, and college attendance.[6] But so has everyone else; thus it is the size-able gap between boys of color and their female and white counterparts that has been most troubling. At the same time, the moral panic may draw attention away from the racial inequities that place black girls in a better position than black boys but leave them at a disadvantage compared to their white counterparts.

After decades of attention to improving the academic prospects of girls, we are finally grappling with what it means that so many boys of color are floundering in our schools and languishing in our juvenile justice system. Obviously, this is not simply a matter of gender but of race, ethnicity, poverty, and class. Reducing the problem to biological differences between male and female students obscures these significant factors and serves to reinforce peer cultures of masculinity that may ultimately disadvantage boys in school and society.

Of course, not all boys of color are endangered or imperiled, and many girls are also struggling in school and society because of racism, poverty, and sexism.[7] And white children, both girls and boys, are far from off the hook when it comes to "trouble." Nor are these troubles new. Many boys of color were at risk, endan-gered, and imperiled well before the turn of the twenty-first century. Why, then, the sudden attention to this problem, which is neither new nor unique? With few jobs available for unskilled males, zero tolerance policies in the schools, and a societal preoccupation with college degrees, the academic failures of many males of color has become impossible to ignore, calling out for both analysis and policy interventions. And the soaring numbers of boys of color whose lives have been damaged over the past twenty years by escalating prison rates is a phenomenon we cannot afford to ignore.[8] This moral panic serves its purpose, then, if it means that we become newly aware of phenomena that have been decades—or even centuries—in the making. If it can inspire us to do something constructive about the problems boys of color are facing, even better.

There is no doubt that many boys of color are challenged in a society where higher education is vaunted, decent blue-collar jobs are sparse, and the racially discriminatory dispensation of suspensions and expulsions lead to incarceration, joblessness, and other social problems. Boys of color have the lowest graduation rates of any group and disproportionally high rates of placement in special education. Their greater presence in remedial classes contrasts with their relative absence in Advanced Placement and honors classes.[9] The school suspension and expulsion rates for African American males are especially disturbing. Data from 2007 demonstrated that 54 percent of all male African American high school students had been suspended or expelled, a rate nearly double that of their white counterparts.[10] Youth of color make up approximately 35 percent of the total youth population, but 66 percent of those committed to incarceration facilities— the vast majority of them male.[11]

Urgent social problems demand immediate solutions. Politicians and activists determined to make a difference have little time to deliberate or consider the complexities of existing research. In 2006, the U.S. Department of Education modified Title IX regulations, which had previously required public schools to be coeducational, a move that enabled schools to establish same-gender schools and classes, as long as they were "substantially equal." This change, which aroused the ire of feminists and other critics, was instigated largely because of the anxiety occasioned by the "boys in crisis" discourse. Since then, at least 506 same-gender classes or schools have sprouted up across the nation.[12]

Classrooms and academies for African American males have proliferated not only in public schools but also in the many charter schools that have sprung up to remediate problems of urban education. At a 2007 conference for principals of schools for black males, attendees zealously promoted the use of teaching methodologies expressly designed for boys. The principal of the Capitol Pre-College Academy for Boys in Baton Rouge, Louisiana, had reorganized the classrooms in his school so that boys could move about the room at will, which he claimed tapped into boys' unique "tactile-kinesthetic" strengths. Another not-so-new innovation, clickers—a technology in use in many classrooms that allows students to quickly "vote" on the correct answer—was said to cater to boys' inherent "competitive spirit."[13] Some educators even call for teachers to arouse boys' "warrior spirit" to motivate them to be better scholars. Some of these programs capitalize on centuries-old assumptions about boys' inherent instinctual qualities to redeem them.[14] Educators celebrate middle-class (though possibly Afrocentric) masculinity as a tool for turning so-called deviant masculinities into more acceptable ones. Providing appropriate male role models, creating regimens and rituals that are reminiscent of the orderliness of military life, and crafting educational strategies based on what are thought to be boys' essential natures: these programs present "teaching" proper masculinity as one of the key to boys' success in academics and life.

But Pedro Noguera, the author of *The Trouble with Black Boys*, worries about the paucity of research undergirding these new programs for boys: "What constitutes best practice in these schools? We really don't know enough to go around creating a lot of those right now. It could be that just creating a great school is the answer."[15] And a great school, it could be argued, is responsive to the needs of individual children—both boys and girls—and does not require organizational principles that universalize the natures of particular groups of children.

In contrast, popular books such as Michael Gurian's *Boys and Girls Learn Differently* simplify contemporary science to appeal to educators and parents. Invoking authoritative-sounding and seemingly incontrovertible "brain science," books such as this one reinforce what we think we already know about boys.[16] But popular science often stretches the data to make claims that merely reinforce common sense. In fact, most academic research presents a nuanced account of the impact of biology on girls' and boys' learning styles, recognizing that our current understanding of the intersections between biology and culture are limited and that there are tremendous variations within groups of boys and girls.[17]

Although biological influences may put some boys at risk for school failure and delinquency, they cannot overshadow the signal importance of the social construction of gender, which shapes both how schools treat boys and how boys engage with school and other social institutions. If the most significant problem facing boys was that they were boys, white middle-class boys would share the prospects of boys who are impoverished or from groups that continue to experience discrimination and segregation. Grown-up boys, white middle-class men, are at the top of the heap when it comes to many professions and employment (despite steady, if uneven, gains by women). Gender matters, as do race, ethnicity, and class, but in much more complicated ways than we might at first imagine.[18] Serious research on the specific issues facing boys of color may offer better solutions for accommodating children's needs in our public schools, making it possible to engage in socioeconomic, psychological, and cultural interventions that make boys' failures at school—and indeed those of all children—less likely.

As I read the account of the conference for principals of schools for African American boys, I was transported back to the early twentieth century, when educators reasoned that immigrant and poor boys were more "concrete" than girls, not as interested in abstractions, and in need of educational methods that were specifically geared to their boyish natures. Then, as now, many educators based their solutions for the academic difficulties of marginalized boys on cultural ideas about boys that have existed for centuries. This tendency to universalize the qualities of girls and boys (we are less likely to do so with girls today, a legacy of the recent feminist movement) acquired particular salience during the nineteenth century, as scientists scrambled to find biological justifications for gender roles. Like the boy crisis, the "boy problem" of the early twentieth century generated sensational media, cultural anxiety, and concentrated reforms in education and juvenile justice. Reformers used the terms *boy problem* and *boy nature*, indicating a belief in a universal essence of boyhood that could be both problematic and valuable. Although nineteenth-century science was almost purely speculative when referring to "boy nature," much of today's scientific expertise on the differences between girls and boys is at best ambiguous and at worst represents "repackaged stereotypes," as the American Civil Liberties Union claims in its report for the Department of Education on single-gender education.[19]

Today's discussions about how to best help boys to succeed echo a century's worth of claims about boys, their needs, and the best way to educate them. At the turn of the twentieth century, angst-ridden educators railed against the fact that even middle-class Caucasian boys were lagging behind their female peers in primary and secondary schools, blaming female teachers and the "feminized" school for boys' academic failures.[20] They did not worry about the females who excelled academically but faced closed doors in higher education and professional employment except in such feminized occupations as nursing, teaching, and home economics. They feared instead that the nation's industrial workforce and political leaders were not being adequately prepared for their inherently masculine roles. Although schools did not become single gender or radically reorganized, organized athletics, vocational education, technical schools, and evening continuation schools for working boys were geared toward attracting and maintaining the vast influx of working-class and immigrant boys into the public school system.

It is not primarily the average middle-class boy, or even the well-behaved immigrant boy, who is the subject of this book. Rather, this is a history of the "bad boys" and "problem boys" whose fate occupied a whole new profession of boy workers at the end of the nineteenth century. These boys—almost exclusively poor, immigrant, and migrant—skipped school, behaved badly when they attended, and sometimes landed in special education classes and reformatory institutions. The problems they posed led to sustained innovations in public education and juvenile justice.

With the explosive growth of urban poverty in the nineteenth century, indigent and seemingly homeless boys spurred the first calls to action. Reformatories, orphan trains, boys' clubs, and even compulsory education arose in part to rescue boys from the streets and to channel their energies into productive and manly citizenship. When schools failed to attract or accommodate the most difficult boys, a new form of schooling arose: special education. At its outset, special education was developed as a corollary to compulsory schooling: a repository for students with behavioral problems, truants, and slower learners more than a system predicated on the identification of a medically verifiable disability (although the fluidity of certain categories continues to bedevil the system). In virtually every city I have studied—including Chicago, Detroit, Cleveland, and Philadelphia—approximately two-thirds, sometimes more, of the children in special education were boys. This figure persisted throughout the twentieth century and is almost identical to figures today.[21]

Truant, disorderly, and slower-learning boys have constituted the most schooling-averse population with which educators have had to contend.[22] Solutions to the problem of boys who either did not fit into or threatened the typical classroom have ranged from exclusion and attrition to changes in the curriculum to commitment to residential school programs and reformatories. Boys suffered severe disciplinary measures for minor violations of school order and were sometimes segregated from their peers in separate classes. Boys in general also had far greater autonomy and access to public space than their female counterparts, and some used their liberty to further cultures of delinquency and masculinity that put them at odds with both school officials and society. The advent of compulsory schooling in the mid-nineteenth century thwarted boys' freedom to explore public space and imperiled their ability to work for wages, leading to new efforts to propel the ever-visible boys of the street into schools, reformatories, recreation programs, and other institutions developed specifically for boys.

Believing that boys were obstreperous, restless, and practical by nature, educators crafted curricula for problem boys that were divested of any pretense of a classical education. They pushed for manual and vocational educational curricula in the public schools, hoping that such programs would pull boys off the street. Educators loosened graduation requirements and watered down the academic curriculum to keep boys in school longer and to improve dismal dropout rates. The most difficult youth were placed in separate all-boy classes, often with male teachers and a practical ungraded curriculum. The ideal of the common school was diminished, many historians have argued, by the differentiation of the curriculum based on race, ethnicity, class, and mental ability during the early twentieth century. It is important to recognize, however, that gender was also a component of this differentiation process.[23] And if some twentieth-century boys reaped—and continue to reap—the best advantages that American education had to offer as a result of all this sorting, others languished in suboptimal programs and classes deemed for losers and slackers.

Age as well as gender has shaped the experiences of male youth. During the nineteenth century, children as a group emerged as a powerful symbol of not only innocence but also innocence despoiled. Homeless children, immigrant children, working children, children who appeared to live their lives on the street, children who seemed old beyond their years: these children became the subjects of reform, as well-meaning men and women sought, first through charity work and later through professions in the social sciences and education, to change society by changing children. Theories of childhood espoused by the French philosopher Jean Jacques Rousseau and the pioneer psychologist G. Stanley Hall infused many reform efforts. These theoretical understandings of boys merged with more commonsensical approaches in ways that naturalized boys' opposition to school and society as a nearly normal developmental pathway. Thus in schools, classes, boys' clubs, and even reformatories, many experts sought to capitalize on their beliefs about boy nature as they sought to alter their behavior. But reformers often found their efforts stymied, as boys clung to systems of meaning and belonging that they found congruent with their own realities. Stung by the harshness of their living conditions and the hostility of school officials and law enforcement, so-called bad boys used the weapons in their arsenal—their identification with an alternative, yet meaningful, masculinity—to protect their sense of selves and to secure mastery of their environments.

Boys will be boys, so the saying goes, and the standard meanings behind that expression informed every endeavor aimed at rescuing the boys of what nineteenth-century reformers termed the "dangerous classes" from illiteracy, lawlessness, and poverty. Through sometimes inspired and sometimes awkwardly implemented programs, reformers tried their best to entice poor boys to trade in their youthful working-class masculinity for more conventional forms of middle-class masculinity. In so doing, they often devised programs that reinforced rather than replaced forms of masculinity that were situated in opposition to women, so-called effeminate boys, racially different "others," school, and society. School failure and delinquency, coded as problematic in the larger society, were normalized within the problem boys' peer society and, to some extent, by the reformers as well.

The stories of boys who moved in and out of special schools, classes, and delinquency programs first animated this book. As I sat in the Chicago History

Museum archives, I stumbled upon sad and troubling ethnographies of delinquents who had grown up in the city streets, whose young lives were checkered
with special education and institutional placements, and whose antics—whether
minor or horrifying—appeared almost understandable in the context of their
troubled lives. These stories revealed both the personal impact of reform and the
social contexts in which boys showed their discontent with the institutions that
governed their lives. Living in the congested streets of inner-city neighborhoods
in Chicago, Detroit, Philadelphia, and other Northern cities, many of the boys
whose stories are told here were first- and second-generation immigrants, nearly
all from poor or working-class backgrounds. I have limited my exploration to
the urban North, in part because these were some of the major centers of immigration, population explosion, and consequent innovations in schooling and
juvenile justice. As a resident of the Midwest, I was first captivated by the remarkable resources on this topic in the city of Chicago, a place that at the turn of the
century represented some of our most dire social problems and some of our most
exciting innovations in education and social science. Other Rust-Belt cities, such
as Detroit and Cleveland, had similar, if smaller, demographic challenges. Cities
such as New York, Philadelphia, and Boston also appear in this narrative, insofar
as they lend weight to my claim that similar challenges, ideologies, and solutions
were being explored in a range of Northern cities during this period.

Children of German, Irish, and Scandinavian ancestry ran the streets and
caused a ruckus, but many of the children who captured the attention of educators and reformers in the 1920s and 1930s had parents from Italy, Poland, Russia,
and other countries from Southeastern Europe and the Jewish Diaspora. These
bad boys, as they were frequently called, had much in common, from fragile family structures to powerful masculine peer bonds that competed with the authority of parents and the schools. When school administrators and reformers were
faced with rising numbers of African American boys on the same city streets
in the 1940s, they often commented that their problems were virtually identical
to those of poverty-stricken ethnic youth from an earlier era, failing to recognize
the glaring differences in the status of the two groups. For the purpose of this
book, I have limited my attention in this later period to African American, rather
than Latino or other, youth of color. This choice was partially a question of space
and time: although Latino youth were clearly becoming a presence on the city
streets in many urban cities, I found that I was unable within the parameters of
this book to recapture their stories in any detail. Had I written this story based
on archives in Los Angeles or San Antonio, Mexican and Asian youth would
surely have a prominent place in this book. Similarly, the experiences of African

American boys living in the South were undoubtedly different from those of the Northern youth I profile in this narrative. Even with these caveats, however, the tale I spin has relevance in a period when the racial and gender achievement gap is not limited to the urban North, and the solutions we are devising to close those gaps have national implications.

There have been many histories of how the Irish, Italians, and Jews were "whitened" during the course of the twentieth century. This book extends that narrative by showing how immigrant children who were marginalized in school and society were also whitened as the century progressed, in juxtaposition to African American children, whose prospects for success were thwarted at every turn. Ultimately, it became possible for some troublesome (white) youth to transcend a delinquent past and secure a union job, join the Civilian Conservation Corps in the 1930s, or benefit from the G.I. Bill, possibilities that usually evaded African Americans.[24] The early twentieth-century beliefs about the latent inferiority of many immigrant groups dissipated as Italians, Poles, and Jews were whitened and moved out of immigrant enclaves into more prosperous working-class sections of the city and the suburbs. Thus as many European immigrant boys were lifted out of poverty, the boy problem became primarily a problem of boys of color.

Situating the boy problem in the context of the development of compulsory and special education, I document the efforts of cities such as New York, Philadelphia, and Boston—pioneers in juvenile delinquency and education in the nineteenth century—to teach, control, and contain the boys of the street. All three cities were dealing with the problems endemic to urbanization in the nineteenth century: population expansion, immigration, rampant poverty, and escalating crime. The growth of an ideology that children needed to be protected from the stresses of adult life was accompanied by the increasing prevalence of children on the street, who were viewed as not only impoverished but also corrupted by their exposure to adult crime and immorality. Although both boys and girls of the so-called dangerous classes merited the attention of the reformers, in their rationales for the establishment of reform schools, compulsory education, and the infamous orphan trains, they invariably invoked the threat to society posed by the roving armies of uncivilized and lawless boys. As my story shifts in the late nineteenth century, the book emphasizes the Midwestern cities of Detroit, Chicago, and Cleveland, places that were experiencing the stresses of immigration, explosive population growth, and mandates to compel children to attend school. Newly minted urban professionals in education, psychology, and sociology brought the full weight of their expertise to bear on the inevitable problems that schools experienced in trying to get working and wayward children off the streets and into school. Chicago, the inaugurator of the juvenile court in 1899, was the pre-eminent leader in child welfare and the site where many theories of delinquency were invented and embodied in reform efforts. It also houses the richest narrative sources and thus provides a focal point for this study.

Boys from the ages of seven to fourteen, an understudied group in the history of childhood, are at the center of this story. Many crime prevention programs, such as the Boys Clubs, concentrated on this age group in hopes of channeling boys' energies into productive activities to forestall delinquency. Although many states raised the age of compulsory education to sixteen during the 1920s and 1930s, in actuality most truancy programs focused on younger boys, the group presumed to be most at risk for dropping out of school—and also, not inciden-tally, the group thought to be most capable of redemption. At the end of the nineteenth century, the age of entry to many reform institutions ranged from six to eight, but this number moved up to ten or twelve during the early twentieth century, because of changing views about the types of nurture most appropriate for boys at different ages. Many institutions established at the turn of the century catered to boys under the age of fourteen, when they were no longer required to go to school; by the late 1950s most of these same classes housed adolescents. In a vivid reminder of the shifting meanings of boyhood, younger boys were now coded as "innocent," in contrast to more menacing older teens portrayed in films like *Rebel without a Cause*.

The structure of the book is both topical and loosely chronological. The first chapter investigates the rise of reformatories for boys, orphan trains, and com-pulsory education in the nineteenth century. Institutions presumably developed for the generic child were in fact constructed out of pressing concerns about boys in particular. Many reforms for girls, such as the girls' reformatories, were copycats of institutions first developed for boys. Indeed, the very different as-sumptions under which they operated throw into relief how central beliefs about boys were to the operations of these institutions.

In the second chapter, I turn to newly emerging ideologies about boyhood that merged science and common sense in the nineteenth and early twentieth centu-ries. In an era of institution building for youth, boys' clubs, organized athletics, and the recreation movement all attempted to transform youthful and some-times unruly antics into organized and purposeful activities. Building on a base of beliefs about the inherent savagery of boys, these reforms aimed to allow for both the taming and expression of boys' latent impulses as a means of arresting delinquency. YMCA worker Henry Gibson coined the term *boyology* to describe the so-called science of boys that provided the theoretical basis for much of this program building.

The subjects of compulsory and special education form the basis of chapters 3 and 4. Proponents of compulsory education were not only dismayed by the intractability of low-income children, whose families needed their wages, but by groups of boys who willfully evaded school to have the freedom of action and access to public space to which they had become accustomed. Schooled in the company of other boys and their uneducated parents, their value systems often clashed violently with that of school authorities, creating the new crime and label of truancy.

By the early twentieth century, special classes for children, what we have come to know as special education, became increasingly ensconced in urban school districts. Chapter 4 examines how special classes originated in the need for special spaces and teaching methods for children who did not easily fit into the regular classroom, particularly unwieldy boys. By the early twentieth century, however, when measuring intelligence became a central practice of modern educational system, schools developed two strategies for dealing with children deemed to be slower learners. So-called ineducable children were often forced into institutions, where little if any academic instruction took place. But educators also created classes for children considered subnormal or backward in their intelligence or academic achievements. These classrooms often became dumping places for children who were mainly thorns in the side of their teachers. Boys once termed incorrigible or bad were now anointed with the language of handicap—transforming what had once been deemed moral problems into medical ones.[25] Many urban school districts also devised residential and day schools that attempted to remediate truant and disruptive boys with methods that fused punitive and rehabilitative approaches.

Both the culture of schools and boys' peer cultures of delinquency contribute to academic failures and unwillingness to attend school. In chapter 5, I explore the alternative delinquent worlds that boys devised as well as the programs that child welfare workers developed in attempts to transform boys' lives and return them to school. Based on the idea that it was essential to tap into masculinity, including boys' instinctual propensity to form gangs, programs such as the Chicago Area Project—which would have long-lasting implications for youth development work—implicitly justified these inclinations and upheld the ethnic, racial, and gender boundaries that were a key component of gang formation.

Although most of the subjects of reform in the early twentieth century were the children of European immigrants, African Americans had been migrating North during the same period, first in a trickle, later in a deluge. As a result of segregation, racism, and, at least at first, smaller absolute numbers, African American boys did not receive much explicit attention from child welfare institutions until the 1940s. In chapter 6, I consider the boy problem through the lens of African American boys who migrated north and found themselves frustrated by the lack of opportunities in the cities of their dreams. As the population of African Americans swelled during and after World War II, African American children in general received greater attention. These children were grossly overrepresented in special schools for troubled boys in large cities, as they were in the juvenile justice system, spurring outrage among community leaders as early as the 1940s.

But when civil rights in education rose to the top of the national consciousness in the 1950s, these debates focused on race as the most significant issue affecting children's life chances. Gender was also a relevant civil rights issue but one seen almost entirely from the perspective of girls. Although African American boys were still significantly more likely than their female peers to be behind in grade level and placed in special education classes and reformatories, there was little to no attention to boys' relatively poor school performance. It was mainly when boys joined gangs and became a more visible threat to urban populations that reformers stepped in to try to transform the culture of the gang—using techniques very similar to those developed by urban reformers working with European immigrant boys a generation earlier. The salience of race during this period far overshadowed that of gender in explaining the life chances of children of color.

In the epilogue, I survey the most significant transformations in both the juvenile justice and special education systems in the 1960s and 1970s. In the 1960s, African Americans began challenging the disproportionate placement of black children in classes and institutions for the "educable mentally retarded." As in the 1950s, the crisis appeared to be about blackness, not boyness. New labels such as cultural disadvantage and cultural deprivation were used to explain the academic deficits of many poor children, and compensatory education stepped in to attempt to remediate minority children's school deficiencies. In 1975, the Education for All Handicapped Children Act was passed. This act, which was later revised as the Individuals with Disabilities Education Act (1990), began the process of ensuring appropriate safeguards for children in special education programs. Mainstreaming, and later inclusion, became the guiding principle for dealing with children deemed special, whether by virtue of behavioral, social, intellectual, or physical challenges. Despite these changes, the problem of boys' overrepresentation in both special education and juvenile justice systems continues unabated. The recent demands that schools be more accountable for children's learning outcomes has brought the poor academic performance of many African American and working-class boys to the fore.

Many of the contemporary arguments about the lack of fit between boys and public schools are based on little more than centuries-old assumptions about the nature of boys. This book suggests that some of our assumptions about what is best for boys who are not doing well in school—single-sex education, male teachers, "tough love," special classes, and a more "practical" curriculum, building on pre-existing male peer groups—are rooted in a gendered past. They need to be explored rather than hastily implemented with little forethought or historical reference. Early twentieth-century attempts to solve the boy problem through vocational and basic education curricula may arguably have contributed to the very problems that current educational policies seek to correct.

Like girls, boys are not a homogenous category. The problems of our most troubled youth lie at the intersections of gender, race, and class. We should be examining the cultural processes and social constraints at work in relegating these boys to the margins of education and society, and we should make use of some of the very same tools that we have developed to help us better understand the lives of girls and women. Instead, we continue to promote programs that falter for want of a deeper probing into the premises undergirding both the problems of and the programs for boys. Failure to deal with the underlying problems of poverty, discrimination, and peer cultures of masculinity have thwarted reforms in the past and will continue to do in the future, unless we change our thinking about the boy problem.

CHAPTER 1

Schooling the "Dangerous Classes"
Reforming Boys in Nineteenth-Century America

"At ten years of age the boys are all thieves; at fourteen the girls are all prostitutes," a journalist charged in an article entitled "The Street Arabs of New York," published in 1873.[1] Beneath the sensationalist reportage, there lay a grain of truth: crime in New York, including pickpocketing and prostitution, had increased exponentially during the previous two decades. In New York, the terrifyingly fast escalation of immigration, population, and poverty, along with the family disruptions caused by the Civil War and its aftermath, contributed to what appeared to be an endless proliferation of wayward and homeless children roaming the streets. Among the ten thousand children under the age of fourteen speculated to be "adrift" on the streets of New York, according to Edward Crapsey in his *The Nether Side of New York* (1872), were countless boys "rapidly preparing for the almshouses, prisons, and gallows" and hundreds of girls "who have before them the darker hollow of prostitution."[2] These juxtapositions starkly revealed the different types of danger that unsupervised boys and girls on the street embodied for nineteenth-century New Yorkers.

Most children who roamed the street, though, were not so easily encapsulated under the rubric of thieves or prostitutes. Instead, they occupied a more ambiguous space in the nineteenth-century city as beggars, scavengers, and street peddlers who claimed the right not only to earn but also to play and to appropriate for themselves the pleasures of the city. The fate of the city hinged on the upbringing of the children of those slum-dwelling adults referred to by Charles Loring Brace as "dangerous classes." It was boys, however, who seemed the greatest threat, a ubiquitous presence on city streets, in gambling halls, and taverns. Frightened by the spectacle of what seemed to be hordes of lawless male youth roaming the city, reformer Edward Everett Hale testified to the "tremendous power in the hands of these boy ruffians of our large towns, to save or to ruin."[3] But the salvation of boy ruffians was not to lie in the hands of the boys' parents—

who were viewed as hopelessly inadequate and immoral, if they were not absent altogether—but in new institutional reforms that would afford boys the education that they were lacking at home.

Adults have always been apt to exaggerate the depravity of youth, who perennially seem to be the worst generation that history has ever witnessed. Such exaggeration notwithstanding, unsupervised and poverty-stricken children in mid-nineteenth-century American cities attained a newfound visibility. New York experienced particularly breathtaking population growth, expanding from a population of around sixty thousand in 1800 to over three million by century's end.[4] By 1870, nearly half of New Yorkers were foreign born. Combining these immigrants with migrants from the American countryside, a majority of New Yorkers were from somewhere else by the second half of the century.[5] Poor, immigrant, and migrant families crammed into unsanitary and poorly constructed dwelling spaces, contributing to slum conditions second only to those seen in London. Although New York epitomized the challenges of population expansion, other East Coast cities, particularly Philadelphia, Baltimore, and Boston, experienced similar pressures and developed reforms similar to those of New York.

Complicating matters for New York's boys, this population explosion was taking place during a moment of transition in employment and wage practices. Traditionally, working-class families had either voluntarily indentured their teen sons into apprenticeships or had been forced to indenture them by the supervisors of the poor.[6] Although the system could be exploitive for the youth, it offered supervision for the teen, reduced economic pressures on families, and provided a modicum of education and instruction, leaving a gap as it went into decline throughout the nineteenth century.[7] Although most nineteenth-century child labor was actually performed on farms rather than in cities, a phenomenon that no one seems to have found disturbing, from a child's perspective, working in a factory offered certain adult freedoms, such as engaging in leisure and recreational activities that were unavailable to agricultural laborers.[8] Children also participated in such street trades as blacking boots and selling flowers and newspapers, where they exerted considerable autonomy, free from the intrusions of adults. Still others, especially those under the ages of twelve or fourteen, were not involved in gainful employment of any sort. Seemingly homeless, aimless, and up to no good, these "vagrants," "vagabonds," "street arabs," "gutter snipes," and "street urchins" became the fodder for a steady flow of treatises exhorting the public of the dangers that would ensue unless the state took responsibility for educating the children of the poor.

The city streets were the playgrounds of the poor, and boys especially claimed public space as their own. The visible signs of tarnished childhood lent them-selves to portrayals in histrionic Victorian literature that measured the children of the poor against emerging middle-class ideals of childhood. Instead of residing in the protected space of the nursery, clothed in starched collars and white lace, street children scampered about, lived for the excitement of the theater and the gaming rooms, and purloined food and fuel when they could. Both boys and girls begged passersby to share a few pennies with them, their ragged and dirty cloth-ing causing well-off adults to avert their eyes. Pretty young girls nudged prosper-ous businessmen, entreating them to buy their flowers, while rough young pugs dashed down alleys with the wallet they had just snatched. Such children were not only morally endangered by profligate parents who drank and gambled and whose sexual partnerships were not always enshrined in law, but by the corrupt city landscape that provided temptations galore for unsupervised youth.[9]

The dangers, both real and imagined, that these boys and girls posed were deeply gendered. Girls and boys occupied distinct spaces, played different roles in the city streets, and embodied danger differently. The tarnishing of girls' sexual virtue was the worst possible fate that reformers could imagine. And although some voiced concerns about the despoiled innocence of girls involved in street trades and beggary, most public commentary was launched at the supposed sex-ual exploits of teenaged girls. These girls were presumed to be temptresses, able to ensnare a virtuous man in their trap. Reformers therefore focused on the plight of the sexually experienced teenaged girl, whose moral transgressions threatened to throw her outside the pale of respectable womanhood and doom her to a life of penury, isolation, and possibly even insanity and death.[10]

Unlike girls, boys did not need to achieve puberty to pose a threat. Boys as young as seven or eight joined older brothers and friends in multi-age bands that claimed the city streets as their territory; many learned the tricks of petty thievery at a young age.[11] Even when boys reached the age of puberty, they were only uncommonly charged with sexual crimes and were rarely imagined in terms of sexual danger. If endangered girls risked personal doom, boys posed more of a peril to society. As potential threats to property, civility, and public order, boys were more likely to be committed to penal institutions at younger ages than girls, even when they had committed no crime more serious than vagrancy. Uncivi-lized boys symbolized danger to the republic. In the wake of the disastrous draft riots of the 1860s, observers reported that its leaders and major culprits were youth (whom they termed boys) from the ages of fifteen to eighteen.[12]

Yet in spite of the grave danger posed by unsocialized boys, commentators were generally more optimistic about the potential fate of errant boys than that of girls. Narratives often portrayed street girls as pitiable, while boys embodied more danger but also more promise. A boy who committed a crime against property was redeemable, but a girl's virtue, once lost, was gone forever. Popular accounts often displayed admiration for the cunning, street smarts, liveliness, and entrepreneurship of the ubiquitous and picturesquely described newsboys and bootblacks. The natural charm, spunk, and innate goodness of the iconic Ragged Dick, the bootblack in the Horatio Alger series, for instance, ultimately enabled him to prosper and put his vagabond life behind him.[13] No such piquant touch entered into the depictions of girls of the street, who were generally portrayed as pitiable, depraved, or both.

Reforming Boys in the Institution

The nineteenth century was an era of institution building as a means of dealing with crime, poverty, and familial and personal dysfunction in the urban environment. New York, Philadelphia, and Boston, among the nation's oldest, largest, and most diverse cities, led the way. During the nineteenth century, the significance of children and their nurture rose to the fore, with an intensified focus on proper child rearing among the middle class. Many reformers sought to ensure that not just the middle class but all children were appropriately sheltered, educated, and socialized. The public school was the most universal of institutions founded during this era to address these concerns, but more specialized institutions such as almshouses, orphanages, reformatories, and mental hospitals also emerged as venues for the care, containment, and control of deviant and dependent populations.[14]

The first juvenile reformatories, which were termed houses of refuge or reformation, opened practically simultaneously in New York, Philadelphia, and Boston in the 1820s. Prior to the establishment of these facilities, child offenders were sent to prison, while vagrant or dependent children were either put out to work with another family (placed out) or put into almshouses. English common law held children over the age of seven criminally responsible, but juries were reluctant to commit the youngest offenders to adult prisons, wondering whether it was proper to throw youngsters in with hardened adult criminals.[15] At the same time, however, reformers contended that some youth were getting off scot-free when charged with minor crimes because judges did not want to send them to the miserable facilities for adults. The state had much to gain, one advocate said, "when it has convicted a boy of stealing a pound of sugar,—if that conviction result in his receiving the best discipline the State can give him, in place of the neglect of drunken parents."[16] Believing that the seeds not only of delinquency but also of poverty lay in early childhood socialization, the Society for the Prevention of Pauperism in New York City resolved in 1823 to establish the House of Refuge for "vagrant and depraved young people" to, in the words of historian Robert Pickett, "scotch pauperism at birth."[17]

With the advent of these institutions and the newly expansive delinquency statutes that accompanied their creation, children who were guilty mainly of the sin of lacking or evading adult supervision became susceptible to confinement. The houses of refuge embodied an unprecedented self-consciousness about the role of the state in socializing youth. Historian Michael Katz characterizes the reform school as the earliest example of "state-wide compulsory education," driven by the need to compensate for the inadequate and immoral parenting of the poor.[18] Fearing dependency, reformers were more willing to subsidize institutions for children than to provide funds to ensure that their families could adequately care for them. In Philadelphia, as Priscilla Clement shows, Quaker reformers with good intentions had initially sought to protect young delinquents from hardened criminals in the House of Refuge, but the new reform school, which housed children for the most minor of infractions, soon resembled a prison "where boys and girls, mainly between the ages of eight and ten, were incarcerated for about a year, given some schooling, and required to work eight hours a day under threat of punishment."[19] Presumably rehabilitated by such close supervision, the youth were indentured upon their release.

The New York House of Refuge followed a similar plan, intending to commit "boys under a certain age, who become subject to the notice of the Police, either as vagrants, or homeless, or charged with petty crimes."[20] Along with punishing children who were guilty of minor crimes, the Boston House of Reformation, founded in 1826, was charged with receiving "all children who live an idle or dissolute life, whose parents are dead, or if living, from drunkenness or other vices, neglect to provide any salutary control over said children."[21] Although the institutions were not exclusively for orphans, like orphanages, they included children whose public activities indicated a lack of proper parental care and supervision. In the 1850s, Boston and New York passed truancy laws that enabled the commitment of youth who were neither in school nor employed, further widening the net of the potential institutional population.[22] In his overview of juvenile reformatories of the nineteenth century, historian Steven Schlossman demonstrates that up to 80 percent of the nineteenth-century reform school population was guilty merely of being "wayward, incorrigible, or vagrant."[23]

In its earliest years, the New York House of Refuge seemed to serve more as a referral center for apprenticeships than as a purely punitive institution. Boys sent to the refuge may have been picked up by the police, but parents and guardians also often played a role in placement. There were many stories similar to that of F.G., an eleven-year-old boy, whose father was dead and whose remarried mother had left her son in the care of his grandmother, who sold goods in the open market. F.G. ran about in the streets and docks, "picking up old copper and lead at the Dry Dock." He would disappear from home for weeks at a time, only to be found sleeping in some hayloft or alley. He was not sent to the refuge, however, until he absconded with the money his grandmother had given him to purchase some items for her. After a brief stint at the institution, F.G. was indentured to a blacksmith where he ostensibly learned a trade and became a solid citizen.[24] Parents and guardians often utilized institutions for their own purposes when they were either unable or unwilling to properly care for and supervise their growing boys. Clearly, the coerciveness of poverty led many to these solutions, but the idea that someone other than the parent might be qualified to steer young men to adulthood was commonly held, whether in the form of wealthy families sending their boys to boarding schools or poor families seeking institutional help or apprenticeships.

Most refuge inhabitants were boys, who constituted a more palpable menace to society if left unchecked. Although all three institutions admitted girls, albeit with separate dwelling spaces, boys greatly outnumbered them, and eventually separate facilities would be built to accommodate girls. In the early refuge annual reports, where such organizations traditionally justified their endeavors, girls appear to have been an afterthought. The New York House of Refuge, for instance, articulated in its mission statement that it was primarily for boys but that girls who were "too young to have acquired fixed habits of depravity" might also have a place. Young women of notorious sexual virtue were excluded, because they might have an unwholesome influence on the other inmates. One justification for having girls under their roof, however, was that they could provide needed household labor.[25]

Girls and boys experienced different types of regulation in the reformatories. For instance, it was common to set different ages of mandatory release for the two genders.[26] In the New York refuge, both boys and girls were committed for indeterminate sentences, but although boys could be committed until the age of twenty-one, girls were to be released at eighteen.[27] This was similar to the terms of most indenture laws, which allowed girls to be released by contract at eighteen, boys at twenty. These different terms no doubt expressed the patriarchal presumption that girls must be free to marry at a younger age and that younger women were appropriate spouses for older men. Boys, in contrast, were supposed to stave off marriage until they were financially responsible and able to adopt civilized norms of behavior.

Girls' infractions, which were primarily sexual, were perceived as assaults against women's nature. Even the bad boy, however, was deemed to be acting within the bounds of boy nature and therefore was capable of redemption.[28] The wayward, incorrigible boy had indulged what was most positively boyish about him. Normal boys could be adventurous, reckless, entrepreneurial, and eager for physical challenges, qualities that had been perverted in delinquent boys by improper environment and training. These same impulses could be productively channeled into seamanship, entrepreneurship, or farming. Boys entertained prospects, at least in theory, but girls who had sinned had fewer options: domestic service or marriage.[29] According to B. K. Peirce, who compared boys and girls at the New York House of Refuge, "The proportion of girls who seemed when they left the House to take a decidedly virtuous course has not been so large as that of the boys. Vice gives a woman's nature a more terrible wrench than man's . . . Her opportunities to rise are not comparable with the boy's, who finds a hundred doors opening before him, while she finds nearly every honorable door closed." When Peirce talked about his graduates becoming ship captains and wealthy oil merchants, he was undoubtedly exaggerating their prospects, but he gave accurate voice to the very real limitations that girl graduates faced in making their way in the world.[30]

Many reformers believed that the street smarts that vagrant youth had cultivated could easily be converted into more respectable forms of learning. Nathanial Hart, early superintendent of the New York House of Refuge, believed that "the ability which would have made ingenious rogues, renders them apt scholars."[31] Even so, physical labor was clearly prioritized over schooling—in part because administrators hoped that boys' work would subsidize if not pay for their confinement, in part because work was viewed as an appropriate punishment, in part because it was believed that such labor would arrest impulsiveness and help shape manly men, and, last but hardly least, as a form of training in some occupation. The harshness of the conditions under which boys labored, however, could be extreme. In Boston, a scandal erupted when a fourteen-year-old boy charged with only truancy was buried in a bank of wet clay upon which he was digging in 1864.[32] And, in reality, many of the skills boys learned—brush making, cane making and basket weaving, for example—were not easily transferable into paying occupations.[33]

It was not until the 1850s that separate state institutions for girls would be founded, based on very different premises about the appropriate treatment and discipline of girl offenders.[34] It was a given that boys and girls would provide different kinds of labor, engage in different forms of recreation, and receive different types of schooling. Females were considered to be the "gentler sex" and their "delicate" constitutions merited milder treatment.[35] When the first girls' reform school was built in Lancaster, Massachusetts, in 1854, it was also the first such institution to adopt what was termed the "family" model of treatment. Instead of housing all of its inhabitants under one roof (the congregate type of institution), the Lancaster Industrial School for Girls gave each girl her own room and placed thirty or so of them in a cottage under the supervision of a "motherly" matron.[36] The cottage system, sometimes termed the "family reform school," was soon thereafter adopted in boys' reform schools, but it is significant that it emerged from the first girls' reformatory.

Punishment was also gendered. Although some reformatory administrators disavowed corporal punishment, the sentiment that the so-called bad boys would not behave without it was pervasive. Prohibitions against corporal punishment were stronger for girls in most venues. For instance, while the New York House of Refuge did not preclude corporal punishment, the regulations stated that "if it should ever be necessary to inflict corporal punishment upon *females* [emphasis in original], it shall only be done in the presence of the Matron."[37] At the Lancaster Industrial School for Girls, corporal punishment was technically forbidden.[38] Tim Hacsi's account of nineteenth-century orphanages includes evidence that boys were whipped more frequently than girls in many institutions.[39] Accounts of the most brutal beatings in the reform schools almost always focused on boys, and, in debates about corporal punishment in the public schools, proponents inevitably invoked the specter of the bad boy in their rationales.

As historian David Rothman eloquently states, "The descent from the rhetoric to the reality of juvenile institutions is precipitous."[40] The Boston House of Reformation, established in 1826 as a humane alternative for vagrant and minor offending children, quickly garnered a reputation for hardened inhabitants and harsh treatment.[41] Administrators had originally intended to separate the mere truants and vagrants from those who had committed robberies and assaults, but this clearly did not happen as promised.

The New York refuge started out with humane intentions. But when reformatory personnel were confronted with runaways, thieves, and violent aggressors, they often resorted to standard prison discipline. The heavily ingrained presumption that the most brutal boys could only be kept in line by brutal methods of discipline ultimately held sway. Whippings, solitary confinement, and balls and chains were run of the mill in many reform institutions. Boys learned to steel themselves against crying when physically chastised so as to not provoke the scorn of their peers. Elijah DeVoe, a disgruntled ex–assistant superintendent at the New York House of Refuge, railed against the severe punishments inflicted on boys in the institution, even while he critically reflected on his own response to a boy who defied him: "I therefore struck him several times with a rattan, and calmly repeated the order. He would not obey. I continued to apply the rattan; stopping after every two or three strokes to renew the command, until I dared to proceed no further. He would not yield. I then took him from the shop where the scene occurred, and put him in a cell, first satisfying myself that I had done him no permanent injury."[42] Broken bones or gaping wounds might attract attention, but physical punishments that fell just short of serious injury were more commonplace.

Violence spawned violence. Boys at both the New York and Philadelphia Houses of Refuge stabbed guards, and one in Philadelphia burned the refuge cane-making factory to the ground.[43] When the state of Massachusetts sought to create a more humane alternative to the House of Reformation by creating the Massachusetts State Reform School for Boys in 1848, it too rapidly lost its bearings. In 1859, a fifteen-year-old boy who had been sentenced for a minor robbery set a fire that leveled two-thirds of the building. A subsequent investigation demonstrated deplorable conditions for the inmates: boys living on bread and water, languishing in dark and musty cells, and manacled to the floor.[44] In 1866, the Wisconsin Reform School, which initially had promised to practice "affectional discipline," was burned down by a group of young arsonists, including an eight-year-old, who may have been retaliating for their terms in solitary confinement with balls and chains.[45] Prison personnel were also guilty of perpetrating acts of violence that only came to light in the case of an exposé or a lawsuit brought by a parent. Just two years after the opening of the Chicago Reform School in 1867, a guard was so enraged by a thirteen-year-old who laughed at him that he whipped him hard enough in the head to kill him.[46] Even if boys had the potential to transcend their ignominious past, they first needed to have the "devil beat out of them." Instead of providing young boys with an opportunity to become respectable, law-abiding citizens, reform schools appeared to exacerbate the violence they sought to curtail.

Disposal as the Solution to Dependency

The scandalous fire at the Massachusetts State Reform School, along with other reformatory atrocities, provided the opening for Charles Loring Brace's infamous

The Best Method of Disposing of Our Pauper and Vagrant Children, penned in 1859, which urged the "placing out" of the children of the dangerous classes with good Christian families in rural America.[47] Brace, who first sent trains of children west in 1853, decried the institutionalization of delinquent and dependent youth, which, he claimed, was doing nothing but churning out more confirmed criminals. Brace aimed to drain the city streets of vagrant, dependent, and mildly offending youth by sending them to the rural hinterlands, where they would be removed from the corrupting influences of the city and trained to respectable citizenship. Later the trains that would transport these youngsters to rural America would come to be called the "orphan trains." During the early years, most of the occupants were older boys, looking more for work than for permanent homes. Brace's so-called emigration scheme curtailed, if it did not extinguish, the growth of public institutions for dependent and delinquent children in the mid-nineteenth century.

Brace was unhappy not only with reform schools but also with orphanages, most of which cared for children with at least one living parent, termed "half-orphans," and which were burgeoning in the late nineteenth century. Between 1850 and 1870, more than a dozen orphanages and juvenile asylums were opened in New York, a trend that was duplicated in many other cities on a smaller scale.[48] Like the reformatories, orphanages were deeply gendered institutions. Although there were sometimes separate institutions for boys and girls, boys predominated in the coeducational facilities. For instance, the New York Juvenile Asylum, founded in 1851 as an alternative to the House of Refuge for dependent and semidelinquent children under the age of twelve, had a huge preponderance of boys.[49] Boys, especially younger boys, were viewed as more difficult to place with families than girls, who were perceived as more pliable and were more often sought as domestic servants. Administrators at the Boston Children's Friends' Home, established in 1833, accepted boys only until they reached the age of seven but took girls up to the age of twelve, exhibiting a belief that boys were more difficult to govern than girls and required more commodious living arrangements because of their level of physical activity. They complained that they were forced to send many young boys to the almshouse because there were few families or employers who were willing to indenture boys under the age of ten.[50] When the Boston Children's Aid Society was founded in 1865, it announced its purpose as taking from the streets "boys, from seven to twelve years of age, who are living in such exposed and neglected circumstances, as to be likely to fall into vicious habits," while saying nothing about girls.[51]

Although adoption was not common in the nineteenth century, when individuals did seek to adopt, they usually preferred younger children; it is likely that they more often sought girls than boys. When the first group of forty-five orphans was brought from the New York Children's Aid Society to Dowagiac, Michigan, in 1853, of the entire group only one small girl was *adopted*, as Brace noted in italics in his report.[52] Brace's emphasis on the one adoption suggests that legal adoption was far from the norm, yet perhaps especially desirable. The first annual report of the Washington, D.C., City Orphanage in 1865 boasted that, in addition to its indentures, "2 kind ladies have each adopted a little girl as her own child."[53] Reformers with the Massachusetts Society for the Prevention of Cruelty to Children observed in 1889, when adoption was becoming more palatable, "Parties are sometimes ready to adopt children, especially if attractive. Boys under ten are not often called for."[54] Boys over the age of ten were more often sought for their labor than their emotional value as children. It may have also been that older boys who had proven their character and work habits might be a more suitable choice for an heir to a family with no biological son. By the turn of the twentieth century, in contrast, adoption had become a more desirable option, and agencies were complaining that they could not meet the demand for infants and toddlers, particularly girls.[55]

Although Brace's emigration scheme of placing out presumably homeless children to families in rural areas in the Northeast and the Midwest was not unprecedented, he popularized the concept. In terms of sheer numbers of children transported, the Children's Aid Society that he founded in 1853 was unparalleled. By 1929, the society had sent approximately 250,000 children to new families in the West.[56] Brace was a notorious and incredibly effective reformer whose distress over the fate of street children, especially boys, galvanized reformers and sparked changes in child welfare practices throughout the country. In his sensational account, first published as a journalistic series and then a book, *The Dangerous Classes and Twenty Years' Work among Them* (1880), Brace articulated the anxieties of well-bred New Yorkers about the chaos wrought by poverty and immigration. He traced New York's crime, corruption, and political unrest to the inadequate nurture of the boys of the dangerous classes:

> All the neglect and bad education and evil example of a poor class tend to form others, who, as they mature, swell the ranks of ruffians and criminals. So, at length, a great multitude of ignorant, untrained, passionate, irreligious boys and young men are formed, who become the "dangerous class" of our city. They form the "Nineteenth-Street Gangs," the young burglars and murderers, the garrotters and rioters, the thieves and flash-men, the "repeaters," and ruffians."[57]

The scandalous political corruption in New York, along with a succession of riots starting with the Astor Place riots in 1859, the terrible Draft Riots of 1863, and the Orange Riots of 1870 and 1871, appeared to be stark evidence that something had gone dreadfully wrong in the rearing of male citizens. Reflecting on the Draft Riots, Brace exclaimed, "The rioter of 1863 is merely the street-boy of 1853 grown up!"[58]

Although the Children's Aid Society assisted girls as well as boys, Brace was far more captivated by the problems of boys, both because of their potential perils and their promise.[59] A boy gone wrong could derail democratic institutions, whereas the girl who came to a "sad end" mainly harmed herself.[60] Yet Brace found the typical street boy to be a rather charming and insouciant character whose life had its pleasures as well as its difficulties. Enchanted by evolutionary theories, Brace at times identified with the "savagery" that he projected onto the boys he was saving. He acknowledged that even he found "scarcely a greater pleasure of the senses than to gratify 'the savage in one's blood,'" as the boys of the street regularly did. Noting that many boys had drifted from their original placements, Brace contemplated, "Probably as a sensation, not one that the street-lad will have in after-life will equal the delicious feeling of carelessness and independence with which he lies on his back in the spring sunlight on a pile of dock lumber, and watches the moving life on the river, and munches his crust of bread."[61] But Brace proposed that boys exchange the grand adventure of the streets for the grand adventure of traveling west on the railroad to make a new future for themselves.

Brace's first charitable venture was to establish lodging homes for newsboys—facilities that would eventually become recruiting grounds for the orphan trains. For a small sum, newsboys received a warm bed and nourishing meals, in addition to sermons and lectures on morality and deportment, which at times elicited more catcalls than prayerfulness. The population housed at the newsboys' lodging homes rose exponentially in the years from 1854 to 1858, ultimately sheltering more than three thousand boys in two different homes throughout the year. Brace was both appalled and enchanted by the inhabitants of his homes. Although often dirty, profane, and capable of all manner of petty crimes, the lodgers' minds could be "exceedingly sharp and keen," "their wits sharpened like those of a savage." He was moved by the newsboys' light-heartedness, describing them as a "happy race of little heathens and barbarians" who could be "generous to a fault" with each other. Horatio Alger was so inspired by the newsboys that he even moved into the lodging home for a time to gain inspiration for his novels. But, however charmed Brace might be by some of their antics, he noted that such a "mass of wild young humanity" threatened mainstream society.[62] However pleasurable, such freedom from discipline and restraint would ultimately lead to the political and economic problems that seemed about to overtake the city of New York.

Ideally, Brace wanted to see the boys placed with upstanding citizens, parental substitutes who could teach the boys Christian manners and morals while benefiting from their labor. An avid critic of institutions, Brace firmly believed that children needed the guiding hand of individuals truly interested in their welfare. Moreover, the experience of the newsboys' lodging homes had taught him that the urban environment was not conducive to the development of healthy manhood. Indeed, the idea that the cityscape was the worst possible venue for reforming either delinquent or predelinquent boys became a recurrent theme in the child-saving movement. Placement in individual homes removed boys from the deleterious impact of the peer society of boys, which condoned if not celebrated challenges to lawful society.

The orphan trains, inaugurated in 1853, appealed to multiple constituencies: New Yorkers, frightened about the spectacle of street children; rural farmers in need of labor; and older boys, girls, and even some men and women in search of opportunities away from the streets of New York. Historian Clay Gish has determined through quantitative analysis that the great majority of children placed on Brace's trains were older boys from ages fourteen to seventeen looking for work. Gish argues that the boys saw the trains as an employment opportunity as much as anything else, an assumption they demonstrated by frequently leaving their initial placements to find better work elsewhere.[63] According to Peter Holloran, the Boston Children's Aid Society sent three times as many boys as girls on the orphan trains. He hypothesizes that boys might have been perceived as being more useful, while older girls were seen as "sexually dangerous."[64] Brace's earliest appeals made clear that finding work was the primary function of placing out. In his circular addressing farmers, mechanics, and manufacturers in rural New York, he appealed to readers to help him find work for children: "These boys are, many of them, handy and active, and would learn soon any common trade or labor. They could be employed on farms, in trades, in manufacturing; and many an intelligent lad might be saved to society from a life of theft or vagrancy."[65]

Girls, by contrast, were eligible only for housework and did not receive as much attention in the fliers advertising orphans. A similar advertisement sent to Ohio farmers and mechanics did not mention girls at all but instead focused on the labor potential of the boys: "there are now scores of poor boys constantly in our office, able-bodied and willing to work."[66] Historians of the orphan trains have also suggested that the continuing need for domestic labor in New York may have curtailed girls' desire to leave their familiar surroundings to find jobs similar to what they already had. Brace may also have been uncomfortable with grow-ing girls' sexuality, Marilyn Holt speculates, believing that they may have needed protection.[67]

The orphan trains, it is argued most persuasively by Linda Gordon, not only had the potential to move children up the class ladder but could also transform the racial status of such dubiously white ethnicities as the Irish, who suffered from serious stigma in the city.[68] However degraded these children might appear initially, Brace claimed that the children he placed had all of the latent capacities of children from more prosperous homes, thus contributing to the incipient be-lief in adoption as a mode of moving up the class ladder. Brace quoted the speech of one newsboy to his peers, who repeated his claim that only in rural America could boys transcend their origins: "Do you want to be newsboys always, and shoe-blacks, and timber-merchants in a small way by sellin' matches? If you do you'll stay in New York, but if you don't you'll go out West, and begin to be farm-ers, for the beginning of a farmer, my boys, is the making of a Congressman and President . . . I want to be somebody, and somebody don't live here, no how."[69] The children of New York's dangerous classes needed to go somewhere else in order to be "somebody."

And in fact, Brace's ideology was not completely misleading. Some of the or-phan train boys did make good, and two even became governors: John Brady of Alaska and Andrew Burke of North Dakota. Of course, the two, both of whom were placed in 1859, had very different stories, which suggests the range of boys' experiences. At age nine, Burke had been placed with an Indiana family. At twelve, he left to be a drummer in the Civil War and wandered from job to job before settling in North Dakota. Brady, however, had been placed with an upper-class family in Indiana, which offered him everything a scion of the privileged classes might receive, including an education at Yale's Union Theological Semi-nary.[70] Despite the different trajectories of such successes, these stories helped to perpetuate the idea that boys might best escape the perils and pitfalls of their origins by going west.[71]

Compare Brady and Burke's stories with that of Kansas Charley, a notorious juvenile delinquent poignantly brought to life in an account by historian Joan Ja-cobs Brumberg. Charley was a child of desperate poverty whose parents had died and who spent some miserable years in the New York Orphan Asylum before he was shipped out on an orphan train at the age of twelve to be placed with the first of several families. The placements did not take for various reasons; some fam-ilies were abusive, others were kind. After these failed placements, Charley was caught stealing and ended up in reform school. After reform school, he became a vagabond, hopping trains throughout the West and Midwest, where at the age of sixteen he murdered two boys he had befriended who refused to share food with him as he starved. The fate of the "boy murderer" briefly became a cause célèbre among progressive child savers who believed that Charley's rough beginnings and eventual starvation had led him to his dastardly deed. Despite the outcries of progressive reformers, Charley was eventually executed. Charley's case was by no means representative of a typical orphan train rider, but it does demonstrate the many things that could go wrong when boys, especially the less resilient, were left on their own to find their path.[72]

The potential for abuse among orphan train riders was real, as there were very few procedures in place to ensure that the children on the orphan trains received proper care in their new homes. In reality, many older boys moved from placement to placement before setting out on their own. A lack of clarity about the roles of guardians and children in their new lodgings was inherent to the process. Brace asked that caretakers treat the child as "a member of the family," and families were required to provide some schooling, but this relationship was complicated by the labor exchange that was also a part of the bargain, especially for older children. Newspaper circulars announced the "distribution" of orphans at railroad depots, and some children later complained of being poked and prodded for their anatomical fitness before being chosen or rejected.

Whereas the early orphan trains comprised primarily older boys looking for work, by the turn of the century they increasingly carried greater numbers of younger children and a more equitable balance of girls to boys. Families were encouraged to raise younger children "as their own," although they were expected to furnish wages to older children. Something akin to adoption became the purpose of families seeking one of those darling children who had arrived at the local railway stations.[73] Parents were seeking children for their emotional value rather than for their labor.[74] By this time, however, reformers were growing wary of the processes by which these new families were being forged. By 1929, the orphan trains were history. Reformers had to find new solutions to the problems of child poverty and dependency.

The orphan trains were only one example of the new institutions for dependent children that proliferated in the second half of the nineteenth century. In addition to orphan or half-orphan asylums, industrial, trade, and farm schools were formed, some of which degenerated into prototypical reform schools, others of which had more success educating and training poor youth for a respectable existence. A variety of institutions, all of which were directed at poor or delinquent children, opened under the rubric of the term *industrial school*. Industrial schools were primarily meant for homeless and even errant boys, but they were not meant to house dangerous delinquents. Their purpose was to provide shelter and training for unsupervised youth so that they might graduate into respectable adulthood.[75]

For instance, the Cleveland Industrial School was founded in 1857 by the Children's Aid Society. At first it served both as a day school for those children "unsuited to the public schools," but it also operated as a placement agency for homeless youth. In a column entitled "Lost Boys at the Industrial School" (1863), the *Cleveland Daily Herald* posted advertisements for young boys who had been found wandering the streets in search of housing and employment. Ten-year-old Frank Band, whose face had been deformed by the kick of a colt, was the son of a widow who took in washing. He told the school personnel that his mother wanted him to go live with a family and work. Henry Road, age seven, hailed from Cincinnati and claimed that his mother had given him five dollars to ride the rails; he had no desire to return home.[76] Perhaps some parents sent their boys off in the direction of the industrial school, knowing that a place might be found for them if they showed up at the door. When the boys' families were found to be in absentia or unwilling or unable to care for their children, school personnel sought placements with families in the surrounding areas.

Although initially the school mainly took in youth briefly and then apprenticed them, as the numbers of applicants rose, administrators decided to operate a residential facility for dependent and delinquent youth. As was the case with many such ventures, approximately half of the boys' time was spent in school with the other half working. Initially, the school was reluctant to take boys older than fourteen, and at least half of the institution was composed of boys under the age of ten. As the century wore on, however, and more stringent child labor and compulsory education laws changed the definition of childhood, the age of the Cleveland School's occupants crept up. Later the school became reluctant to take boys younger than twelve, who were deemed to be in need of more individual care than could be offered in an institution. However, many industrial schools continued to take boys younger than fourteen throughout the early twentieth century.[77]

One widely publicized but short-lived response to the problem of incorrigible and vagrant boys was the ship school movement, which originated in Massachusetts and New York. Both states had passed stringent truancy laws in the 1850s, but each was running out of spaces in the reformatories as the problem of vagrancy increased. Not only were police rounding up incorrigible boys but parents were also begging the state to take their unmanageable sons off their hands.

Massachusetts responded to the need for additional institutions in 1860 with the establishment of the Nautical Reform School for minor offenders; New York followed with a similar measure in 1869.[78] In an article about New York's school ship *Mercury*, entitled "The 'Gamins' at Sea" (1871), the author explained:

> Many of the unmanageable boys of this city, such as have been found guilty of petty crimes, or are complained of by their parents as incorrigible, are sent to the school-ship *Mercury*, at Hart's Island, there to be trained for practical seamanship, as well as kept under wholesome control, and prepared for obtaining a livelihood in an honest and useful occupation.[79]

Believing that many boys' wrongdoings had been caused by an excess of adventurous spirits, the ship school seemed just the place to transform wild, unruly boys through indulging their appetites for excitement by travel on the high seas.[80] Their travels would be accompanied by harsh discipline and serious instruction in seamanship. It was said that one or two cruises on a ship school, with ports of call in Sierra Leone and the West Indies, was enough "to quell the most turbulent spirit."[81] San Francisco and other coastal cities such as Charleston also found the ship school idea appealing. Decrying the "recent irruption of ruffianism among the embryo criminals of the city" that had fueled the movement for a nautical reform school in San Francisco, one journalist nonetheless warned citizens about the dismal news he had been hearing about the existing school ships.[82] Accounts of homosexual liaisons; poor sanitation, health, and nutrition; severe physical punishments; and numerous escape efforts, both successful and unsuccessful, ultimately served to hasten the demise of the ship schools.

Perhaps as importantly, jobs as sailors were in decline, defeating the goal of training boys for gainful employment. Sometimes it seemed as if the solutions designed to stop delinquency caused more problems than they fixed, creating youngsters who became more, rather than less, criminalized as a result of rehabilitation. Within several years the ship schools represented another failed experiment for boys. Dismay about these failed experiments no doubt strengthened the cause of those who sought to prevent waywardness through a state-sanctioned system of education mandated for all children.

Compulsory Education

In 1877, a conference of prison reformers in Newport, Rhode Island, passed a series of resolutions about how to prevent crime, the first of which was "how to secure a suitable education to all the children of the state." The reformers lauded the goal of compulsory education, arguing that society needed to provide a "gradation of institutions . . . from the cradle to the grave," beginning with the common school, to stamp out delinquency.[83] By the 1870s, many would agree that securing a proper education for all children, including the neglected "street urchins," was a major crime-control measure. Citing study after study showing that much higher percentages of prison inmates and paupers than their lawful counterparts were illiterate, compulsory education advocates remained convinced that only the public school could reduce crime.[84]

Common schools had come into existence in the early nineteenth century, and by midcentury most urban areas had thriving public schools (even if many children still failed to attend). Charity schools predated the expansion of more encompassing public education in some Northern cities, such as Philadelphia and New York, both of which provided a free education to the poor in the early 1800s.[85] Middle-class children were often taught at home or in private schools, but many school districts worried, as did Baltimore educators, about the children of the poor. Growing up in ignorance, mingling with the "dangerous" elements, these children occupied a "sort of middle ground; neither elevated to the Public School or to the level of the House of Refuge." This class, they argued, is the one "to which the work of education should be immediately addressed."[86]

The main challenge launched against compulsory education was that the government would undermine parental authority. The prevention of crime and pauperism, however, was a persuasive counterargument, especially in areas plagued by rising numbers of immigrants and increasing poverty. Advocates for compulsory education sometimes invoked the threat that unschooled male citizens posed to the republic. In Wisconsin, a compulsory education bill was advanced in 1867 to "provide against ignorance and crime, and to secure the benefits of general education to the people of Wisconsin." The director of the state reform school testified on behalf of the bill, complaining of the children who "grow up to manhood in ignorance and under the blind guidance of vicious passions and depraved appetites." If this group of children were not afforded the advantages of a liberal education, the writer continued, citizens could expect "riot and arson . . . the upheaving of an infuriated and degenerate populace."[87] A proponent in New York similarly argued that compulsory education could be a powerful antidote to the dangers unleashed by immigration, expressing a hope that the power of knowledge may hold some sway "over the ignorant swarms of the lowest forms of European life that are flooding our country."[88] This theme was further developed in George Leib Harrison's reflections on state charitable institutions, where he also spoke of the urgent need for education, especially for the boys of the street:

> This large army of neglected children, growing up in idleness, ignorance, vice, and crime, who are not only destined to increase our taxes, to endanger our property, and disturb our peace, to infest our highways with mendicancy, pillage, and violence, to crowd the docks of our court-rooms and fill our almshouses, jails, and penitentiaries, but who are soon to exercise with us and over us the sovereignty of the elective franchise, marching up to the polls with added thousands of new recruits every year—*these* are the cancerous source of what is probably the greatest peril to which our Commonwealth and free institutions are exposed.[89]

Arguments for women's education had been couched in terms of the need to nurture good mothers who would rear respectable citizens, whereas males would not only need to be good breadwinners for their families but would also directly shape the nature of the republic. Harrison's comments held an undercurrent of regret at the expansion of the franchise, but, like it or not, universal white male suffrage was here to stay. Given that the parents of these boys were not to be trusted, the best that could be done was to attempt to mold the character of the budding boy citizen in the public school classroom.

It was this failure of nurture on the part of parents, in fact, that further necessitated state action. The president of the Philadelphia Board of Education made clear in 1876 that one of the key purposes of the public school was to instill virtuous citizenship:

> It is patent to every observer that where there is an aggregation of the ignorant and criminal classes, the laws regulating suffrage are frequently violated. The most effective remedy for this pernicious evil is the school. It is the nursery of the good citizen; regulates his will and action by certain fixed principles, informs and disciplines his mind, and excites and fortifies his self-respect.

And he further exhorted his readers, "Can we afford to permit an army of youth to grow up prey to vice and the lowest barbarism, because parental prejudice, lack of authority, negligence or greed, are interposed between the children and the school?"[90]

Yet it had also been the case that the poor were either shunned or, in some cases, even denied entrance to the public school. Some school districts established minimum standards of clothing; children without proper attire were fearful of attending and in some cases excluded.[91] In 1838, the Boston school system attempted to resolve this dilemma by organizing "intermediate" schools—which David Tyack characterizes as a form of "de facto segregation"—for children who were overage, immigrant, or the victims of "misfortune or neglect," hoping to alleviate the stresses on common school teachers and to encourage parents to bring children to school who might be embarrassed by their intellectual deficits or shabby clothing.[92]

As school districts increasingly adopted age grading in the mid-nineteenth century, the problem of children who did not fit into the regular classroom was magnified.[93] This reform, which appealed to middle-class parents with its promise to move children through a carefully sequenced curriculum, simultaneously made it difficult for schools to accommodate children who did not fit easily into standard grades: children who lagged academically, disrupted the classroom, or attended only sporadically. High rates of attrition and nonattendance on the part of difficult and backward children were tolerated, because some city schools could not house all of the children eligible to attend. The expulsion of troublemakers and children with intellectual deficits was also a practical measure that kept school populations more manageable.[94]

In reality, teachers had much to endure in managing extremely large classrooms, which—even if graded—often harbored children of various ages, abilities, and degrees of English proficiency. Physical chastisements involving rods, rulers, and whips were not uncommon both in rural and urban areas and most frequently involved male teachers and male students. In one-room schoolhouses, Jonathan Zimmerman shows, violence was a common occurrence, a finding that is not surprising given the vast range of ages attending the one-room schools and the tenuous qualifications of teachers who may have been the same age as some of their own pupils. Troublesome boys had plenty of pranks up their sleeves: plugging the chimney, throwing buckshot on the blackboard, and doing everything they could to disrupt the classroom environment. Some teachers sent boys out to pick their own switches so that they could receive their beating.[95] But when teachers were more violent than either the boys or their parents thought just, boys sometimes retaliated. Among the more extreme cases were those that involved actual deaths, as in the case of Robert Bailey, an Illinois teacher who was killed when the seventeen-year-old pupil he was punching pulled a knife on him.[96] In another farming community in Connecticut, where, according to the paper, "the big boys were disposed to make trouble for their young teacher," the teacher had whipped several of them, including one who was nearly his own age. The "malcontents," as the newspaper article called the boys, attempted to exact revenge by donning masks and assailing their teacher on the street after school.

The teacher, having seen the boys from a distance, grabbed a club and killed one of the young men by striking him on the head.[97] In short, the nineteenth-century ungraded schoolroom could be a violent and unruly space, despite the nostalgia so frequently ascribed to it. Incidents such as these also suggest that antagonism to school was not purely an urban phenomenon.[98]

It is possible that corporal punishment was less commonly used in large urban school districts, where schools were more closely monitored and classes were more apt to be age graded. Still, many nineteenth-century school districts continued to defend the practice. Some female instructors (perhaps loathe to employ such punishments) were lauded for their ability to maintain order through gentler means of discipline, but when things went awry many sent boys to the principal's office, where the presumably male administrator was usually more comfortable with dispensing physical punishments. The superintendent of the Detroit school district admitted in 1876 that corporal punishment was commonplace but suggested that they might dispose of it in the regular classroom if they could put the truants and incorrigibles in separate classes. In annual reports, complaints abounded of rough older boys who intimidated teachers, such as the sixteen-year-old who chewed tobacco and spit on the floor of the classroom. When the female teacher complained of his behavior, the principals insisted that she physically punish him. When she approached with the rod "he 'squared off' at her, after the manner of a prize ring," at which point the principal himself charged at the boy and a chase ensued.[99] Administrators used these types of stories both to defend their use of corporal punishment and to underscore the necessity of creating special classes for troublemakers.

Debates in the New York and Boston public school systems about the use of corporal punishment make clear the gender and class assumptions that were embedded in this practice. In 1864, the New York Board of Education, which had maintained separate classes for boys and girls, tried to phase out corporal punishment, especially because a number of parents had protested the beating of their children in school. An investigation revealed that, in 1864 alone, there were a hundred thousand cases of corporal punishment in male grammar and primary schools. After a bylaw was passed seeking to curtail the practice, the numbers initially diminished, although out of 3,438 documented cases, only 26 were female. The most persistent advocates of the practice were male grammar school personnel, who argued that such punishment enabled teachers to maintain discipline and thus helped them to teach more effectively. In fact, they argued that boys who were not so disciplined could become juvenile delinquents, be expelled from school, and be sent to the reformatory. It was in the best interests of the boys, they argued, for them to be physically disciplined so that they might remain at school and receive a proper education.[100]

The Boston debate over corporal punishment in the schools in the early 1880s displayed more clearly the class- and gender-based assumptions behind the practice. In 1880, the school district resolved that corporal punishment should be used exclusively for *boys* in grammar school but not in the upper grades. No one questioned the right to physically chastise younger boys, but an extensive minority report was filed, justifying the practice for older boys. The authors insisted that the gentle means of discipline that might work with middle-class children would be inadequate for those who live in "miserable abodes": "moral suasion, repeated advice and pleasant talk does not work with such boys." Teachers could more easily manage larger classes if allowed to use corporal punishment, they argued. They contended that if they were forced to abandon physical punishment, the school might need to expel boys who could not be disciplined by verbal chastisements, which would "practically nullify the State Law relating to children growing up in ignorance and crime." Failure to physically restrain certain types of boys would promote lawlessness and licentiousness.[101] Only brute force could subdue the wild passions that animated the bad boys who inhabited the slums of the city.

Not only did teachers and administrators worry about bad boys, but, with the advent of compulsory education laws in the 1870s, middle-class parents, who began to use the schools in greater numbers, became concerned about their children sharing classrooms with the unwashed masses. An 1878 *St Louis Globe-Democrat* editorial against compulsory education laws argued that the question was not entirely "how to drive in the street Arabs, but how to make those that are in comparatively harmless to those with whom they associate . . . whereby the vices bred in the slums may not be caught by the children bred of a decenter parentage."[102] Thus was born a strong argument for separate ungraded, industrial, and evening schools for children of the poor.[103]

There had already been spirited debates about the dangers coeducation posed to girls by forcing them to endure the antics of ruffians. For instance, the superintendent of schools in San Francisco worried that it would be dangerous to mix "delicate and refined daughters" with "rude and depraved boys" in the same class. It was in urban school districts, where the poorer and respectable classes mingled, that the fear was most pronounced. The principal of the Girls High and Latin Schools in Boston contended that in more "homogenous" communities, the dangers that "coarse natures" posed to girls at school might not be so profound.[104] Ultimately, coeducation won the day, mainly because of finances and beliefs about the benefits of educating boys and girls together, but educators were determined to find other ways to protect children from the worst of the trouble-makers.[105]

By the late nineteenth century, school administrators had organized un-graded, disciplinary, or truant classes, many of which were exclusively for boys, to accommodate the unruly masses in the public schools. Simultaneously with the passage of compulsory education legislation in 1876, Cleveland established ungraded classes for boys "whose habits and inclinations were detrimental to others."[106] Michigan's Compulsory School Act of 1883 authorized school districts to "do something towards correcting the evils of truancy and youthful incorri-gibility," which included efforts to curb truancy and separate classes for trouble-makers. In 1883, Detroit began its first "truant school" as mandated by the leg-islation, defining its purpose for the "reckless and vicious boys who infested the streets."[107] In 1890, a delegation of Chicago citizens petitioned the school district to erect classes for the "neglected" children who had "become so lawless and undisciplined" that they created "great disorder in the schools in which they are currently enrolled." Viewing the special classes as transitional, the superinten-dent of compulsory education argued that such children could be placed in the ungraded class "until the danger of disturbing the discipline of the school might be removed."[108] The lack of a gender signifier in the term *ungraded* is mislead-ing, however, because in Chicago and many other cities the classes were almost entirely composed of boys.

In ungraded classes, the usual academic expectations and requirements were waived in favor of education in the rudiments of literacy and manual education. Some classes were merely holding tanks, but the Boston administrators claimed that, once they brought "ungovernable" boys into manual training classes, they would transform the "dunces" and "wild boys of the street" into courteous and proficient craftsmen.[109] Assuming that mastery of a more bookish curriculum was beyond them, these boys still needed to prove themselves capable if they were to develop a healthy sense of masculinity. Reformers were convinced that such schooling—focused on training the hands and heart, as well as teaching the ABCs—was an essential crime prevention measure.

But even ungraded classes could not hold boys who skillfully eluded truant officers, whose escapades kept them on a constant collision course with the po-lice and teachers, and whose parents were deemed incapable of keeping them on the straight and narrow. By the end of the century, public expectations held that boys under the age of fourteen should be in school rather than on the streets or at work. Yet the task of actually corralling the boys of the streets into schools and institutions seemed nearly insurmountable. Truant officers spent their days combing the streets, even while realizing that the schools did not have room for all of the unruly youth who evaded school. Nor did schools have the resources to bring children who rarely attended school up to grade level with their age counterparts. Parents were often uncooperative, secretly or not so secretly viewing the school as a suspect institution, a usurper of parental authority, or an expensive waste of time for boys who could be out earning money.

Whether or not their parents approved of schooling, it was clear that there were powerful communities of boys in city neighborhoods who wholeheartedly resisted the mandate to attend school. They rebelled at being stuck in public school classrooms where they were expected to observe polite manners, be deferential to their teachers, and labor for hours on end over boring school subjects. Together they dodged truant officers and police; when they did show up at school, they frequently taunted teachers and principals, who had strong incentives for either expelling them or consigning them to institutions. Although the transformation of boys was seen as central to the project of social renewal, boys as often eluded as benefited from reform. With a growing recognition that boys of the dangerous classes would not be easily corralled into schools, reformers created new spaces that would provide greater opportunities for boys to be redeemed through the expression of their boyish natures.

CHAPTER 2

The Nature of Boy Nature

Education and Recreation for Masculinity

"Being a boy," popular writer Charles Dudley Warner concluded in his book of the same title, first published in 1877, was something to aspire to. Some were fortunate enough to live in the country, where they could express their "animal spirits," enjoying halcyon days of fishing and tramping about the woods or engaging in such manly activities as pushing a plough. Warner did not bother himself about boys for whom pushing the plough allowed for few opportunities to linger along tranquil waterways, such as African American sharecroppers and overworked hired farm hands. But city life was simply not the ideal venue for the expression of essential boyishness. Under idyllic rural circumstances boys could experience the wonders of boy nature: "one of the best things in the world is to be a boy; it requires no experience though it needs some practice to be a good one."[1] Although all boys possessed boy nature, only some were fortunate enough to have the experiences that would allow them to embody true boyish masculinity.

Inspired by their own nostalgic reminiscences of boyhood, anguished about the forces of civilization that seemed to be eroding typical boyish pursuits, or appalled and captivated by the adventurous lives of the boys of the street, late nineteenth- and early twentieth-century writers revealed an almost religious reverence for boy nature. Amid growing urbanization, immigration, poverty, and labor unrest in the nation's cities, reformers sentimentally sought to resurrect a vision of boyhood that was distinctly rural and unfettered by the demands of city life. These theories of boys and their nature were distinctly unbiblical, casting doubt on, if not completely eradicating, the Calvinist belief in original sin and the need to "beat the devil" out of unruly boys. Whether reformers were seeking to bring boys to God, to better develop their masculine characters, or to save them from the almshouse and the penitentiary, they increasingly sought to derive their methodologies from their perceptions of the inherently adventurous and unruly nature of boys.

Jean Jacque Rousseau's *Émile,* a tale about the development of a young boy who exemplified the author's ideas about the proper nurture of children, resonated with nineteenth-century writers and reformers, who appreciated the effort to salvage boys' native natures from the dustbin of Christian children's literature that valorized moral earnestness and propriety. Rousseau's Emile was simultaneously granted liberty to express his childish urges and hardened to the environment, so that he could grow up to be a free man. Rousseau acknowledged that boys and girls were essentially the same prior to puberty but argued that their educations must differ because of their divergent future lives.[2] Rousseau pitied the overly civilized boy who was forced to comply with the demands of society before maturation had taken hold. His future spouse Sophie was to be trained to mask her real desires to make her more appealing to men. Rousseau's ideas about the importance of honoring childhood as a stage of life where children should be sheltered from the demands of civilization would be applied to many reforms for children, both boys and girls.[3]

Insofar as girl nature was romantic, girls were posed as selfless icons whose virginity remained untouched. In keeping with Rousseau's Sophie, most writers viewed girls as being in training for their future roles as wives and mothers; few sought to preserve girlhood as a period of life that was distinctively different from womanhood, except in terms of sexuality. For girls, compliant behavior was a sign of incipient womanhood, but just the opposite was true for boys, who, in their lack of compliance, demonstrated some of the essential traits of boyhood.

More and more, middle-class writers and reformers spoke of a "boy problem" to express a wide range of social ills thought to negatively impact boys, especially boys of the so-called dangerous classes. The problem was not so much errant boys themselves but society, which had failed to structure child rearing and education in ways that catered to boys' needs. Emerging theories of boy nature underpinned a slew of reforms and new organizations devoted to both privileged and deprived boys: the Boy Scouts, the Young Men's Christian Association (YMCA), "muscular Christianity," boys' clubs, the playground and recreation movements, and organized athletics. These reform movements transformed boys' existing peer networks into organizations that would produce respectable men, rather than dangerous ruffians. Ironically, however, the reforms could also facilitate and reinforce a form of masculinity defined by physical prowess and the patrolling of ethnic, racial, gender, and age boundaries. Meant both to restore middle-class boys to manliness and to rescue street boys from depravity, education through recreation was by no means the quick fix that reformers dreamed about.

Science and Boy Nature

Even if he was smudged beyond recognition from street dust and spoke in an unfamiliar argot, the corner newsboy or bootblack still offered reformers glimmers of the universal boy, one who might grow up into respectable, and presumably cleaned-up, manhood. Street boys of European ethnicity, even those from such stigmatized groups as the Italians, held all the latent potential to become solid working men and soldiers, rather than gangsters and thieves, if reformers could only unlock the key to their natures. By universalizing the concept of boy nature, reformers asserted that there were inherent masculine instincts that might transcend race, class, and ethnicity. This certainly held true for European immigrants, who were at least "white by law" and held the potential to become white by custom as well.[4] It was much more exceptional to find references to African American boys in discussions of the universality of boy nature. In an editorial for the journal *Work with Boys* (1916), which defined itself in opposition to all that represented feminization, the editor declared, "We write in these pages suggestions about boys' clubs, big clubs or little clubs, for big boys or little boys, black boys and white ones, red, yellow, and raw green country boys. Boy nature is pretty much the same all over."[5] Yet this pretty theory was rarely put into practice or even accepted by most reformers. The idea that at least boys who were "white by law" possessed the same nature minimized the pronounced differences in not only the experiences but also the opportunities accorded boys of different class and ethnic groups. This rhetoric opened the doors of citizenship, at least for white ethnic boys who—by virtue of the universality of boy nature—could have access to the privileges of male citizenship.

Boys were more than just the male variant of the human being, according to the new thinking; they were a species unto themselves, with unique age- and gender-related qualities. Just as anthropologists were smitten with the prospect of studying the strangely foreign habits and customs of non-Western peoples, so social scientists were becoming enthralled with the particularities of boys' instincts, propensities, and cultures—albeit with a respect bred from familiarity and nostalgia. According to scholar Kenneth Kidd, "the boy became an anthropological subject," and the students of boyhood religiously categorized what they viewed to be the essential characteristics of young males.[6] Writers even found analogies to the study of animal species. Leonard Benedict and Amzi Clarence Dixon, who wrote *Waifs of the Slums and Their Way Out* (1907), a plea for boys' clubs, made a parallel with zoology: "boys, like fish, must be studied; their habits, their tastes, and their peculiarities must be ascertained."[7] Josiah Flynt, who went through a period of "tramping" before he turned into a sociologist, studied "outcast" boys in the 1890s and admitted that he was just as fascinated by "vagabonds, rowdies, and criminals" as were some who studied the peoples of Africa and Siberia, an odd statement given his experience.[8]

Although the idea that the growing boy manifested savage or primitive qualities was not new, by the mid-nineteenth century many writers and theorists tried to turn what was once considered a negative feature of human existence into a developmental stage that was to be simultaneously cherished and directed. Warner claimed that "every boy who is good for anything is a natural savage."[9] Thomas Bailey Aldrich's enormously popular memoir, *The Story of a Bad Boy*, which was serialized in the periodical *Our Young Folks* in 1869 before being issued as a book, was an important articulation of the idea that "real" boys—who were boisterous, mischievous, and pugilistic—were having unnatural Victorian ideals of deportment forced down their throats.[10] Aldrich contrasted his own obstreperous boyhood with that of the refined boy who featured as a moral exemplar in Victorian tales: "I call myself a bad boy partly to distinguish myself from those faultless young gentlemen who generally figure in narratives of this kind . . . I was a real human boy . . . and no more like the impossible boy in a storybook than a sound orange is like one that has been sucked dry."[11] Some writers, such as Mark Twain in *Huckleberry Finn*, first published in the United States in 1885, juxtaposed civilization to primitiveness, so that the superiority of an untamed boyhood threw into light the corruption of civilized society.[12]

Scientists captured such popular notions about the true nature of boys in their explanations of human development. Biologist Ernest Haeckel was the first to articulate the theory of "recapitulation" in 1874—the idea that the development of the individual mirrors the history of the human race. This idea was repeated and embellished upon in many subsequent writings on boy nature, which insisted that boys manifested in their development the various stages in the development of humankind—from savagery to civilization. Girls' savagery was never all that savage, though, and girls were never termed "little savages" unless they had clearly veered beyond acceptable standards of femininity.

The recapitulation theory was most famously articulated by G. Stanley Hall, the well-known developmental psychologist, whose massive two-volume opus, *Adolescence* (1904), was considered to be almost a bible for twentieth-century boy workers (although, like the Bible, it is not clear they read it, even if they referred to it).[13] According to the new evolutionary logic, the instincts that enabled savage peoples to survive persisted in modern peoples, and educators and social scientists argued that boys must be allowed to both express and harness these instincts before they attained civilized manhood. This was a rather stark divergence from earlier conceptions of the inherent viciousness or depravity of children, which called for stringent applications of discipline and religion in order to restore them to righteousness. Many reformers now argued that boys most pass through different cultural epochs, including savagery and barbarism, on their way to manhood, re-enacting more primitive times. If boys bypassed this epoch, they could turn into sissies; if they never evolved beyond this stage, they could become hoodlums and hooligans. Playing Indian was all very well and good in its place; if the phase was prolonged, however, the boy who exemplified Mohawk Brave might be perennially driven by instincts rather than respectable codes of behavior.[14]

According to this theory, white ethnics might have an opportunity to move beyond savagery toward civilization. African and Native Americans were seen primarily as examples of unevolved races where savagery was a permanent, rather than a developmental, characteristic. Theologian Walter Fiske gave as an example a fictional boy who embodied both civilization and savagery. Boys, he contended, vacillated between the boisterous "Jimmy" and the prim and proper "James." The resolution of this dichotomy was to take shape in the form of the manly "Jim": "let him be the boy savage and barbarian if need be, when Nature seems to indicate it; and then be done with it, and give Jim, *the white man* [my emphasis], a chance."[15] Jim became a white man through the process of development, but reformers also held out the possibility that youth who many regarded as racially distinct, such as Italians and Jews, could become true Anglo-Saxons if their primitive instincts were properly channeled, leading to respectable manhood.

A new cadre of reformers who deemed themselves "boy workers" enthusiastically devoted themselves to boys in churches, settlement houses, the YMCA, the Boy Scouts, and boys' clubs, among other places, and sought to make use of this evolutionary logic. Eager young college graduates, seminarians, and sociologists in the making, these mostly middle-class young men devoted themselves to bringing up boys to be respectable men. Boy workers spawned their own organization, the Federated Alliance of Workers with Boys, in 1898 and even published a journal that promulgated their ideas, *Work with Boys: A Magazine of Methods.*[16] YMCA boy worker Henry W. Gibson went so far as to coin the term *boyology* in his book of the same title, urging that the science of boyhood be incorporated into Christian evangelism.[17]

Evangelical boy workers sought new ways of reaching not only middle-class boys, tired of Sunday school and church, but the little outlaws of the street.[18]

The movement for "muscular Christianity," as it has been called, started in the pulpits in the 1880s as a way to bring boys and men back to church through a more virile message. Groups such as the YMCA, founded in the United States in 1851, initially sought to evangelize by providing young urban men with services but later expanded its mission to younger boys. Eventually, the YMCA began to see exercise and even body building as central to its reform efforts.[19] With leaders such as Luther Gulick maintaining that spiritual development was premised on physical development, the YMCA, sometimes reluctantly, moved toward its reincarnation as a recreation center for boys.

The muscular physical body, once seen as the product of meaningful labor and not necessarily appealing from an aristocratic point of view, now became a personal project and the keystone of moral fitness. Proponents of muscular Christianity seized on masculine qualities, once attributed to bad boys, as the qualities of all normal boys. For instance, William McCormick defined real boys as "uncouth," "rude," and "ungracious," while describing the boy who was "too pietistic" as "abnormal."[20] The emotional characteristics of masculinity had been more starkly defined as antithetical to femininity in the rough working-class culture of New York City in the nineteenth century, while many genteel New Yorkers embraced a more androgynous ideal of manliness.[21] This line of thinking shifted at the end of the century, as the arbiters of culture turned against what they found to be the feminization of religion, culture, school, and society.[22] Using this line of thinking, the adventurous ragamuffins of the streets were in some respects more normal than the stereotypically overly civilized effeminate boys, ostensibly the darlings of female Sunday school teachers.

A number of reform movements, first directed at boys and later granted to girls, sought to give boys access to the opportunities that reformers believed their natures craved: playgrounds, camping, organized athletics, scouting, and boys' clubs.[23] Many organizations were initially designed for middle-class children, but urban reformers also found ways to capitalize on this rhetoric and build organizations of their own. Through boys' organizations, such as the Boy Scouts, it was hoped that boys whose inherent boy natures had been stifled by too much civilization might be toughened up a bit. Urban reformers, however, used boys' clubs to modify boys' exuberant boisterousness and even unlawfulness by steering them into more acceptable but still masculine pursuits.[24] In all of these endeavors, organizers sought to build on boys' pre-existing peer networks and native impulses to devise programs that both catered to and sought to modify boy culture.

Recreation, Play, and Delinquency

If, by *play*, we mean taking the opportunity to turn even the most adult of activities into opportunities for mischief and amusement, then children from nearly every culture and period have played. Play, suggests historian Howard Chudacoff, is the "spontaneous, joyous activity of children," which, at its best, is not overly constrained by adult monitoring.[25] Nineteenth-century reformers intent on saving poor children from the deleterious impact of their social and familial environments, however, had something more specific in mind. These "child savers" imagined a certain type of play as the birthright of every child and theorized that its absence contributed to stunted development and juvenile delinquency.[26] This type of thinking infused the child labor movement as well. Advocate Howard Braucher contended:

> We know the longings of the poor boy for a good time. Men who have known in their childhoods the depths of poverty and the cruelty of child labor tell us that it was comparatively easy to live on scanty food . . . The hardship lay in the fact that they had to work while other boys of their age were at play. To miss the childhood games is far worse than to grow hungry and cold.[27]

In their assumption that they knew what was best for children, child savers overlooked the appeal of work to poor and immigrant children. Child labor could be abusive, but many children, both immigrant and otherwise, took pride in their work and their ability to help sustain their families or fill their own pockets with spending money.[28] Labor did not entirely preclude play, especially for the many children under the age of fourteen whose work both on and off the streets was casual, intermittent, and provided many opportunities for socializing and merriment.[29] For instance, it was reported that Italian boys in Chicago during the 1890s could often be found "romping the streets or loitering." Still, they would get up at 2:30 a.m., sell newspapers, and spend the rest of the day "shining shoes, playing tricks in the street or dozing in some hallway."[30] At the same time, child laborers from immigrant families could not help but become cognizant that American middle-class culture regarded childhood as a special time of life that should be protected from the cares of adulthood. This did not necessarily mean that these children wanted to attend school or to adopt middle-class forms of play, but that many avoided overly structured forms of work, when they could, and saw their wages as a means of embellishing their own childhood, either in addition to or instead of helping their families.

Yet there were also some immigrant families who did not share the American reverence for play, who expected their children to contribute responsibly to the family wage economy or to attend school. Memoirist and Jewish immigrant Daniel Blaustein was taught that play was a "waste of time, a frivolity." Many immigrant parents did not view childish amusements as an end unto themselves, as did many American reformers; in fact, they were concerned that the penchant for play and recreation was driving children from their homes and traditions.[31] But some immigrant parents still found playgrounds and recreation centers to be safer, more appealing spaces for children's activities than the streets, especially when they lived in homes where there was little space for the physical play that most boys enjoyed.

Reformers at once vaunted, envied, and bemoaned the exuberant play life of urban boys. When such play did veer into delinquency, advocates of recreation were loath to blame youth themselves, developing a sharp critique of urban society for failing to provide poor children with opportunities for healthful and legitimate forms of recreation. Writer Frank Tracy Carlson demonstrated the shift in moving from more moralistic to environmental conceptions of the causes of delinquency that took the onus not only off youngsters themselves but off their families. The problem lay in the very nature of boys: "There is no such thing as a bad boy," he insisted. "Vice is misdirected energy."[32]

Carlson's sentiments were echoed by Pauline Goldmark in her study of boyhood and lawlessness in New York's immigrant West Side (1914). Her descriptions of boys' street life were remarkably similar to those captured by the memoirs of immigrant boys who grew up in New York and Chicago in the beginning of the twentieth century. In these accounts, the neighborhood and the peer group exert a powerful influence on the texture of boys' lives, an influence that is sometimes even more important than family and school. On the West Side, the street functioned as both spectacle and a space where play and petty crime intermingled: "now a funeral, now a fire; craps on the sidewalk; a stolen ride on one of Death Avenue's freight trains; a raid on a fruit stall; a fight, an accident, a game of 'cat.' "[33]

In fact, it was boys' play, which could be physically dangerous as well as illicit, that propelled many reformers' efforts. Boys played numerous types of ball games on streets and in alleys, gambled, displayed their gymnastic feats to admiring audiences of children and onlookers, and utilized whatever neighborhood spaces they could to find fun, such as swinging "like orangutans" from the telephone wires at the Chicago Loop, an activity that allegedly led to a number of fatalities.[34] Others, according to Josiah Flynt, carved out spaces for themselves, like one gang that holed up in a cave in a cabbage patch at the end of the city, "where they smoked, read dime novels, told tales, and planned mischievous raids." Flynt described the Chicago Loop as "one of the most congested business districts in the world . . . full of children playing and working and loafing in the midst of danger."[35] But although many described boys' illicit play in somewhat salacious detail, others worried that children either did not know how or did not have the opportunity to play. For instance, a study of children's play in 1913 conducted by the People's Institute of New York found that most children were engaged in "idling" and "watching others play," a finding that may have missed the social learning and interactions that were meaningful to children who hung about on corners observing and chatting with their friends.[36]

Boys' play also appeared to be curtailed by the growth of cities and crackdowns on juvenile delinquency. Goldmark contended that there were forces that opposed "boys' ownership of the streets." Playing ball on the street, one of the most popular of boys' activities, was illegal well into the twentieth century. In New York City in 1909, according to the juvenile court's annual report, practically one-half (5,733 out of 11,494) of the children who were made to appear at court were prosecuted for such trivial infractions as playing ball, building bonfires, and playing other normal boyhood games such as "shinny" in the street.[37] Drivers argued that the streets were for driving rather than for marbles, stone throwing, or ball playing, so when youth "exercise childhood's inalienable right to play, the boy finds himself colliding with the rights of property."[38] Reformers complained that children living in one- or two-room tenements did not have enough room to play at home, even if their parents were attentive, and that the "unbridled freedom" of the street was a most tempting, if dangerous, alternative.

The amount of public space available for children's recreation was also in decline. This was especially the case for boys, according to sociologist Anthony Rotundo, who argues that society had traditionally afforded boys, but not girls, access to physical space fairly free from the intrusions of adults and respectable codes of behavior.[39] Throughout most of the nineteenth century, in many urban areas, patches of woodlands and marshes could be found that were perfect for the unfettered and imaginative play that many boys enjoyed.[40] Of course, the street was an equally popular venue for amusement, but street play was becoming increasingly dangerous because of the congestion caused by streetcars, delivery wagons, and, later, automobiles. As building proceeded apace, green space, vacant lots, and even alleys disappeared. "Every inch of the city is utilized by factory, store, street, or railway track," argued Woods Hutchinson about Chicago at the Annual Playground Congress. Backyards were increasingly rare.[41] In Michael Gold's semiautobiographical novel *Jews without Money*, the young protagonist lamented the shrinking space for children's play on New York's East Side and yearned for a bit of grass, complaining of the lack of "air, space, weeds, elbow room, one sickened for space on the East Side, any kind of marsh or wasteland to testify that the world was still young, and wild and free." When he and his friends did find a place to play in a vacant lot, they soon lost it to city planners building a new parkway.[42] Gold's protagonist wondered why the cops, who hung out in saloons and cavorted with loose women, seemed to have it out for the boys:

> Why, then, did they adopt such an attitude of stern virtue toward the small boys? It was if we were the biggest criminals of the region. They broke up our baseball games, confiscated our bats. They beat us for splashing under the fire hydrant. They cursed us, growled and chased us for any reason. They hated to see us having any fun. (44)

Fleeing and tricking the "coppers," as they called them, became another element in their fun: but one that could quickly turn ugly if kids were picked up to spend the night in juvenile detention.

Boys' play spaces were not used only for innocent fun but as battlegrounds for ethnic rivalries and places to stash stolen goods. If boys played in authorized venues under appropriate adult guidance, so the thought went, they would be less likely to come into conflict with the authorities. Carlson theorized that when boys experience too much restraint from police, parents, and schools, the "natural and inevitable result, if the child is normal, healthy and vigorous, is attempted evasion of rules and regulations."[43] An advocate of expanded recreation spaces for youth, Alan Burns related an anecdote about how some boys, having been forced out of a vacant lot by the big boys, decided to play ball on the street when a driver accosted them and "warned and reprimanded the boy at the same time by a cut from the lash of a long whip." "The boy's cry of rage and resentment" could contribute to antisocial behavior and juvenile delinquency, he reasoned.[44]

Liberal reformer Jane Addams, who had been instrumental in the creation of the Chicago juvenile court, attempted to deflect blame from youth for their misdemeanors in her *The Spirit of Youth and the City Streets* (1920), arguing that young people's natural animal spirits had been stunted both in the home and in the community. She shifted the blame onto neglectful and "degenerate" parents; irresponsible leisure businesses that preyed upon youthful weakness, such as pool halls; and communities that failed to provide adequate resources for structured recreation. Addams was quite willing to excuse youthful misdeeds, in contrast with today's zero tolerance attitudes toward juvenile delinquents, and explained many crimes as emanating from a childish "spirit of adventure."[45] Both girls and boys, especially those from immigrant families, had been freed from the traditional controlling forces of home and community, many of them spending money of their own on disreputable forms of leisure and debauchery, including dance halls and alcohol.

Boys, Addams argued, were particularly possessed of "primitive instincts" that propelled them to adventurous activities. Curiosity and a desire to make things happen often sent them to "juvie"—for instance, "setting fire to a barn in order to see the fire engines coming up the street" and "stealing thirteen pigeons from a barn."[46] Even murder could be explained this way, as in the case of Pfister, a boy from an Irish gang who called a boy from a Polish gang, Niecgodzki, a coward. Once Pfister saw that Niecgodzki was carrying a gun, he challenged him to a fist-fight. Instead Niecgodzki fired and killed Pfister: "what might be merely a boyish scrap is turned into a tragedy because some boy has a revolver."[47]

An account of a brawl that took place under the auspices of a New York boys' club in 1905 also reflected the assumption that violence was an unfortunate but not wholly unexpected corollary to boys' play. With the headline "Killed by Play Policeman," the *New York Times* told the sad story about a boy killed at the Flatbush Boys' Club. The boys had been playing cops and robbers in the club's gymnasium when a boy referred to as Hines, one of the robbers, resisted arrest by Driscoll, who played a policemen. At that point, Driscoll withdrew a gun from his pocket and shot Hines square in the head—a purely accidental incident, according to the paper, as the shooter did not know that the gun was loaded. Contrary to recent opinion that young people today are especially violent, the degree of casualness with which the killing was treated is notable. Nothing was written of the dangers of youth carrying guns, and the writer even found it possible to discuss the incident as resulting from a "boyish prank."[48] The ethos that "boys will be boys"—meaning inherently disposed to violence—was used as a rationale for even some of the most devastating of occurrences.[49]

Ultimately, Addams blamed society for offering boys the "cheap heroics of the revolvers found in the pawn shops," along with other tawdry and illicit pleasures, without offering more wholesome activities to fulfill their need for adventure. Thus she excused boys who thieved and pilfered so that they might get theater tickets, even when they stole from her own beloved Hull House settlement.[50] The desire for adventure was basic, especially for boys, and it was up to settlement houses such as Addams's to supply them with opportunities to "jump out of the humdrum experience of life" without having to turn to drink, drugs, and crime. Recreation enthusiasts such as Addams believed that they could prevent delinquencies, inculcate respect for authority, and guide and direct children's development through the provision of specially constructed and supervised activities and play spaces for children.

Clubs for Boys

Although much has been written about the Boy Scouts, an organization that prospered among the middle class during this period, "mass boys clubs," as some have called them, had the most impact on the lives of inner-city boys during the late nineteenth and early twentieth centuries. The mass boys' club movement was specifically aimed at serving urban youth and curbing delinquency—themes that still reverberate through what is now called the Boys and Girls Clubs of America (significantly, the national organization did not add *Girls* to its title until 1990).[51] Unlike the more structured and labor-intensive Boy Scouts, the boys' clubs have emphasized informal recreation, inclusive membership, easy access to facilities, and looser governance structures.

Urban boys' clubs evolved out of mission work in the post–Civil War era but became a more broadly based movement by the end of the nineteenth century. The "street boys' movement," as it was termed in the journal *Work with Boys*, was careful to distinguish itself from groups such as the Boy Scouts and the YMCA, which were devoting themselves to middle-class boys. In "A Sketch of the History of the Street Boys' Club Movement in America," William Byron Forbush contrasted his constituency in unflattering terms with the boys who frequented the YMCA: "You and other societies take from us the cream and leave us the skimmed milk . . . Your work is largely constructive, to win boys to Christ and build up the church. Our work is preventive, to keep boys from prison and crime and build up the state by building up good citizens."[52] In other successive editions of the journal, writers would allude to the scouts and the YMCA as being for the "desirable" and "good" boy, code words for children from respectable white middle-class families who were not, at least initially, meant to be the focus of mass clubs for urban boys.

Although girls clubs, the Girl Scouts, and the Camp Fire Girls would follow in the wake of these activities for boys, club workers were convinced that in girls the "instinct" for club loyalty was not so easily awakened and that it was difficult to get them to enlarge their social activities beyond the immediate family. Girls' clubs "do not come up to the standard of boys' clubs," which, Charles S. Bernheimer and Joseph M. Cohen suggested, was the opinion of all those who observed such clubs. Unlike boys, who form gangs, they said, girls form "sets" that were by nature "exclusive" and "undemocratic" and did not lend themselves to the kind of parliamentary procedures they recommended for boys.[53] Boy workers ardently believed in the potential of the boys' club to promote republican virtues, always measuring girls' cultures and characteristics against what they viewed as the more volatile but ultimately more promising culture of boyhood.

In supervised boys' clubs, organizers sought to reel in already existing groups or gangs of boys in order to form more respectable boys' organizations. But, even while working with pre-existing groups, reformers' first efforts were more driven by the Gospel and their own staunchly held ideas about manliness and the proper behavior of youth. Still, throughout the entire history of the boys' club movement, there were many competing aims and ideas of what were the best methods of "holding" and guiding boys. Were methods aimed at instilling discipline and character through exacting rules of comportment and activities designed to develop boys' appreciation for the finer things in life the best? Or should reformers take their bearings from youths' inclinations, help to foster self-government, and provide the kind of recreation they most enjoyed? For the most part, early boys' clubs stressed moral guidance and bending boys to enjoy the recreation leaders deemed appropriate. In these first clubs, the idea that only male workers could lead boys or that more clearly delineated masculine pursuits such as athletics should be primary was not yet the party line.

Over time, however, the vast majority of boys' clubs would be structured in accordance with reformers' premises that "holding boys" was best accomplished by bowing to the ethos of the peer group, providing specifically masculine role models and guidance, and "giving boys a good time." As they progressed, advocates of boys' clubs promised to base their work with boys not only on the psychology of boys but on the "psychology of the boy mob or gang," which they would put to use in organizing group activities. Instead of the rigid discipline of school and church, clubs were "elastic" and self-governing, utilizing boys' native tendencies to form groups and choose "natural leaders" among their own ranks based on physical prowess and courage. Organizing clubs that put to use the values and virtues of the masculine peer group eventually would be adopted as keys to the organization of boys' clubs.

The picture of the nineteenth-century boys' club that early reformers drew on was radically different from what the movement would later come to signify, as the budding ethos of masculinity, rather than manliness, took hold.[54] Nineteenth-century manliness was a more androgynous ideal that melded courage and strength with tenderness and gentility. As historian Gail Bederman and others amply demonstrate, eventually middle-class men would embrace aspects of working-class masculinity as a way to recapture manly virtues that had been lost in the industrialized, and what they considered to be increasingly feminized, world.[55] As boys' clubs evolved, they moved from stressing the virtues of manliness to adopting the tenets of masculinity—a rougher ideal that equated manhood with stereotypically male characteristics.

What would later become the Boys Club of America, institutionalized in 1931, traces its origins to a club founded for needy boys in Hartford, Connecticut, by charitable women in 1860.[56] Although women, as key players in the settlement house movement and in child welfare, had been deeply involved in the early boys' club movement, they became increasingly marginalized as the clubs emphasized the need for male leaders to model manliness and later masculinity. The shift toward masculine leadership was reflected in an editorial directed against the Woman's Christian Temperance Movement's objections to the use of military drills in boys' clubs in 1895. In defending military drills, one leader claimed that such techniques were superior to the "sugar-coated" pills dispensed by well-meaning reformers trying to "surreptitiously" improve boys. Military drills, the author contended, inspired order, respectability, and passion for the soldier's life: apparently, the outcome that some believed best combined masculinity and responsibility.[57]

New York established the first citywide boys' club network in 1901, which originated in 1876 when budding mogul E. J. Harriman rented a space for boys in the Tompkins Square tenement district where boys could play games, amuse themselves, read, and put on little shows. Legend has it that the club was begun after a bunch of young "ragamuffins" commenced throwing stones at the Wesleyan Mission. Unable to deter the youngsters, the woman in charge invited the children in for coffee and cake during a momentary lull in catcalls. After that, she arranged for the boys to have a room where they could play games and participate in "innocent enjoyments" rather than the vandalism that had previously preoccupied them. Harriman supplied the funds to expand the club, which was distinct in that it did not evangelize or require dues and that it accepted all boys, regardless of race or nationality.[58] Attempting to restrict the dangerous autonomy of the peer group, Harriman and other organizers hoped to reel boys in only to transform them.

Many early boys' clubs were premised on the need to "refine" and "cultivate" manly men, not through military drills and aggressive physical competition, but through activities that would now be thought of as "feminine," such as dramatics, singing, and reading aloud. The St. George Boys' Club hoped that it would provide space for street boys who had no "cheerful homes" to be under "more refining influences."[59] Charles Stelzle had been a child laborer and a member of St. Marks' Boys Club in New York in the 1880s before becoming a reformer himself, eventually publishing *Boys of the Street: How to Win Them* in 1901.[60] Stelzle recommended that boys' club headquarters should be decorated with fresh flowers and beautiful pictures to give boys a taste of refinement. He believed that boys' adventurous street life had deprived them of their ability to appreciate "quiet consecutive work or enjoyment," which he hoped that the boys' club would instill in them.[61] Thus, in early clubs, reformers tried to offer boys spaces that resembled in miniature the men's club of nineteenth-century gentlemen.

Journalists depicting the new clubrooms described paneled libraries with oak tables where boys could find an array of magazines for youth, fantastic tales of heroism, and the newspaper, along with more sedate literature. Leaders hoped that such libraries would appeal to the "intellectual side of the boy." Board games such as dominoes, backgammon, and checkers "lead minds to think, eyes to see, hands to do" and also crowd out "vile and unworthy thoughts and acts," according to Frank Mason, secretary of the Bunker Hill Boys Club in Boston.[62] Clubs sponsored theatrical events, glee clubs, and Punch and Judy puppet shows. What these boys needed, leaders believed, was not only an uplifting space in which they could engage in wholesome recreation but the presence of a nurturing, as opposed to a specifically masculine, role model. One organizer of New York boys' clubs argued that the most important factor in boy work was "love and sympathy of which they get so little elsewhere, and which will do more than anything else ever can to counteract the dangerous influence of the street."[63] Some clubs extended this notion even further by attempting to rehabilitate the entire family, utilizing so-called friendly visitors to go to boys' homes to both investigate their living conditions and offer advice to parents on how best to guide growing boys.

It seems likely that the varnished spaces described in journalistic accounts did not retain their elegant appeal for long, however, as boys claimed the spaces as their own territory. Frequent depictions of the boys of the street took note of their "animalistic" characteristics. Alvin Sanborn, organizer of a Boston boys' club, objected that when clubs opened their doors to the masses, the boys "remind me more of herds of wild horses than anything else." Sanborn tried to instruct other boys' club leaders on how to transform the wild horses into a disciplined group, by the use of "rigid discipline, force, or persuasion." Upon inviting local street boys to come to his room and enjoy books, papers, and games, a group was more than happy enough to come but "they would not apply themselves to anything . . . They shifted rapidly from games to papers, papers to books, and books back to games." Sanborn tried to restrain such shiftlessness and make boys apply themselves to one game at a time. Still, games were commonly disrupted by "a bit of bad luck, a boast, a flash of envy." In the end, whatever Sanborn's accomplishments were—and he claimed that he inculcated better discipline and sportsmanship—the varnished space of the boys' club was ultimately transformed by the street culture that boys brought with them into these spaces.[64]

Early boys' clubs also drew heavily on the energies of women such as club leader Winifred Buck. But as time went on, women were slowly shut out of the boys' club movement. Some of the principles upon which they and some male leaders operated—for instance, the objection to military drills, the reluctance to subject younger boys to the discipline of competitive athletics, and the benefits of such refining influences as reading, art, and music—would be cast aside as remnants of an overly feminized age. The emerging culture of masculinity had little room for the nineteenth-century concept of manliness. Twentieth-century masculinity defined itself by its opposition to all that was feminine and sought to instill characteristics that were viewed as uniquely male.[65]

But regardless of their methods or approaches, when reformers reeled in the boys of the street, boys often upended the intentions to reform them. In the 1890s, for example, a writer for *Scribner's Magazine* described a boys' club trip to Staten Island to see a Buffalo Bill show. All was initially well on the boat, with the captain adopting a paternalistic attitude to the throng of youngsters. The boat trip home, however, was another story, with the boys rapidly tiring of the games they were playing on their two-hour journey. Bored with the brass band hired to accompany them on the trip home, one youngster "attempted to release his pent up emotions by sticking a button into the trombone," which had the effect of practically strangling the man, according to one reporter. When the musician made a "wild dive" at the boy, who defended himself with a chair, a full-fledged brawl ensued, with "chairs flying, the band-men swearing, and the boys yelling like steam whistles." Interestingly, the journalist telling the story did not seem to place blame on either the boys or the organization but seemed to view it as a colorful episode in the development of boys' clubs.[66]

Perhaps the Chicago Boys' Club, which federated a number of individual boys' clubs in 1901, thought they could avoid the sometimes chaotic, occasionally violent, atmosphere of some of the first mass clubs for street boys by injecting more structure and explicitly defending the use of religion as a means of reform. Formed in 1901 by John F. Atkinson, who wished to do something for the city's "street waifs," the group set out to reform "heathen from foreign lands," as well as racial minorities. The club had a diverse membership composed of 30 percent Jewish, 30 percent Italian, and 15 percent African American youth, with only 3 percent of involved boys having native-born parents during the first six years of its work.[67] Harking back to earlier practices, the Chicago organization was—at least at first—intent on conveying a message of muscular Christianity, bragging about the manly prayerfulness of its camp boys and considering all children, whether Jewish or Catholic, as potential converts to Protestantism.[68] In their promotional material they testified to the possibility of yoking the "real boy," who was by nature masculine, to religion.[69] Although the word *sissy* traditionally had been an epithet used by boys to insult their peers, increasingly male reformers, psychologists, and others were using the term to negatively characterize boys who did not exhibit the masculine qualities of real boys. Capitalizing on what they thought to be the true nature of boys, organizers hoped to instill a healthy reverence for God, along with the character traits deemed essential for a lawful and productive manhood.[70]

The Chicago group made it their mission to serve boys who had been neglected by existing social agencies, such as the YMCA and the churches. Using language that would return in the late twentieth century, the group's organizational literature referred to the "the underprivileged boy." *The Boys' Club Manual* (used beginning in the 1920s) explained that a Chicago boys' club organizer had been traveling on a railroad coach with members of organized labor. As they chatted, the phrase *privileged classes* surfaced again and again, and it occurred to the worker that the children his organization served were "under-privileged" in terms of education, recreation, and opportunity. This term might also have seemed less pejorative than those holdover labels from the nineteenth century: *street boy, waif,* and *urchin.*[71] In the years to come, the nationally federated Boys' Clubs of America literature would make central its claim that it catered to the "underprivileged boys of the crowded city," stretching its goals to include those who had suffered the "disadvantages of limited education, of unfavorable environment and of prejudice growing out of religion and race."[72] Believing that appropriate interventions could offset the damages wrought by these disadvantages, boys' club leaders were much more optimistic about the forces of nurture than their more eugenically minded peers.[73] This attitude presaged the efforts of educators and reformers of the 1960s to reconceptualize the reasons for the weak academic performance of children living in poverty.

Now termed a "deficit" approach to education, defining youth as underprivileged fails to take into account the aspects of their own culture that children valued.[74] For instance, in Chicago, as elsewhere, the amusements clubs offered often failed in the competition to "win the boys of the street." Arriving in Chicago at the age of six in 1919, Italian immigrant Anthony Sorrentino remembered his gang and their unorganized activities as the source of his fondest memories as a child:

> Our small gang usually played in the streets, alleys, or backyards. An old basement or coal shed refurnished by our talents would constitute our clubroom. Sometimes the clubroom would be built on empty lots by the boys with boards acquired by devious means. An old kerosene lamp or stove furnished a little heat to thaw out the place. The clubroom was usually full of smoke, damp and smelly, but it was adventure . . . The settlements and community centers did good work, but the fact was that the rank-and-file kids of my neighborhood went there only occasionally. They played basketball and ping pong and made handicraft articles, but the time spent on them was infinitesimal compared with the hours spent on the streets and alleys in random "unsupervised" activities, which were always stimulating and attractive.[75]

Just as the reformers imagined, Sorrentino's little gang got involved in various escapades, from smoking to begging to petty thievery. Rather than admiring the leaders of industry, he and his friends admired local gangsters. Although Sorrentino eventually made good and became a leader in juvenile justice and community activism, his story testifies to the enormous appeal of boys' unstructured play life.

Early boys clubs, as we have seen, did not solely focus on physical recreation but also provided a range of services, including industrial training. Proponents Benedict and Dixon acknowledged that their boys were not meant to enter the ranks of the professions but instead to become carpenters, printers, or day laborers who would fill their "humble stations with honor" instead of becoming the "saloon-keepers, the gamblers, the tramps, and the 'bums' of the future."[76] In other cities across the nation, too, some clubs focused on working (as opposed to idle) boys, hosted savings clubs, offered classes in writing and bookkeeping, and even sponsored employment bureaus. Most reformers did not expect youth to become the captains of industry, or even middle-class professionals but hoped to instill the morality that would enable them to become solid law-abiding working men, able to support a family with their wages and steer clear of the penitentiary.

In Chicago, as elsewhere, boys club advocates struggled with identifying and attracting the "right" boys for their services—unsure as to whether they wished to serve the most delinquent or the most promising of the city's boys. In 1908, using newly emerging social scientific methodologies, the Chicago Boys' Clubs employed a map of the city and delinquency figures to determine the most "contested and needy district" for establishing a facility.[77] But even while envisioning their activities as helping the "neediest" boys, the board of directors exhibited prejudice toward Italians, with some complaining that the Italian boys "scare off" boys of other ethnicities from attending, and others commenting on the difficulty of securing cooperation from Italian families. Of course, as long as boys' clubs espoused Protestant evangelism and ideologies about boys and recreation that were counter to traditional beliefs, Italians were unlikely to welcome the ministrations of boys' club workers. As a result, eventually the Chicago clubs recognized that "American" boys found their programs more appealing than did immigrant children.[78]

By the 1920s, the Chicago clubs had abandoned the proselytizing and cut down on the industrial training, instead focusing on a message of serving the underprivileged and preventing delinquency through the provision of recreation. The Chicago Boys' Club's promotional literature featured comments by a North Side policeman claiming that a 50 percent decrease in delinquency between 1923 and 1928 could be attributed to the boys' club work—a claim that would be tested and found wanting by other delinquency researchers.[79] Ethnic group leaders sometimes complained that, by supplying places where boys might play games and socialize in the evening, boys' clubs loosened family connections and encouraged youth to spend more time on the streets. Boys' club advocates, though, contended that, for most of the boys they served, homes themselves were deleterious: "boys' club workers recognize that however desirable it may be to have boys spend their evenings at home . . . there are in most communities homes lacking not only everything that interests a boy, but homes that are a positive hindrance to the boys' mental, moral and spiritual growth."[80] Espousing the view that youths' homes were inadequate places to cultivate youthful virtue, reformers offered not only schools but also recreational sites as more suitable places for socialization.

As boys' clubs evolved in many urban locations, however, they found themselves kowtowing to boys' penchant for pleasure and physical activity. Increasingly, it was the physical spaces, such as gymnasiums and basketball courts that they boasted about in their publications. In fact, their facilities for exercise and organized athletics consistently served as the biggest draw of urban boys' clubs. Club leaders delighted in the fact that, when they built gymnasiums and pools and provided boxing equipment, boys lined up to get in. Seeking to drum up funding, John Witter, the superintendent of the Chicago Boys' Club, asked the members of the chamber of commerce to imagine the excitement that gets around when "a club house is to be opened, athletic teams organized and a swimming pool built."[81] The boys themselves, as consumers of recreation, mandated that such games would be the centerpiece of club offerings. Boys' desires to engage in such play fit in well with the growing tendency among boy workers to equate physical strength with mental toughness and masculinity, a theme most famously perpetuated in Theodore Roosevelt's speeches and essays on the strenuous life and the American boy. "What the foundation is to a great building, the body is to well-developed manhood," a boys' club leader claimed.[82] Boxing, a sport increasingly popular with urban youth, and team sports, which rewarded team efforts to defeat an enemy, fit in well with this vision.[83]

By the 1930s, the rhetoric of boys' clubs had altered significantly, with the emphasis on the physical body being paramount—a focus that boys enthusiastically embraced. But the boys, it must be recognized, used these organizations instrumentally. The spaces that the organizations created became more important than the programs that were offered. Even boys (such as my second-generation Irish American father who grew up in Wilmington, Delaware, in the 1930s) who did not identify as belonging to a boys' club played basketball at the boys' club gym, used the swimming pool, or frequented the camps that the clubs increasingly sponsored.

Typically, both publicly and privately funded reform efforts must justify even projects that simply improve people's lives, such as providing glasses or attempting to remediate other health problems, by referencing the greater public good that the project will serve. Boys' club organizers claimed that they could address not only delinquency but also worker unrest and labor turnover by ameliorating the problems of underprivileged boyhood, surely a winning appeal in a city like Detroit that pioneered industrial discipline.

Yet boys' club workers clearly did not seek to overturn existing social relations. Instead, as had other boy workers before them, they hoped to prevent working- and lower-class boys from falling into lives of criminality and dependency. Many historians have deemed these types of organizational efforts as attempts to "socially control" youth. It is too simplistic to conceive of boy workers' efforts as attempts to maintain the social structure. Many boy workers had themselves experienced the chaotic lives of their young charges and earnestly sought to secure social advantages for them.[84] Surely some supported the aspirations of the working class, who sought more control over their lives through union organization. And even if controlling the working class was central to the aims of some club promoters, boys themselves used the organization more instrumentally: for most, belonging to the boys' club meant that you had access to basketball courts, swimming pools, and perhaps some contacts that would help you find work.

Playgrounds, Recreation Centers, and Masculinity

Boys' clubs were not the only recreational spaces deemed pivotal to the transformation of troubled youth. As masculinity became increasingly premised on
the cultivation of the male physical body, athletics and recreation spaces such as
playgrounds emerged as central sites for the expression and harnessing of boys'
masculine instincts and as means of deterring delinquency. Playgrounds started
quietly enough with the establishment of small sandlots for young children in
Boston in the 1880s; by the turn of the twentieth century, they had developed
into more comprehensive urban spaces. With widespread public support, playgrounds proliferated as a guarantor of crime prevention, safety, socialization,
Americanization, and a "good time" for children.[85] Urban planners, politicians,
women's groups, and other proponents of municipal reforms joined hands in
reshaping urban space to include government-sponsored recreation for children.[86] Children must have access to lawful recreation, the child savers opined;
without it, their bodies and psyches would suffer, and they would seek illegal
means of amusing themselves.

Although settlement house workers and reformers such as Jane Addams and
Jacob Riis were at the forefront of calls to establish playgrounds, the movement
itself was not entirely driven by the reformers. It additionally derived support
from neighborhood constituencies and even youth themselves. Historian Ocean
Howells, for example, has discovered solid neighborhood support for playgrounds in working-class neighborhoods in San Francisco. He quotes from a
petition for a playground or place to play ball signed by 2,500 youngsters in a
working-class district of San Francisco: "every place we start to play rubber hose
or bat the wicket we are generally stopped by a policeman."[87] In New York, historian Steven Riess has found evidence of dissenting voices among the Jewish community in New York, with some petitioning for a playground in 1901 but others
arguing that accessible space should be used for housing rather than play.[88] In any
case, playground leader Henry Curtis claimed that hundreds of children lined up
at the gates when New York City opened its first playgrounds, so much so that it
was sometimes necessary to close the door on newcomers.[89]

There was a considerable difference of opinion, however, between many of the
reformers—who insisted on the need for adult-supervised play—and children
themselves, who often wanted a place to play free of the mandates of grown-ups
to amuse themselves in a particular fashion.[90] Even the U.S. Congress rejected
a playground appropriation bill on the premise that too much intervention in
children's play was like a human trying to teach a fish to swim. Reformers such as

Curtis were concerned that, without adult guidance, the playgrounds could, and often did, degenerate into yet another example of street society, where the "bully and the street loafer" reinforced the value of status hierarchies based on age, physical prowess, and gender. Such playgrounds were, according to Curtis, "some of the worst places in the city for the children, so far as morality and social ideals are concerned."[91] The problem was, argued Curtis, that the so-called undirected playground was in fact "controlled by the unsocial members of the community," that is, older boys.[92] And though Curtis did not make the point, the spaces simultaneously reflected and reimposed age and gender boundaries. Usually enclosed with iron fences to block off the dangerous elements of the street, playgrounds typically featured different areas for boys, girls, and younger children, with boys often claiming far more than their fair share of space.[93]

Although the movement for playgrounds in both Chicago and New York started off with facilities attached to settlement houses, by the early part of the twentieth century, agitators had garnered support for public recreational spaces. By 1914, the New York Board of Education had established thirty-eight recreation centers with the foremost purpose of promoting athletics but also sponsored clubs, games, libraries, and study rooms for children.[94] In Chicago, providing suitable recreation for the children of the poor became a major focus of reform and received astounding support; by 1916 the city had fifty-five playgrounds or parks under public administration, many of them in districts where immigrant populations resided. The largest of such parks, such as Armour Square and Ogden Park, included gymnasiums, swimming pools, and social centers for club meetings and parties.[95] These larger recreation centers served multiple purposes and constituencies, but boys, particularly those under the age of sixteen, were the largest constituency of the South Side gymnasiums, according to a 1907 study.[96] One journalist hopefully, rather than satirically, termed the recreation center a "gang headquarters," which would transform boys' peer networks through the provision of supervised leisure activities. In his vision, "instead of shooting craps or stealing apples from crippled peddlers, the slum children occupy themselves with less vicious, and eventually they find, more enjoyable activities."[97]

As part of their effort to organize the playground, reformers praised the value of team sports. No other activity designed to harness boys' energy in a positive direction had the staying power of organized athletics, which served multiple purposes beyond strengthening boys' physical bodies. In high school, boys clamored for athletics as an independent venue for the expression of peer culture, and educators theorized that school-sponsored sports might stanch drop-out rates. In recreation centers, reformers found that they could use something boys enjoyed to develop qualities deemed essential to manliness: physical prowess, bravery, competitiveness, and group loyalty. Luther Halsey Gulick had been a pioneer in advancing the role of athletics in the YMCA then resigned to become director of New York City's Public School Athletic League in 1903.[98] Gulick believed that supervised athletic competitions would teach boys respect for the law and that the peer group of the team would play a key role in instilling social conformity among its members. A contradictory figure, Gulick supported the limitation of Eastern and Southern European immigration while also viewing playgrounds and athletic competitions as venues where ethnic tensions would be dissolved through the ethos of sportsmanship.[99]

Prior to the development of competitive athletics for non–college age students, boy experts considered gymnastics to be the most appropriate sport, both because it required only a minimal amount of space and because it developed boys' bodies at their own individual pace. In 1891, however, one of Gulick's protégés James Naismith, confronted by an "ennui of wintertime" among a group of uninspired gymnastic students in Springfield, Massachusetts, invented the game of basketball. The team sport grabbed hold of reformers and boy workers alike. Boys loved the game, it had minimal space requirements, and it could easily be supervised, particularly if conducted inside.[100] The game proved so popular with the boys that it helped to transform YMCA facilities into athletic arenas. Basketball courts were one of the centerpieces of nearly every park and recreation center built for children in the ethnic districts of cities such as New York and Chicago for decades to come. And whereas reformers had initially believed in the importance of rule-bound, adult-supervised play, the game easily lent itself to more casual forms of play. In this way, boys used the game for their own, not the reformers', purposes. Some basketball courts even became central to the perpetuation of forms of peer culture based on values antithetical to those of the reformers, with menacing toughs frightening girls and younger boys from even approaching the hoop.

Gulick, one of the founders of the Playground and Recreation Association, wrote *Philosophy of Play* (1920), which depicted play as an embodiment of primeval masculine instincts.[101] Along with George E. Johnson, who wrote *Education through Recreation* (1916) and was superintendent of the Pittsburgh Play Association, Gulick argued for the instinctual basis of male athletics.[102] Gulick loudly proclaimed that his work built on the scientifically established principle that all boys possessed the "gang instinct" once they reached the age of ten or so. The imagined gang instinct led boys to found groups of peers whose influence over boys was nearly insurmountable unless productively channeled by adults.

According to G. Stanley Hall, who wrote the preface for reformatory principal J. Adam Puffer's *The Boy and His Gang* in 1912, "the gang spirit is the basis of the social life of the boy."[103] School athletics, Gulick argued, could "convert the gang instinct from evil into righteousness," which he thought to be the "root of masculine altruism."[104] Although the loyalty of the gang was primitive, Gulick argued that modern society still needed the "power and barbaric virtues of manhood" that prevailed in the gang. Through organized athletics, clubs, and other activities that capitalized upon the gang, reformers could transform these "barbaric virtues" into acceptable forms of masculine bonding and aggression.[105] But, as historians of athletics have shown, competitive athletics was only partially successful in its aim of deterrence, with many successful athletes found among the ranks of the delinquents.

In his championship of organized sports, Gulick described boys as being essentially competitive and pugilistic, going so far as to say that "the desire to throw straight and hard" was an "instinctively masculine desire" that girls did not possess.[106] Johnson agreed, arguing that, because girls' ultimate destiny was motherhood and running and throwing were not key to their survival in the evolutionary past, athletics did not test their essential femininity as it did for boys' essential masculinity.[107] Unlike boys, whose fundamental instincts were thwarted by contemporary civilization, girls' domestic instincts were allowed expression through doll play and caring for younger children. Boys, therefore, were more in need of organized opportunities to enact their evolutionary requirement to compete and engage in supervised activities where their physical prowess could be on display.

Despite the belief among some reformers that girls suffered no lack of organized play, a girls' branch of the Public School Athletic League was established only two years after the formation of the parent organization. Even as she encouraged girls to exercise, the organization's head, Elizabeth Burchenal, was gravely concerned that girls be protected from the competitive and pugilistic nature of boys' athletics. She insisted that girls would never regard sports as the "breath of life," as many boys did, and that athletics for boys—but not for girls—was an inheritance of primitive pursuits. Athletics for boys embodied "fighting," but for girls the key was "fun."[108] In fact, the league banned individual and interschool competition for girls, which they thought might impair girls' delicate reproductive systems, and focused on dancing, gymnastics, swimming, and other sports deemed to be less detrimental to girls' bodies and psyches. Although by the 1920s women were beginning to gain some recognition for their participation in women's sports in college and adult athletic competitions, these exploits were viewed with suspicion, and much opposition to interschool athletic competition remained among parents and educators alike.[109] As with many other innovations for boys—boys' clubs, competitive athletics, camping, and the Boy Scouts—new ventures for girls followed in their wake but operated under very different premises. It rarely went the other way: activities developed for girls were not appropriated for boys.

Advocates for organized athletics similarly articulated a need to develop age-appropriate forms of competition. At the outset, competitive athletics was meant to be the province of young men. It was not until later that it would become a central component of the high school experience, in large part as a result of young men clamoring for a realm of their own. Many reformers believed that less competitive games were more appropriate for preadolescent boys, because their mental and physical bodies were still fragile, partially formed, and not up to the demands of more structured competition. In settlement houses reformers often noted that younger boys resisted rule-driven games, and in some cases the female leaders of boys' groups themselves believed in less organized forms of sports for preadolescent boys. In fact it was not until 1939 that the Little League for boys ten and over was established. By this time, the trend toward encouraging more competitive single-gender pursuits for young boys had taken hold. Nonetheless, although reformers of the late nineteenth and early twentieth centuries continued to champion gymnastics and other types of calisthenics for younger boys, they also took advantage of new sports such as basketball that could be casually enjoyed in a smaller urban environment.[110]

Neither playgrounds nor recreation centers were panaceas for the problems that urban boys faced, nor did they come close to bringing the majority of the city's inhabitants under their tutelage, as many studies showed. The new spaces, such as Chicago's gracious Lincoln Park and its beautiful beaches, became popular escapes for boys where truancy, street play, mischief, and fighting abounded. Yet the movement for organized recreation had a profound influence on the public discourse about delinquency. It imagined play and recreation as central to children's lives and viewed the lack of opportunities for wholesome and organized play as central to delinquency. Rather than viewing "badness" and incorrigibility as inherent in degenerate children, spokespersons for the movement placed the onus on society for failing to afford children the proper conditions for developing both morally and physically.

There were some striking paradoxes in the effort to reform boys by accessing boy nature. In catering to the boys' peer culture, reformers often set up arenas for the demonstration of some of the more damaging demonstrations of masculinity. These spaces were moreover often used to avoid school and engage in delinquencies that had previously been performed in other spaces. Although recreation enthusiasts frequently insisted on the need for diligent recreation supervisors, when money was an issue, they were one of the first things to go. The boys' clubs, recreation centers, parks, and playgrounds designed by reformers to protect and guide boys often became the sites of conflicts and even violence around gender, age, class, race, and ethnicity. Although reformers envisioned recreation as a means of overcoming national antipathies, noting how "a Russian Jew, a Frenchman, a Swede, and an Irishman" had joined a local basketball team, African Americans were notably absent from these activities, and many athletic clubs divided along ethnic and religious lines.[111] Recreation enthusiast Joseph Lee observed that, when athletic games were not monitored carefully by adults, they could easily lead into "neighborhood jealousies, race prejudice, mob violence, perhaps wars" because of the excitable emotions that were stimulated by intense physical activity.[112]

Conflicts at parks and playgrounds frequently centered on ethnicity, neighborhood, religion, and race. For instance, historian Steven Riess tells the story of a group of Jewish boys playing ball in Chicago's Douglas Park—located in an area that straddled the Jewish North Lawndale neighborhood and the Polish West Side—who were attacked by thirty Polish boys on a particularly hot day in 1921.[113] Ethnic groups often clashed, but when African Americans started to move into neighborhoods that either housed or bordered on enclaves of European immigrants, the clashes grew more violent and at times escalated into riots. There were few playgrounds or recreation centers in predominantly African American neighborhoods; most such spaces were in the borderlands, but significant barriers kept African Americans from crossing into them. Some public swimming pools were apparently more welcoming: at Chicago's Union Park Pool, for instance, it was said that up to 40 percent of the swimmers were African American during the 1910s. But although small children were likely to intermingle in the same waters, black and white adolescents and grown-ups swam in separate parts of the pool.[114]

In a report on "colored school children" in New York, authored in 1915, the writers documented the poor recreational opportunities available to African American children in neighborhoods such as Harlem. Of the many recreation centers in New York, virtually none were located in African American areas of the city, and the white ethnics who attended those that were in the borderland areas, such as St. Cyprian's Parish House, were opposed to including black members. Some recreation directors wished to make their centers inclusive spaces, but their constituencies of white male youth were powerful forces in denying entry to nonwhite members. Some directors did not want "trouble," arguing that having separate spaces for African Americans was the only way to secure equity, while others seemed rather naïve in wondering why the African Americans who lived just a few blocks away neglected to use their facilities.[115]

There were practical obstacles to providing recreation for African Americans as well. Because organizations like the New York Public School Athletic League required dues, few youth could afford to participate. Others were dissuaded from participating because of a race riot at a nearby high school. Children, both boys and girls, tended to avoid the clubs provided for them either because they were too busy helping at home or earning wages. Other parents objected to their children traversing the streets at night to attend clubs, especially if they had to walk through dangerous neighborhoods to attend. Not only were African American communities denied access to existing resources but those that were available seemed to have been designed without careful attention to community needs.[116]

Chicago, which had strenuously sought to provide public recreational activities for young and old alike in the form of parks and beaches, demonstrated most vividly the contests over recreation in the form of the disastrous Chicago Race Riot in 1919. Only the Twenty-Fifth Street Beach on the South Side was designated for African Americans, whose population had grown during the Great Migration and who competed for jobs and housing with the Irish, Poles, and Italians, especially in the stockyard district just west of the South Side. Although Chicago did not legally segregate public recreation, one beach that independent observers described as "narrow, limited, and unattractive" had been reserved for African Americans by Chicago's ethnic athletic clubs for young men, who informally policed the recreation centers, beaches, and neighborhoods.[117] African American teenager Eugene Williams and his friends had built a raft to float about in the waters beyond Twenty-Fifth Street, into so-called white waters, unaware of rising racial unrest caused by the presence of several African Americans on the Twenty-Ninth Street Beach. After a white man systematically hurled rocks at the floating teens, who were not expert swimmers, he finally hit and dislodged Williams from the raft. He subsequently drowned.[118] Once reports that the youth was dead traveled to the black beach, African Americans requested that the man who had thrown the rocks be arrested. When the policeman refused, African Americans retaliated with violence, immediately after which Chicago's worst ethnic gangs went on a rampage that, in its wake, left twenty-three African-Americans and fourteen whites dead and dozens of businesses and homes burned and vandalized.

After the disastrous occurrence, the city charged a commission with a fact-finding report designed to survey the state of race relations in the city. The report is noteworthy in what it tells us about the state of segregated recreation prior to the riot. The Armour Square Park, located in what was by all accounts a borderland area three miles south of the city's central Loop, with a high concentration of Italians whose turf was being encroached upon by the expanding African American population, seemed to be one of the hot spots in the city. It had one of the best recreation centers in the area, with a pool, showers, and gymnasium. In 1913 a secretary of the Wabash YMCA brought nineteen African American boys there, where they played a few games and then took showers in the field house. While they had been showering, a crowd of white boys amassed outside. When the African American youngsters began to exit the building they were "assailed with sandbags, tripped, walked over, and some were badly bruised." They took refuge in local saloons and houses and were only able to walk home after the police had been called in. In 1915, an Episcopalian priest tried again to bring a group of African American YMCA youth to the center to play basketball, but both the youths and the priest were beaten up on the way home. White gangs similarly terrorized African American youth in Ogden Park in 1914 when they made use of the showers. Even the director of the center was beaten with brass knuckles by one of the angry youth, and though the offender was brought into court, he got off with no more than a reprimand. There were other incidents less violent but equally damaging to the boys' sense of self, for instance when white boys refused to wrestle with African American boys in the clubs or when directors denied African American boys the use of showers or permits to play baseball. These ongoing acts of discrimination and terrorism meant that African American parents were reluctant to allow their children to go to playgrounds and recreation centers in borderland areas, even when directors made special efforts to publicize their activities to the community.

These contests over recreation left a significant gendered blueprint. If gangs of white youth were apt to demonstrate their masculinity and ethnic consciousness by policing the boundaries of white space, then African American youth would also seek to demonstrate their masculinity by defending their own turf, taking a stand against the forces that would seek to constrain their recreational opportunities and abilities to move through public space. Paradoxically, these sites of recreation, meant to revitalize and curtail the excesses of boys' masculinity, became the venues for the expression of a form of hypermasculinity that defined itself through the control of space at the expense of those of different ages, genders, ethnicities, and races. The ability to move through public space freely, without harassment, was one of the hallmarks of boys' emerging masculinity, a characteristic shared by adolescent boy cultures of virtually all racial and ethnic groups. In 1922, when the report on the Chicago Race Riot was released, it was noted that organized gangs were the province of white ethnics, rather than blacks.[119] Eventually African American youth would also bond around their race and masculine identities by forming groups and gangs that were premised on their right to counter violence with violence and to protect their right to access public space. Although the recreation movement surely enhanced opportunities for some youth, it paradoxically had the potential to exacerbate the ethnic and racial components of the boy problem.

CHAPTER 3

The Perils of Public Education
Truants, Underachievers, and School Leavers

In 1905, Frederick, a destitute ten-year-old likely of German parentage, was committed by the juvenile court to the Chicago Parental School, a residential institution run by the board of education for truant and incorrigible boys. His second-grade teacher described him as bright and well behaved; her only complaint was that he always lagged behind the others because he never came to class. When asked what he did instead of going to school, the boy eagerly detailed his adventures: "I jumped the cars with other boys. I used to catch a freight and ride way out. I used to go down on S. Water after bananas. Then I used to go down to see the stores. I know where Siegel Coopers, The Fairs, and the 5 & 10 cant [sic] stores are. Sometimes we would catch a trailer and go out to Lincoln Park to see the animals and go swimming."[1]

Frederick's story was not uncommon, and it challenges the assumption that the only reason youth did not attend schools was so they could work. Urban neighborhoods spawned vibrant peer cultures of boys whose adventurous exploits helped to counter the deprivation and poverty that some experienced at home. Frederick, for instance, shared a basement tenement flat with five other children and had already lost three of his siblings to death. Urban schools could be dismal, overcrowded places, where drills and boring recitations were the bill of fare.[2] Although some truants engaged in petty thievery and other unlawful activities, other male youngsters engaged in activities that might otherwise be respectable if they were not required to be at school. A variety of pleasures, including visiting consumption palaces such as the Siegel-Cooper department store, hitching free (if unlawful) rides on streetcars and freight trains, and peering at the animals in public zoos ultimately proved more tantalizing than school for some youngsters.[3] Although better-off Jewish families often made valiant efforts to ensure that their sons at least attended primary school, even if they were yanked by their shirt cuffs by their older brothers to school, some poor parents, whether native born or ethnic, were not as convinced of the virtues of public education. Their efforts to ensure compliance may not have been as vigilant, even when their children's contribution to the family economy was minimal or nonexistent.[4] Perhaps this was the case with Frederick, whose mother simply told the truant officer, "I could not make Frederick go to school."[5]

Compulsory education was one strand of a much larger program of Progressive Era reform that sought to bring the strong hand of the state to bear on the social problems that were enveloping the nation in an era of immigration, urbanization, and poverty. Education was seen as an arena where science and morality might combine to transform ignorant and unsocialized poor and working-class children into upstanding and productive citizens. Education reformers increasingly believed that advanced schooling was central to preparing youth for citizenship and participation in a modernizing society. This "civic socialization," as Michael Olnek terms it, was central to the project of assimilation and integrating new immigrants into republican citizenship.[6] Recreation and boys' clubs were purely voluntary affairs, yet both child labor and compulsory schooling laws increasingly sought through legal means to ensure that children spent most of their days in school. As schools became more accountable for producing educated children, nonattendance, grade retardation, and school leaving became significant policy issues for all children, especially boys.

The "boy problem" in public education seemed a real and potent peril at the turn of the century, and not just for the street arabs and urchins who continued to be a visible presence on the city streets. Dramatic publications emphasized, then as now, that even upper-working- and middle-class boys were at risk, although the bold print of book headlines, such as Leonard Ayres' *Laggards in Our Midst* (1909), obscured the ethnic, economic, and racial variables that underlay the disturbing statistics. Ayres's book dramatized the plight of boys in general, who were 13 percent more likely to be behind in grade and 17 percent less likely to complete high school than girls.[7] Similarly, renowned educational psychologist Edward Thorndike reported for the U.S. Commissioner of Education in 1917 that girls were more likely than boys, by a significant margin, to enter and graduate from city high schools.[8] Many reformers, including Ayres, attributed boys' learning problems to the schools themselves rather to boys' biological deficiencies. In an italicized conclusion, he intoned, "*These facts mean that our schools as present constituted are far better fitted to the needs of the girls than they are of the boys.*"[9] In an age when men were deemed intellectually superior and more fit to run the country, the data appeared devastating. Several historians have shown how the "fear of feminization" spurred an elaborate debate about the inadequacies of public schools for boys.[10]

At issue in some of these debates was the question of whether schools were adequately equipped to deal with "boy nature." Many educators assumed that, if even native-born middle-class boys were faltering in school, then something must be wrong with the system itself.[11] The fear of feminization and the boy problem were two sides of the same coin, with some commentators worrying that female success would come at the expense of boys. Psychologist and child study advocate Earl Barnes, among others, worried about the repercussions of feminization in the halls of academe, journalism, and even society itself in an essay for the *Atlantic Monthly* entitled "The Feminizing of Culture" (1912). Barnes observed that it was "inevitable that women should invade fields where formerly only men were found," especially journalism, education, and the arts, where their "emotional" and "child-like" sensibilities threatened to trivialize American culture. He offered statistics not only about the rising rates of women attending high school but also about their increasing attendance at postsecondary institutions, which had once been masculine preserves. For Barnes and others, the most worrisome statistic was that of the rising numbers of women teachers. Driven by the need to save wages, big cities increasingly hired women teachers, so that, by the second decade of the twentieth century, women made up almost 90 percent of urban teaching staff. Barnes asked his readers to consider the potential political implications of this trend: "Does it not seem strange to bring up boys and girls, who are to be the future citizens of a democracy, under the exclusive leadership of people who have never been encouraged to think about political life or allowed to participate in it?"[12] How could women teachers instill in students—especially boys, who would eventually obtain the franchise—the skills and attributes deemed necessary for a successful democracy? The very future of American political institutions seemed to be at stake.

Barring such hyperbole and sexist rants about the problems of female teachers, there *were* larger numbers of girls than boys attending high school at the turn of the century, although only about 10 percent of American youth attended high school at all.[13] Aside from a growing if limited trend toward educational equity for girls, girls seemed—quite simply—to gain more advantage by attending high school than did boys. Before the 1930s, boys could receive on-the-job training in many types of economic enterprises, while girls who sought remunerative labor other than domestic service, dress making, or millinery, required education to become a teacher or secretary.[14] Most ethnic bad boys, in contrast, did not even conceive of going to high school at the beginning of the century; just getting them through grade school was a challenge. For instance, in its study of thirty-seven cities in 1907, the Dillingham Commission found that only 1 percent of immigrant youth went to high school, compared to 9.1 percent of the children of native-born white fathers.[15]

The solutions reformers devised to entice boys and their parents into schools relied on the same sorts of assumptions about boy nature that animated earlier attempts to redeem potential juvenile delinquents. Psychologist G. Stanley Hall and his legions of supporters chastised modern educators for attempting to stamp out boys' natural instincts through artificial methods of education, thereby contributing to behavioral problems and academic failures. Hall contended that the "progressive feralization of boys, the growing hoodlumism, etc., which all admit and complain of, is directly connected with the feminization chiefly of the school."[16] Many reformers and educators agreed schools were churning out truants and delinquents by failing to take the nature and needs of boys into consideration.[17] Boys, it was argued, needed to exercise their talents in productive ways if they were to regain the sense of accomplishment provided by work. Manual and vocational education methods—long the schooling of choice for predelinquent and delinquent boys—were championed in part because they promised to remediate the gender gap in public education at the turn of the century. School athletics and other extracurricular activities came to be seen as significant enhancements to facilitate boys' greater engagement with the high school curriculum and build loyalties that would stem their exodus from school.[18]

Because truancy and noncompletion of school were problems experienced by both middle- and working-class boys alike, many of the solutions to these issues advanced in urban education served multiple constituencies. One innovation was "limited segregation" of boys and girls. In 1904, J. E. Armstrong constructed a segregated secondary education system at Englewood High in Chicago that was specifically focused on alleviating the boy problem. Here, subjects could be geared toward the different tastes and inclinations of boys and girls, with a greater emphasis on science and mathematics for boys. Girls' scores declined relative to boys', and the program was shut down when Ella Flagg Young took over the superintendency in 1910, in part because girls and their parents objected.[19] The city of Los Angeles was more successful in attracting boys to high school by erecting a new polytechnic high school in 1904 that offered majors that funneled students into engineering, chemistry, and science programs at the university and immediately attracted a student body that was more than 50 percent male.[20] New technical schools like this one, which attracted both working- and middle-class students, enhanced the prospects of talented boys, while perpetuating the idea that these scientific subjects were particularly well suited to males.

One factor that was overlooked in much of this commentary was the geographic variability of the so-called boy problem. Insofar as the boy problem was presented as universal, it detracted attention from the very real differences in the prospects of boys from different places and racial and ethnic groups. F. E. De Yoe and C. H. Thurber reported that in 1897 boys constituted 42.36 percent of the high school population nationally but only 34 percent in Boston and 35 percent in St. Louis.[21] These numbers hid distinct ethnic, racial, and regional differences as well, as historian Joel Perlmann and others have shown. In some Italian and Eastern European Jewish communities, for instance, girls were less likely to attend high school than their male peers both because their families viewed extended education as wasted on future homemakers and because they hoped that their daughters would contribute to the family economy through household labor or as wage workers in manufacturing.[22] In Chicago's heavily Eastern European immigrant stockyard district, girls were less behind in grade than boys, according to a 1911 report, but were also less likely to complete the eighth grade, despite the fact that boys had access to better employment opportunities. The same report showed that in Boston, African American boys and girls were about equally likely to enter high school, but in Chicago black girls were twice as likely as black boys to attend high school.[23] It was not gender alone but rather the intersections of gender with race, class, ethnicity, and geography that did most to explain differences in children's participation in public education.

In spite of the turn-of-the-century worries about school avoidance, the rapid entrance of students into high school during the early twentieth century was startling. Whereas only 10 percent of American students completed high school in 1910, in the next three decades the figure would rise to 51 percent. As economic historian Claudia Goldin and others have demonstrated, the main reason for this shift was economic; more and more jobs required a high school education. As a more diverse student population attended high schools, they increasingly became differentiated by class, race, intelligence, and gender.[24] Making education more relevant to kids with a palpable distaste for ordinary schooling was undoubtedly one of the aims of reformers who sought to cajole or coerce these children into the schools. But, no matter how many innovations were put in place, reformers of the city were lucky if some of their most difficult boys attended school at all.

Truancy and Compulsory Education

By the turn of the century, most large Northern and Midwestern cities had passed legislation requiring school attendance to age fourteen, yet, in cities such as New York, Detroit, and Chicago, boys, especially those ages ten and over, could often be found hanging about the street rather than going to school. When Jacob Riis, in 1905, chanced upon three "dirty and tough" boys sitting on a beer keg playing cards in a New York City alley at eleven in the morning, their feet "nearly black with dried mud," he got varied answers to the question of why they were not in school. A thirteen-year-old said merely that he did not believe in it, while another child claimed that the schools did not want him because he had no shoes.[25] Was it poverty, cultural differences, or the appeal of the street that kept kids under the age of fourteen out of school? In some cases, it was all of the above.

In 1900, graduating from eighth grade itself was an accomplishment, worthy of a new fancy outfit and a lavish party.[26] As the century progressed, however, more and more children enrolled in elementary school. But, even while elementary schools were expanding and the numbers in school continued to increase, as children passed through the grades there was a decline in attendance that began during what were termed the "grammar school" years (now typically "middle school") from the fifth through the eighth grades. In most cities, grades one through three were fairly well attended. After that, the numbers started to drop, at first gradually, and then precipitously, just before high school. This phenomenon may be explained in part by a larger proportion of younger children in the population, but it is clear that many children stopped going to school as they grew older. In the Chicago of 1911, for example, where two-thirds of the pupils were the children of immigrants, 32,770 children were enrolled in third grade but only 17,940 made it to seventh grade.[27] In New York City, the largest school district in the nation, nearly three-quarters of students were either immigrants or the children of immigrants. The district enrolled 574,655, but of that total number only 2,305 were currently in high school. The slide in attendance started much earlier than high school, however, for, while there were there were 86,841 first graders, there were only half as many seventh graders.[28] In Cleveland and Detroit, smaller cities that also had ethnic majorities in the public schools, the slide was not as pronounced, although a significant drop emerged by seventh grade.[29]

The reasons for the grammar school slide went beyond the expectation that working-class and immigrant children above age ten should contribute to the family wage economy. Regular attendance at school was an ethos that educators sought to inculcate, but in reality many families were not convinced. When barriers to schooling appeared, therefore, families were less likely to force the issue. One factor appears to be the very high percentages of children who were overage for their grade—a factor that contributed to youth's disenchantment with school. Ayres pointed out that a whopping 33 percent of American children were overage for their grade in school, suggesting that the age-grading system that had been introduced in the nineteenth century was far from perfect.[30] How could it be, in school systems where more than 50 percent of the students were immigrants or the children of immigrants and unaccustomed to the demands of the American public schools? The numbers of children behind in grade generally climbed as students approached fifth grade, which makes sense given the greater difficulty of material encountered, the importance of English-language competency, and the increase in autonomy that enabled boys especially to skip school and fall behind in their studies. Immigrants, the children of immigrants, and African American migrants were the most likely to be identified as what educators of the time termed "retarded," or not up the grade level for their age. In Chicago, 42 percent of children in the grammar school grades were judged to be overage, but the figures for Poles, Italians, and Slovaks ranged from 65 to 74 percent. Obviously, these figures put youth from these ethnic groups especially at risk for difficulties both in and outside of school.[31] Few older boys would have enjoyed mingling with and being forced to read subject matter appealing to third graders.

Even though attendance was generally required up to age fourteen, in many cities youth could get exemption certificates if they could prove they were employed. In spite of the onslaught of images bespeaking the pitiable condition of children who labored, some adolescents and perhaps even younger children preferred working to school. In 1913 factory inspector Helen Todd conducted a study of 500 child laborers from ages fourteen to seventeen and was astonished to learn that 412 would rather be employed than go to school. The youth complained that teachers were more punitive than their employers, often slapping and pinching their ears, and that other students called them "Dago" and other ethnic epithets. They also received better treatment from their families when they brought home good wages than when they brought home good grades—or worse, bad grades, which could earn them a beating. Some youth suggested that it was much easier to understand and follow the factory's rules than the school's. Through the money they earned, youth could satisfy not only their parents but themselves, by purchasing a new hat or a ticket to the nickel show.[32] Those over fourteen could work without a permit, but the example they set for their younger siblings might have contributed to the perception of school as a waste of time.

Child labor campaigns increasingly portrayed even boys as "vulnerable" children, whose nurture required schooling rather than labor, and child labor laws increasingly restricted the ability of even willing boys to work.[33] Yet such campaigns often overlooked the inherent meaning that work possessed for at least some boys. Intended to invoke pity, the famous photographs by Lewis Hine for the National Child Labor Committee in the early 1900s include many pictures of besooted and ragged boy miners, glass blowers, and factory workers. Yet the images are complex. Boy workers were often displayed in groups of their peers, evoking a sense of the boys' camaraderie, shrewdness, and even pride. It is clear that, for at least some laboring boys, work was not only necessary but fulfilling. Schools, in contrast, appeared to enforce passivity and erode more traditional forms of adolescent belonging, autonomy, and passages into adulthood. Thus reformers sought not only to discourage child labor and make school attendance mandatory but also to transform the curriculum so that it would be more relevant and appealing to an increasingly diverse student population.

Gender, Ethnicity, and Truancy

One of the biggest changes in schooling from the nineteenth into the twentieth century was not necessarily that more students liked school (although they may have) but that they and their parents grew to understand that children were required and expected to go to school—that school was their job. Compulsory education statutes, which included the prosecution of individual truants and their parents, were not the sole cause of this shift. The decreasing need for child laborers went hand in hand with a shift toward a view of childhood that was at once more and less demanding. On the one hand, it sought to protect children from abusive treatment and such responsibilities of adulthood as gainful employment; on the other, children's lives became increasingly regimented through longer school years, a more stringent attendance regime, and more organized recreation. Younger child laborers tended to engage in work that was fairly unregimented, with free time interspersed between such money-making activities as selling newspapers, shining shoes, or peddling various types of wares on the street.[34] School attendance was far more sporadic in the nineteenth century, when farm labor was cyclical, laws stipulated that children needed to attend only part of the school year, and parents were accustomed to keeping their children out of school for any number of reasons.[35] For children who did not labor in factories, routine school attendance offered a regimentation of childhood that was bound to instigate resistance.

In 1885, a St. Louis high school principal even celebrated occasional truancy for boys: "the boy who never played hookey during his school days is hard to find, for the reason that somehow or another the goody-goody boys all die young and the teachers' pets never seem to pan out into anything remarkable." The two seasons of highest truancy were when the circus came to town and when the hot sun made boys itch to hit the swimming hole. Girls, he claimed, were far less likely to be truant from home and, when they did, were unlikely to be punished. But for boys, he proposed the rattan, especially for those manly fellows who take a whipping in "a manner that makes him the pride of his fellows." Moral suasion was also a powerful force, but the "incorrigibles we get rid of."[36] Although truants could be disciplined, boys who disrupted the classroom routines and challenged teachers' authority—what the principal deemed "incorrigible"—would be excluded. But, as schools faced increasing regimentation and the growing demand that they teach all children, including those most difficult to educate, the principal's premises about the normalcy of truancy, as well as the ease of eliminating incorrigibles, began to break down.

Even with these new demands, however, there still lingered an image of the truant as an archetype of the "real" boy who—like Huck Finn—found more adventure and excitement in exploring the outdoors than the stuffy atmosphere of the schools.[37] This sensibility could be found even in observations of tenement boys. In his preface to a study on truancy in the tenement districts of Chicago in 1905, Chester Sherman Carney claimed that the hero of his study was a "barefoot boy" who has "knowledge never learned in school."[38] Carney, like many others, argued that the gist of the problem lay in the fact that the schools were not adequately equipped to teach growing boys: "one wonders how long it will be till the school will make its studies fit the children, and cease making truants and delinquents in the attempt to pare down and warp boy nature to fit its curriculum."[39] Truancy and delinquency, then, were the end result of a system that sought to foist methods of learning that were out of step with boys' proclivities.

The characteristics ascribed to boys by various students of boy nature put boys at odds with many of the premises of the public school. Truancy was understandable, in part, because boys were naturally averse to being sequestered indoors under the rule of prissy female teachers. School playgrounds and recess were thought to preserve children's health and to allow them to "blow off steam" after long hours of sitting still and learning meaningless facts. But when did playful truancy, a developmental characteristic of boys whose adventurous spirit led them to spurn the repressive atmosphere of the public schools, turn into something more insidious, dangerous even? And what was the difference between the normal mischievous boy who occasionally played hookey and the incorrigibles who were commonly expelled from public schools in the nineteenth century? What should be done about the overage boys who intimidated their classmates with their scornful and sometimes hostile presence? In constructing systems of compulsory education in urban areas, educators worked on two fronts to keep boys in school: first, by constructing a general curriculum that was more appealing to the average working-class boy, and, second, by creating separate systems of instruction for the schooling-averse bad boys and the slower learners who tried the patience and abilities of exhausted teachers. Yet reformers also confronted the interesting paradox that many of the boys who ended up in these special programs were not all that different from the regular boy; indeed, part of what made them bad was what was most boyish about them.

Most educators differentiated, however, between truancy and nonattendance. Truancy was defined as willful absence from school for which no legitimate excuse could be found. Both truancy and incorrigibility were criminal infractions in many places, and mainly boys were charged with these crimes. Boys were accustomed to frequenting public spaces for casual work, leisure, socialization, and petty crime, making it more difficult for them to skirt apprehension by police and truant officers.[40] Because girls frequently excused themselves from school on the grounds of illness or caring for family members, they were rarely characterized as truants, even when their rates of nonattendance were similar to that of boys. Consider the situation in Chicago during the 1913–1914 school year. Roughly the same numbers of boys and girls attended the Chicago public schools, yet, of the 499 children brought before the Chicago Juvenile Court on charges of truancy, only three were girls.[41] Philadelphia's truancy figures were similarly lopsided: in 1925, boys and girls had similar rates of nonattendance, but boys declared to be truant outnumbered girls by eight to one.[42]

Reports abounded that children skipped school because they were working, but reformers also probed for explanations for the many children who neither labored with any consistency nor attended school full time. They found differences between different ethnic groups, with Italians being the most suspicious of public schools and Poles a close second. Although many Jewish families valued education, Russian immigrants were the most poverty stricken and therefore most likely to keep their children working until their families could make ends meet. Sociologist Clifford Shaw and his followers mapped "delinquency areas" of Chicago that spawned truancy and other social problems. In areas of the city such as the heavily immigrant West Side, they claimed, boys' peer groups and gangs supplied forms of belonging and adventure that were lacking at home and at school. Recreation enthusiasts, as we have seen, argued that youth whose need for adventure and excitement was not met by school and society would find other illicit means of seeking pleasure. If social institutions such as public schools were to transform incipient criminals into upstanding citizens, they needed to address these basic psychological issues.[43]

On the street, oppositional boy cultures cultivated disrespect for all forms of authority, including school. In their encounters with their peers outside of the gaze of parents and teachers, boys could demonstrate their incipient masculinity through physical prowess, cunning, and brazen defiance of authority, qualities that were unappreciated in public school.[44] When boys defied their teachers, failed to do their work, or merely demonstrated incompetence, they invited raps on knuckles, trips to the principal, beatings, and public humiliation. In contrast, good students were likely to be taunted as sissies by the tough boys for their deference to the school regime.[45]

One young member of a Chicago gang evinced a common sentiment when he scorned a neighborhood boy who proudly showed off his graduation clothes upon finishing eighth grade: "just because he's graduated today, he thinks his shit don't stink; when I graduated last year, I didn't go around like that all day; I went right home and put on my old clothes, graduatin' didn't mean nothin' to me."[46] Perhaps there was some defensiveness in the student's refusal to acknowledge graduation as a rite of passage. But it was a badge of honor, at least in some quarters, to refuse deference to the school's authority and to look to sources closer to home for self-validation.

Many immigrant parents found American schools to be hostile territory, places where teachers trampled on their authority as parents and urged habits and behaviors that were odd, unsettling, or even immoral. Sending a child to be schooled and socialized by strangers requires a good bit of trust—trust that many immigrant families did not yet have. Without this trust, students were less likely to view the school's authority as legitimate, which contributed to more pronounced truancy and disciplinary problems.[47] Parochial schools that simultaneously modernized and preserved some cultural traditions were one solution, but they too struggled to maintain order and compel regular attendance. Even though Polish children often attended parochial schools that maintained the Polish language and culture, for instance, their distaste for schooling was similar to that of many of their public school peers. They watched their adult male relatives gain success through politics and good working-class jobs, whether or not they had received even the most rudimentary of educations. In her discussion of Polish immigrants in Chicago, historian Kathryn Neckerman points out, "Within the working-class immigrant communities, people did not gain status from displays of education and high culture—quite the contrary."[48]

Immigrant parents clearly displayed ambivalence toward the forms of education being promoted in modern American schools. In his eloquent book entitled *Learning to Forget*, historian Steven Lassonde concludes that American schooling intervened in the traditional path to adulthood valued by parents in the largely

Italian working-class community of New Haven in the early twentieth century.[49] Although the push to get more and more children into high school eventually helped transform European ethnics into full-blown American whites, there were numerous stumbling blocks, and truancy, discipline, and early school leaving remained daunting problems.[50] Many immigrant children found a pathway to success through the American schools, as is testified to by the many memoirs testifying to the positive impact of New York's public education system. But others considered school to be alien territory where they were unfairly demeaned by other students and teachers because of their ethnic backgrounds. Actor Harpo Marx recalled that he finished his schooling at second grade because, as the only Jewish child in his New York City classroom, he was taunted by the Irish kids, one of whom threw him out of the window. Even his teacher pronounced that he would come "to no good end."[51] Anthony Sorrentino, who migrated from Sicily to Chicago's West Side as a six-year-old and later become an organizer for a Chicago delinquency prevention program, recalled his first foray outside of the Italian ghetto via the Andrew Jackson Elementary School, which he experienced as a "strange, disturbing world," complete with "rigid-looking teachers" and a punitive principal.[52] For these and many other ethnic male school leavers, walking out on school and forging a different way of life could be not only a form of resistance but also a form of self-preservation.

There were, of course, some immigrant parents who wanted their children to attend school but despaired of making them go. In Chicago, Mrs. B. claimed that she once (in 1937) kept her three boys—ages eight, nine, and eleven—out of school because they had no shoes. She also admitted, however, that she could not keep them in school even after they got shoes from the settlement and that they ran the streets until ten or eleven every night, ducking into shows, stealing apples from stores, and getting into all kinds of mischief.[53] Mrs. B. considered herself helpless to enforce the mandate of compulsory education in the face of her sons' resistance to the school regimen.

Parental Schools

For children who simply refused to complete their "jailhouse term," reformers invented a new form of schooling, which they called "parental schools": residential institutions for truant and troublesome boys. Straddling the fence between the prison and the schoolhouse, these institutions were first established in the late nineteenth and early twentieth centuries, mainly in cities where immigrants and their children were becoming majorities in the public schools. Due in part to the fact that more restrictive compulsory education laws were passed, some states passed complementary ordinances to establish special boarding schools for truants and incorrigibles run by the public schools.[54] Parental schools were intermediary spaces between public schools and reformatories for those boys whose infractions, ranging from truancy to vandalism and aggression, were troublesome but did not quite meet the standard for commitment to a penal institution.[55] States that were serious about making attendance a reality viewed these institutions as part and parcel of their plan to coerce all children under the cutoff age into school or an otherwise appropriate institution. Sociologist John G. Richardson contends that although parental schools had much in common with reformatories, they went further to "promote the inclusion of 'juvenile disorderly youth'" within the boundaries of the urban school.[56] Arising in tandem with the juvenile court movement, which sought to bring a more paternalistic perspective to youthful delinquencies, reformers sought (less than successfully) to give life to the concept of the state as more of a parent than a policeman.

Some smaller girls' parental schools were eventually erected, but parental schools were mostly focused on boys, and many of their practices reflected gendered premises about what was best for troubled youth. The gender-specific solutions to boys' academic difficulties, including single-sex schooling and employment of male teachers, that were subjects of debate in the public schools, were prevalent in parental schools: all-boy classes, boy-friendly subject material, and, when possible, male teachers of the "he-man" type who could maintain order and model masculinity.[57] And although using manual and vocational education to entice boys into school was the subject of vigorous debate in the larger educational world, in parental schools the assumption was that these bad boys could not learn without this type of concrete subject material. In parental schools, reformers aimed to provide boys with legitimate outlets for aggression, excess physical energy, and the instinct to form organized peer groups such as gangs. Because, in many cases, boys were actually committed to the parental school, there was often little that differentiated it from a reformatory. Because of their close connection with the juvenile justice system and their residential character, parental schools can be differentiated from special education, which was firmly ensconced within the boundaries of the regular public schools.

Parental schools have barely been mentioned in most histories of education, but they were a noteworthy reform in large cities in the early twentieth century and widely discussed in educational publications as a key delinquency-prevention and school-compliance strategy. By 1915, a survey conducted for the U.S. Commission on Education by James Hiatt found that thirteen city school districts, including many of the largest cities in the Northeast, Midwest, and West, had residential schools for truant and incorrigible boys, and some more than one. By 1930, twenty-four urban school districts housed parental schools.[58] Most of the schools were in larger cities, including Cleveland, Baltimore, Chicago, Los Angeles, New York, Seattle, Cincinnati, Philadelphia, Detroit, and St. Louis. The schools never enrolled a high percentage of any district's boys, but their presence was certainly felt by many truant boys and their families, if only because the threat of the parental school was used to induce school attendance.

One of the last remaining parental schools was Chicago's, which did not close its doors until the 1970s. Dan O'Connell, who lived near the school, remembered his mother warning him every time he drove by the facility in the 1950s, "That's where you'll go if you don't go to school." Using the school as both threat and consequence, teachers, truant officers, police, and even parents played a role in facilitating boys' placements in correctional institutions such as the parental school. In other words, these institutions served not only the state but also parents who sought a stronger arm with which to discipline their sons. In fact, parental schools held out the love of family as a powerful coercive strategy to get boys to toe the line in the institution so that they could be rehabilitated and returned home. The school was far from parental in its treatment of its inhabitants, but perhaps the term *parental school* referred to the fact that it was meant to step in for parents who were unable or unwilling to control unruly boys.

The first parental school was instituted in Boston in 1895 and housed about eighty boys, over 60 percent of them children of immigrant parents.[59] As early as 1850, before schooling was compulsory, Boston had passed an ordinance that permitted courts to institutionalize boys who did not work or attend school and subsequently appointed truant officers to enforce the legislation.[60] Although the law was widely ignored, some truants were kept in almshouses or local jails, including the notorious Deer Island, where the state's most dangerous delinquents lodged. Educators argued forcefully for a complete separation between truants and other juvenile criminals. The Massachusetts secretary of education urged the construction of special facilities that would be termed "parental schools," to make clear the redemptive aspect of the new institutions. The name stuck, and in what would come to seem ironic, the parental school label would be adopted in subsequent institutions, long after the Boston experiment had been abandoned.[61]

In keeping with predominant nineteenth-century conceptions of boy nature, reformers intended the new Boston facility to have recreational facilities where boys could develop their bodies and characters through athletics. Yet there were objections that the school would be too expensive and that an institution with swimming pools and gymnasiums would do more to attract than deter young troublemakers. So even while reformers sought to make the institution more humane and suited to youngsters who had been guilty of only minor infractions, they attempted to assuage the public by emphasizing equally the punitive dimension of the new institution: "We do not wish to make the school too attractive, but to have confinement here made to be a penalty. The boys should be compelled to do unceasing work of body and mind from the moment they enter, and up to the full limit of their strength. It ought to be the aim to make their coming here a dread to them."[62] Drawing on criminal justice metaphors and practices, the school relied on punishment as a deterrence to make boys learn and behave. Boys did, indeed, dread the possibility of being committed to what they colloquially called the "bad boys school"—a phrase that was used to describe parental schools wherever they were founded.

Despite reformers' optimism, the Massachusetts Parental School was a short-lived facility, lasting only fourteen years. During that time it experienced overcrowding, inadequate resources, high rates of recidivism, and concerns about certain "immoral practices" among the boys. The Massachusetts legislature, once unhappy with the confinement of truants at Deer Island, decided that institutionalization should be a last resort and opened instead the new Boston Disciplinary Day School for truants and incorrigibles in 1915.[63]

Chicago, known for its innovative approaches to child welfare, housed one of the first parental schools.[64] Child savers, including women's club and settlement house workers such as Jane Addams, not only succeeded in establishing Chicago's pioneering juvenile court in 1899, but they agitated for and won stricter compulsory education laws and legislation enabling the city to establish parental schools for children who resisted attending school in that very same year.[65] Reformers argued that it would be impossible to enforce compulsory education laws without provision of a residential facility for the "lawless," "undisciplined," and "vagrant" children who either evaded school or disrupted the regular classroom.[66] In 1905, Illinois enlarged its delinquency law to include roaming the streets at all hours of the night, idleness, and obscene language. "With this sweeping definition," according to historian Joan Gittens, "the legislators demonstrated that they were determined to bring all troubled children of the state within the sway of the state."[67] Parental schools offered a means to rehabilitate boys during the course of their commitment—typically lasting between six months and two years—through tough discipline, enforced schooling, and moral instruction. At the very least, the fear of being sent back might be a deterrent to future delinquent activities.

When it opened its doors to truant and incorrigible boys in 1902, the average

age of a youngster committed to the Chicago Parental School was ten and a half, but reformers could not keep them once they reached the age of fourteen and were no longer required to attend school. This young age seems startling to contemporary sensibilities but reflects historical differences in how persons in the earlier part of the century viewed younger boys and the utility of institutions for reforming them. Holding firm to the belief that it was possible to redeem younger boys before they became confirmed delinquents, many were convinced that institutions, rather than families, would be better at setting youth on the straight and narrow path. Yet intrusive state laws and juvenile sentencing, administrators complained, made it impossible to hold boys as long as necessary to change an incorrigible youth into a solid citizen. As the age of compulsory attendance rose, the ages of boys captured within the net of the school also increased, from fourteen to fifteen, then sixteen.

The Chicago Parental School was meant to rehabilitate children like Pasquale, a child of Italian immigrant parents, whose antics left teachers and principals wringing their hands.[68] When he was asked by criminologist Clifford Shaw to recount the history of his delinquent career, Pasquale reminisced about hanging out in alleys during the 1920s and shooting dice with his pals during school hours. When it rained the boys would go to an old flooded lot downtown and float around on a raft they constructed of old lumber. A favorite topic of conversation among the boys was the injustices wrought upon them by educators who scorned Italians, a charge with some validity judging by the disdainful reminiscences of Mr. Hicks, the principal of Pasquale's school, of the "tattered and unwashed" students who populated his building. Pasquale and his friends spent much of their time trying to subvert the school's authority. After throwing his book on the floor and cursing his teacher, Pasquale was sent to the principal's office for a whipping. Corporal punishment was a given for many children, but, when he was sent to the class for slow children, which was deemed the "sub-normal" class, Pasquale's resentment exploded. He and his pals broke into the school at night, destroyed equipment, and covered the principal's office with excrement. Finally, he was brought to court on an incorrigibility charge, where he told the judge "the teachers and principal don't like me, that they didn't give me a break." The judge ignored his pleas, and Pasquale was committed to the Chicago Parental School for Boys.[69]

In addition to truancy, verbal and physical assaults on teachers, other children, and school personnel were common explanations for parental school referrals. In violently flouting the school's authority, boys were asserting a sense of rough masculinity that could be learned not only in the peer group but in homes where, according to numerous case records and accounts of delinquent or incorrigible boys, domestic violence and corporal punishment of children were not uncommon. Growing boys learned that they could use their physical prowess to intimidate teachers and other students and, perhaps, alleviate feelings of inferiority that some, especially Italians, reported experiencing in the public schools (an even larger immigrant group in Chicago, Poles were more protected from this type of ethnic harassment because they often attended Polish parochial schools). Boys also could demonstrate their working-class masculine virtues through violence, for instance, when a thirteen-year-old hit a boy with a club after finding out that the youth was a scab rather than a union man.[70]

In interviews with boys committed to the parental school, most used the word *bad* to describe their activities at home, on the street, or at school; their parents and teachers generally agreed with this assessment. They used the word, with seemingly little shame, to characterize behaviors that put them at odds with parents, teachers, and other authorities, but not their peers. Salvatore's mother had asked the principal to send him to the school because he was bad at home. When asked why his mother thought he was bad, he contended that "most boys aint [*sic*] good at home. That's the way all boys are in Chicago—most of them." In other words, Salvatore claimed that his behavior was normal, at least in his own peer society. Sam attributed his badness to his response to a mean-spirited teacher, who said he was "fired from school—I was bad. The teacher got me sore. She used to make me write a hundred words on the blackboard after school." His teacher further elaborated on his story: "he would not keep his seat, but would run all around the room, and was a constant source of trouble," causing her to neglect the other youngsters.[71] What Sam perceived as vindictive punishment, his teacher viewed as a response to "trouble."

Some boys evinced regret when recounting their badness, but to be a bad boy in Chicago in the early twentieth century was not the worst of all possible plights, at least among the company of other boys. In fact, being bad was one of the most forceful displays of masculinity. *Bad* signified a willingness to stand up to authority, to assert one's independence, to exert one's physical prowess, to prove oneself as a force to be reckoned with, possibly even to demonstrate ethnic and working-class pride. To be a bad boy was to be as unlike a girl as possible. Being bad at school, or on the street, had its advantages. Home was another story, and many regretted the angst their activities may have caused their mothers in particular. And too much badness, of course, could get one sent to the bad boys' school.

In Chicago, any "reputable citizen" was allowed to lodge a truancy complaint that could result in a commitment to the parental school, with little recourse for the boy or his family.[72] Some parents were aghast at the power of the courts to institutionalize errant boys. One Eastern European mother complained, "If I had but known that my boy was going to be sent away to the Parental School I would never have brought him to court . . . You can believe I sure learned fast to hate the American courts after that."[73] Other mothers—divorced, widowed, and working—considered themselves unable to handle unruly boys on their own, given their early-morning schedules and lack of public assistance. This was the case for one mother who hoped for her son to be sent to the New York City Parental School. Mrs. Gilligan told a truancy investigator, "I have to work out more days than not and it's no use to promise he'll go to school, for he won't . . . I only hope he'll [the truant officer] find him on the street."[74] Stanley, the Polish delinquent who was the subject of Clifford Shaw's criminological classic *The Jack-Roller* (1930), claimed that after he'd been brought to juvenile court at age nine, his Polish stepmother "told the interpreter that I was incorrigible and leading her children astray, and that a few years in the reform school would do me some good."[75] Yet other parents complained that instead of steering boys away from a life of crime, boys in the parental school were thrown together with more hardened criminals, making it likely that their delinquent careers would be launched rather than thwarted at the school.

The Chicago school was located on forty acres of farmland in a remote section of the city, with a herd of cattle, individual vegetable plots for the boys, and even a swimming pool. Reformers theorized that providing boys with these types of nonacademic opportunities would engage their restless spirits in a way that schools were incapable of doing. In recounting Illinois' progress in child welfare, Jane Addams boasted of Chicago's "splendid parental school": "We discovered that certain boys who did not get on very well in the ordinary Schools, when they were sent out in the country to this parental school, developed a taste for farming, for stock growing and for all sorts of things, simply because they had something to do with their hands."[76]

So even Addams believed that "hand work" was to be the savior of immigrant and poor boys gone astray, a premise that had enormous staying power. Did it mean that working-class and immigrant boys were less able to do academic work, or did reformers think that boys attached more value to these types of activities? Time and time again, reformers noted that formerly recalcitrant youth lit up when offered a chance to engage in woodcraft or other productive activities, perhaps because they could more readily appreciate the utility of these activities based on their own cultural experiences. The educational program at parental schools embodied typical ideas of progressive and manual education and was composed "less of bookishness and more learning by application."[77] It was a truism in juvenile justice that this type of learning was more suitable for truant and incorrigible boys. As Judge Mack of the juvenile court claimed when sending a youth to the parental school, "Book study is not enough for this boy. He needs a chance to work with his hands as well as with his head."[78] Perhaps Mack was being unduly skeptical about the ability of this youth to master the academic curriculum, but perhaps he was also recognizing in many youth a need for a wider variety of experiences.

By providing boys with schoolwork suited to their abilities, teachers hoped to foster a sense of accomplishment and to encourage basic academic achievements, without setting boys' sights too high. The Chicago Parental School aimed to reform the individual boy, to make him more amenable to learning and discipline so that he could be returned to his home, neighborhood, and regular school. Educators boasted of their pupils' academic progress due to smaller classes and more individual attention, but in reality boys spent a major part of the day involved in such nonacademic activities as agricultural and manual labor. Educators insisted that such labor enabled boys to engage their natural instincts and discharge excess energy that might interfere with schooling. In reality, however, boys were often shortchanged by engaging in grueling labor while their academic progress continued to be stunted.

However well meaning were the premises behind this educational venture, the Chicago Parental School could not shed its institutional character. It shared many similarities with traditional reform schools. As in reform schools, the boys were placed in separate houses (the "cottage system") and given a set of house parents.[79] The boys ranged in age from seven to fourteen; the average length of confinement was seven months.[80] Recidivism proved to be a huge problem. A study done in 1931 showed that slightly over half of the students had previously been in the institution, some of them as many as six times.[81] For many, the parental school was a launching pad for more severe institutional placements, such as the St. Charles reformatory. Meant to be schools and crafted by idealistic reformers who hoped to rescue boys from a life of crime and pauperism, parental schools ended up more closely resembling prisons.

Yet at the outset administrators approached the project with missionary zeal, convinced that they were protecting society and rescuing their young charges from lives of vice and depravity by substituting strict discipline and moral training for the inadequate parenting they received from dissolute parents. During its earliest years, the Chicago Parental School seemed to embody less a technical progressivism and more the kind of older moralism that had exemplified the reformatory movement, which had stressed hard work, cleanliness, and strong morals rather than academics.[82] With nourishing food in their clean and improved bodies, the superintendent claimed that most of the boys had a "better home here than any they have had before."[83] But he also admitted that there were good reasons for them to prefer home to the school: "Boys, almost to a unit, want to go home! Why? Why, because the discipline is strict, the work is unceasing, the restraint (the continuing absence from home) is irksome and the love of home and parents is strong."[84]

This older moralism, however, was also accompanied by an environmentalism that often put personnel at odds with the eugenic thinking rampant in some school districts and psychological clinics in the first decades of the twentieth century. As popularly understood, eugenics implied that many academic difficulties could be traced to an inferior heredity. Parental school administrators, in contrast, held out hope in the power of the right environment to transform boys' lives. For instance, T. H. MacQueary, the Chicago school's first superintendent, argued that only about 5 percent of the boys in his school had physical or mental defects that could account for their disciplinary problems. In a speech given to educators of delinquents and children in special education in 1910, he remarked, referring to one of the famous studies of several generations of criminality, feeble-mindedness, and "degeneracy" in a family, "The Jukes family has been decidedly overworked." Instead MacQueary attributed most truancy to "poverty, lack of parental care and discipline and vicious association" and envisioned bright futures for the youth who were rehabilitated at the school.[85]

MacQueary's environmentalism was shared by many working in boy's reformatories, special classes, and parental schools, as is evidenced by the annual proceedings of the national Conference on the Education of Backward, Truant, and Delinquent Children, first held in 1904. At the 1905 conference, even reformatory superintendents attributed many of boys' problems to the public school itself, which they believed was doing little to meet boys' needs. It must be remembered that at this time reformatories often housed children as young or seven or eight, with truancy, incorrigibility, and petty theft being the most common charges; others ended up there only because they were dependent and had nowhere else to go. Nelson W. McLain, superintendent of the St. Charles School for Boys in Illinois (a reformatory), argued that "the traditional public school has failed to nourish the mental growth or to engage, employ, and direct the physical activities of child life . . . Given the possible and attainable public school there would be few truants," a view that many contemporary educators might share. E. E. York, superintendent of the Indiana Boys' School, agreed that most reformatory boys were "abnormal" but that these "deformities . . . were not of the child's own volition, and not many, if any of them, inherited, but laid upon him by the unnatural conditions of living through which the child was required to pass."[86]

Although influential scientists Henry H. Goddard and Lewis Terman attributed delinquency to inferior intelligence, many leaders of reformatory institutions and psychologists such as William Healy, who worked closely with the juvenile court, were more dubious about the connection or believed that it explained some, but hardly all, cases.[87] Healy, who was a pioneering psychologist for both the Chicago and Boston juvenile courts, argued, "Delinquency and abnormality are not synonymous," and he urged delinquency workers to search for the individual meaning behind each child's antisocial actions.[88] Eugenicists, in contrast, exhorted school systems not to waste their time trying to teach academic subjects to children who were, in their view, uneducable. Many of the leaders of reform institutions and special classes balked at dealing a deathblow to attempts to teach children, especially when their measures of assessing children's natural intelligence were so still primitive.

Despite these flashes of optimism, parental schools sheltered a number of disciplinary practices that contradicted the ostensible mission of the progressive reformers. It was difficult to dislodge the often-unarticulated assumption that harsh discipline was the only way to keep bad boys in line. One might disavow corporal punishment, for instance, as did MacQueary in his 1902 annual report, but still support solitary confinement for twenty-four hours with only bread and milk, at the end of which boys would be required to perform two hours of work or exercise.[89] One punishment that later reformers found particularly problematic was making boys stand with their backs to the pool for hours on a hot day while the other boys splashed and played behind them. Of this punishment, Mac-Queary stated that "it was agony to have to 'stand on line' and listen to the wild shouts of nearly two hundred boys and their exhilarating plunges and not be allowed even to look around."[90] This practice, which MacQueary apparently found acceptable, was decried as unduly cruel by later visitors associated with Chicago's child welfare establishment. Stanley, in Shaw's *The Jack-Roller*, described his first experience of penal justice at the parental school, when he was eight years old:

> The boys all hated the place, the guards were hard-boiled, and severe punishment was inflicted for the least infraction of the rules . . . If you were slack you would be anointed with cowhide, and there weren't any too gentle about laying

it on. The most common kinds of punishment were muscle grinders, squats, benders, standing in corner, whipping, confinement in the "cage," chewing soap, being deprived of food and sleep.

Although Stanley is not necessarily a trustworthy narrator, there is plenty of additional information to confirm his basic account.[91] Much has been written about the evolution of more humane methods of disciplining children during this era, but practice often lags behind ideology. Both at home and at school, harsh punishments, especially for "bad" boys, continued to be employed.

Many administrators firmly believed that harsh disciplinary practices were essential for educators to move beyond discipline to teaching and rehabilitating young troublemakers.[92] Proponents of corporal punishment for boys in the public schools in the nineteenth century argued that it was not only more expeditious but kinder to beat them into compliance than to expel them.[93] Another debate at the Conference on the Education of Backward, Truant, and Delinquent Children exemplifies the difficulty of eradicating this view. On the one hand were those who, like MacQueary, suggested that the boys' own parents had complained that they had "whipped and pounded and beaten him, and the more I whipped the worse he got." Judge Tuthill of the Circuit of Cook County agreed, noting that many boys brought a "skin pad" to school that they wore in the seat of their pants to protect themselves against whippings, which made them even more antagonistic to authority. Others argued, on the other hand, that if they were truly to take seriously the doctrine of in loco parentis, they should physically punish boys, because most parents hit their children. The founder of the George Junior Republic, considered to be one of the most progressive institutions for dependent and delinquent boys because of its system of self-government, said that it would be an "utter impossibility to administer a reformatory institution without resorting to corporal punishment." To legitimate the view that corporal punishment was necessary to maintain order, some cited President Theodore Roosevelt's public support for the flogging of navy men for infractions of military discipline.[94] The premise that stern discipline is needed to "straighten out" young hoodlums continues to be reflected in the contemporary practice of sending difficult boys to military schools and in the ongoing practice of corporal punishment and physical restraints in many public schools today. Yet early twentieth-century administrators underestimated the harm that could arise when legitimated disciplinary techniques slid into abusive practices.[95]

In examining the full range of players in charge of orchestrating boys' lives in these institutions, including the meting out of discipline, probably those who provided the least in the way of written records were those who played the largest role in daily life: "family instructors." These "house parents," who had the charge of as many as thirty to fifty boys (depending on the level of overcrowding) in the cottage, were more guarded and pessimistic about the potential of the boys with whom they worked; they seemed to regard children's characters as less pliable than the authors of annual reports suggested. In a collection of case studies of parental school boys published in 1905, each child was given a short assessment from one of these workers. For instance, nine-year-old Pat was the son of an unskilled Italian laborer, and his teacher at the regular school was exasperated by his violent temper but still considered him a "good boy." His family instructor, however, was more pessimistic: "He's a tough case. We can't do very much for him." Ten-year-old Walter, who was apparently native born, sold newspapers, and smoked and chewed tobacco, received a similar evaluation: "He is a hard case. I doubt if anything can be made out of him." Were these the perspectives of a particular instructor, or did they reflect a more pervasive eugenic or even commonsense sensibility about the origins of boys' badness? At the very least these comments suggest that some individuals viewed children as young as nine years old to be incapable of redemption and unequivocally "bad." Whole families of children were condemned as feebleminded or degenerate. For instance, when the principal of Washington School was asked about the George Karput case, he found George and his two siblings all to be "crack brained." Apparently, George's family instructor agreed with this assessment of his limited intellectual abilities: "He's no good. Dumb: mentally deficient. Nothing good can ever be made out of him."[96]

Of course, not all instructors were so pessimistic about all the youngsters they worked with, nor is it likely that teachers were homogeneous in their outlook. This particular set of records does not distinguish among individual family instructors, so it is difficult to make blanket statements about either the instructors or their young charges. For instance, eleven-year-old Tony's mother was a widow who shelled pecans for a living and who allegedly sought to have her young son sent to the parental school because he was bad at home. His own sister condemned him as a bad boy for whom nothing could be done, but his instructor believed that Tony could be taught to control his temper at the school, although he worried about what would happen once he returned to his home environment. Eleven-year-old Rocco had been charged with both truancy and theft. His father was a widowed Italian day laborer living in a "dreary" two-room flat, who spoke very little English and could not sign his own name. The family instructor found Rocco to be a "good boy" and blamed his "home conditions" for Rocco's delinquencies. But what did *home conditions* mean? Did it mean poverty, bad parenting, tough neighborhoods, or ethnicity? By referring to the home rather than the larger environment, the implication was that parents were largely to blame not only for their children's bad behavior but for the "dreary" conditions of their own living situations. And, in fact, studies of Chicago's parental school boys demonstrate the full range of social problems associated with poverty— including the fact that, as of 1929, 65 percent were from homes that were missing a parent because of divorce, separation, or death. Children in the institution were likely to come from the most poverty-stricken and congested districts of the city, where crime and other social problems were rampant.[97]

An investigation of the Chicago Parental School that took place in 1923 demonstrated that, whatever the original hopes of school administrators, the institution was more like a prison than a school. The African American newspaper the *Chicago Defender* charged that there were "shocking stories of inhuman brutality inflicted upon pupils of the Parental School," including several involving "boys of our Race." An investigation of the school's practices was inaugurated when a white child by the name of James Wright died of strangulation, said to be a suicide but was questioned by the boys' parents. With the support of another family instructor, eleven boys, four of whom were African American, testified that they had been brutally tortured and beaten by family instructors Timothy Shea, his wife, and Archibald Davis, all of whom were white (and likely Irish). Because one child made an error during drilling practice, he was allegedly beaten so badly with a gun that the weapon was broken. Mrs. Shea allegedly broke the teeth of one her charges when she struck him and was also reported to have subjected the boys to "degrading, unclean acts." All of those charged with the crimes were dismissed from the school and subsequently disappeared.[98]

Following the appointment of Orris John Millikin as superintendent in 1923, there were changes in the Chicago Parental School. In his first annual report Milliken claimed that the "cages have been removed" for solitary confinement and "punishments reduced . . . No boy's food is changed for disciplinary reason." Milliken, self-consciously adopting the philosophy of the recreation movement, confessed that the institution had mistakenly required "repression of healthy boy instincts. Our boys should have an opportunity for noise, rough house, and real sport." Milliken's desire to craft an institution more in keeping with boy nature notwithstanding, there were recurrent investigations regarding the discipline and treatment of the boys in the facility in the ensuing years.[99]

Charges of cruelty toward the inhabitants of the parental school were also lodged against the superintendent of the New York Parental School in 1912. This complaint was issued by one of the cottage caretakers, who claimed that Superintendent Hobart Todd had frequently beaten the boys and engaged in other forms of extreme punishment. Todd admitted "slapping" the boys, but denied the other charges. The affidavit also specifically cited the case of fourteen-year-old Gustave Ruoff, whose back was covered with welts inflicted by four other boys who had been assigned to watch over him while he was doing some work on a woodpile as a punishment. Involving boys in disciplining other boys was a common practice of the time, particularly in these types of semipenal institutions, but there is no suggestion that the charge led to changes in this type of self-government.[100]

In spite of such complaints of abuse and brutal punishment, not all boys viewed their experiences at the Chicago Parental School in purely negative terms, especially after MacQueary's tenure had ceased. William, for instance, was first committed to the Chicago institution when he was eight years old, in 1923. Clearly discouraged by his lack of success in school, William preferred the easygoing life of the streets: "I was not so good in school. I was very hard to teach . . . I wanted to loaf around the street and play games with friends . . . I was dumb as a door." William started "bumming school" and eventually was caught and sent to court, where he pleaded with the judge not to send him to the "bad boys place." Once at the parental school, though, William got along well with his housefather, who was a "good guy" and "gave him a lot of breaks." His popularity extended to his peers, who selected him as squad captain. Unfortunately, success in the institution did not translate into success in the outside world. William was committed to the parental school a total of four times, while his delinquent crimes escalated from petty thievery to larceny.[101] Once out of the institution, the streets reclaimed him as one of their own. There is plenty of evidence that many tough boys in Chicago cycled through the parental school, even if it was only for a two-month stint. Although the parental school could hardly house all the difficult boys in the district, it became a common solution to juvenile court status offense cases for boys.

The job of turning truants and delinquents into disciplined and lawful citizens proved more difficult than reformers had envisioned. As is often the case, institutional practices in parental schools soon departed from what more idealistic reformers had originally envisioned. Yet these practices themselves often reflected commonsense assumptions about what was best for troublesome boys—harsh discipline, manual education, and recreational activities that drew on boys' natural peer group organization. With these premises in mind, it is not surprising that institutional practices could become abusive and that peer cultures of masculinity perpetuated in the institution could foster greater delinquency once the inhabitants had departed. Parental schools were a measure of last resort for school districts' most troublesome boys. At the same time, another innovation in schooling that aimed to keep problem boys in nonresidential public schools had a more lasting legacy: special education.

CHAPTER 4

Bad or Backward?

Gender and the Genesis of Special Education

When a Chicago Italian gang leader, the Cat, recalled his school experiences in the 1920s, he remarked disdainfully about his placement in a class for "sub-normals." Cat and the other kids had heard rumors that "the sub-normal room was where the guys was off their nuts," but in his opinion "the ones in this room were just the ones that won't listen to the teachers and get in a lot of trouble." Cat told sociologist Clifford Shaw that there had been one or two such rooms in every school on the West Side, where boys from the neighborhood would congregate and plan their delinquent escapades.[1] Subnormal, incorrigible, truant, backward, maladjusted: a sequence of labels justified the placement of troublemakers in separate classes in urban school districts during the early twentieth century. Even though only a small percentage of children were enrolled in special education, up to two-thirds of the special education population in urban schools was composed of boys—a figure that is similar to today's statistic.[2]

The story of Cat, a boy who cycled through special education classes and the juvenile justice system, was not terribly unusual in the early twentieth century city. Historians of education cannot fail to notice the difficulty that unruly boys caused teachers or the preponderance of boys in special classes.[3] Yet although this phenomenon is in plain sight, the gender implications of these stories are seldom directly addressed. Have historians taken their cue from past educators and re-formers who seemed to take it as a given that there would always be a substantial group of boys who were slower learners, troublemakers, or apt to repel educators' best efforts to teach them? Boys were put at risk not only by their gender, but by poverty, ethnicity, race, and immigration status.[4] Even so, girls who suffered the same conditions were less apt to be singled out for placement in special classes or the criminal justice system. Charles Berry, head of special education in Michigan, speculated in 1926 that when a teacher was asked to identify the mentally retarded she "picks out the ones that are giving her the most trouble, and the two are not always synonymous," leading to an overrepresentation of boys in the classes.[5] Low-achieving girls, who were thought to be more pliant learners, could be more easily integrated into the classroom.

Cat was exceptional in that he moved through his youthful indiscretions to become a full-fledged criminal, while most boys matured into a more settled existence, including marriage and full-time jobs, as they entered their late twenties. Yet Cat's difficulty with school was shared by many of his peers and posed a challenge to urban school districts as they sought to expand their constituency. Cat's story also resonates with those of contemporary boys who cycle through special education, suspensions, expulsions, and the justice system.

Being diagnosed with a special education label during the 1920s did not confer many rights to boys, other than that of having access to an education: a right that many youth would willingly have given up. But insofar as child savers and special educators construed education as one of the rights of childhood, they saw the provision of special education to be of service, not only to teachers and children in the regular classroom, but to the children who inhabited special education classes. By labeling boys who were difficult or troubled as in need of special education, were early public school systems guaranteeing troubled boys rights to an education that boys without such a diagnosis lacked? Instead of being kicked out of school, boys were forced to stay in school: whether for good or for ill it is difficult to conclude.

Instead of expelling children who were difficult, or letting overage, truant, or slower-learning children drop out, special education allowed the "regular school" to function more effectively for compliant students who were at grade level.[6] The misbehavior of some of the boys who posed disciplinary problems, along with their ineptitude with academic subject material, placed them in an ambiguous category that straddled the boundaries between backward and delinquent. Were delinquents bad because they were backward in their school subjects and frustrated and humiliated by their poor performance? Were students of limited intelligence more prone to delinquency by virtue of their inability to discern right from wrong? Did public schools, with their rigid methodologies, contribute to backward and delinquent boys? Or was it the terrible environments in which boys were ensconced—including debauched parents, debilitated housing, and crime-ridden neighborhoods—that produced both delinquency and backwardness? The lack of certainty about what to with unruly and slower-learning youth led to many ambiguous and fluctuating placements in special education—from special schools, to reformatories, the regular classroom and back again. Special education classes in the public schools offered a less draconian strategy than the public parental (residential) schools for truant, incorrigible, and academically challenged boys.

In many urban school districts the first "special education" classes were specifically begun for troublesome youth, many of them boys.[7] By the turn of the twentieth century, classes for children who were deemed intellectually deficient began to emerge. In the 1910s special education categories proliferated, with large school districts offering classes for children with tuberculosis, speech defects, paralysis, and, in some cases, hearing and visual impairments. Yet public school classes for children with behavior and learning problems were more common than those for children with more clearly defined physical disabilities, such as deafness and mobility impairments (a situation which continues to the present). A study for the U.S. Office of Education in 1911 demonstrated that 152 American cities, mostly in the North Atlantic and North Central regions of the country, held classes for children with behavioral difficulties. In contrast, only 91 cities offered classes for physically exceptional children.[8]

Unlike education for the deaf and blind, which was primarily conducted in separate institutions, at the turn of the century few distinct methods or categories existed for teaching children who "vary from the normal type" in their intellectual or behavioral difficulties.[9] In an era when institutions for the so-called feebleminded were sprouting and schools still felt free to expel children deemed uneducable, some parents were pressured to send their children to institutions. Yet there was a more amorphous group of children who were crowding the halls of city schools—some unwillingly brought to school either by their parents or the truant officers and others whose parents desperately implored the schools to provide their children with an education in lieu of sending them to an institution or letting them roam the streets. School districts were increasingly pressured to accommodate these children, who were perhaps not "feebleminded" enough—to use the idiom of the time—to warrant commitment to an institution, under the auspices of the public schools.[10] Advocates of special education argued that public schools had a responsibility to educate, if not all, then nearly all, children and to provide "abnormal" children with an education that was tailored to their behavioral and developmental capacities.[11]

In most urban school districts, ungraded or disciplinary classes were created in the late nineteenth century; special classes for the intellectually deficient followed in the early twentieth century. In smaller classes, teachers tried to engage pupils with individualized teaching plans and offered more practical applied knowledge as the basis of the curriculum. While coeducation had won the day in public education more generally, classes for delinquent boys were nearly always segregated by gender, and, as male and female children deemed of subnormal intelligence became adolescents, they, too, were often kept in gender-segregated settings and offered gender-specific subject material. Of course, the idea that boys learn better in all-boy settings under masculine guidance was widely held, particularly among the upper classes, which sent their sons to all-boy preparatory schools. Although boys of the middling classes and average talents might prosper in coeducational settings, both the most and least fortunate of boys were deemed in need of all-male educational preserves.[12]

Girls were thought to be less capable of higher-order intellectual work than boys, but the most serious academic failures in primary and secondary schools appeared to rest with boys. Boys were twice as likely to enroll in classes for the intellectually inferior, according to a 1918 report by the U.S. Office of Education.[13] Yet, in spite of these large disparities, one has to read official documents closely to even find a reference to the gender discrepancies in special education. Noting that there were twice as many boys as girls in subnormal classes, William McAndrew, director of special education in Chicago, speculated in 1923, "Whether the results are complicated by the fact that girls are steadier, more reliable, apt to stay within doors more largely, and to receive more assistance from their parents and elders or whether there is greater variability among the male of the species is not known."[14] McAndrew combined commonly held assumptions about girls' behaviors with a popular theory that boys had a greater range of intelligence, with boys being both more superior and inferior and girls generally being clustered among the mediocre. The theory was challenged and found wanting, but untested theories about boys' learning styles continued to abound.[15]

One of the few to research the issue, psychologist Ethel Cornell studied boys' overrepresentation in subnormal classes, concluding that there were few differences between boys' and girls' learning aptitudes. Her research led her to believe that that boys' unique ability to manipulate "concrete things in a problem-solving way" was not being well served by the elementary school curriculum. Cornell observed that teachers referred more boys than girls to special education even when both were equally behind in grade level. Boys' different learning styles and greater likelihood of aggressive acting out disrupted the regular classroom, she contended, which made it more likely that teachers would judge them to be less capable of academic mastery.[16] Cornell was onto a problem that would bedevil the system of public education throughout its history: its inability to make room in the public school classroom for individual students with distinct learning styles, including those that may be shaped by gender.

Although children in special education classes were at first thought to be of inferior intelligence, as time went on educators developed new theories about the factors that inhibited children's, and especially boys', learning. These factors ranged from reading disabilities to cultural deprivation and provided the grounding for the development of compensatory education and a system of special education focused on the concept of disability. Although conventional assumptions of boy nature informed many special education schools and classes for boys, these classes also provided a springboard for more wide-ranging investigations into the nature of learning and academic achievement. Many educators vowed to prevent delinquency by remediating boys' academic deficits but all too often found themselves stymied by their inability to sort out the primary factors impinging on boys' behavioral and learning difficulties, whether they be poverty, immigration status, heredity, culture, or some other as-yet undiagnosed learning disability. Similarly, when boys at risk for school failure and delinquency were sorted into separate schools or classes, they often became breeding grounds for future delinquencies, as we have seen in the story of Cat.

The Evolution of Special Education

The Progressive Era, the term most historians use to describe the years from 1880 to 1920, was characterized by massive transformations in industry and technology, the expansion of the national government, and cadres of reformers who sought to both foster and control social change to meet the demands of the new age. Insofar as Progressives were optimistic about the potential for positive social transformation, they set their sights on children, who were seemingly more malleable and able to embody positive social change. There were so many reform efforts aimed at capturing children under the net of wholesome influences that it is impossible to name them all, but it is fair to say that children living in urban neighborhoods offered social scientists a kind of living laboratory where they could study the effects of schooling, club work, and other interventions on childhood development.

In addition to playgrounds, boys' clubs, and compulsory schooling, special education was another Progressive Era innovation that combined eugenic and environmentalist impulses. Psychologist Henry H. Goddard, an influential early twentieth-century eugenicist, championed the idea that most unlawful activity among youth was caused by inferior intelligence, an idea with incredible staying power.[17] Goddard almost single-handedly brought the IQ test to American schools, warned about the "menace of the feebleminded," and sought the institutionalization of those with low IQs. He was dubious about the possibility of rehabilitating juvenile delinquents, tainted as they were by bad heredity.[18] The IQ test enabled schools to label and segregate the "ineducable," "incurable," and "idiots" deemed incapable of rehabilitation into society.[19] Children diagnosed as ineducable were often thrown into institutions, while some educators strove to find niches within public education for the borderline cases in need of special, yet still public, education. Testing was inexact, however, and children who suffered from a range of ills—from neglect to misbehavior—were mistakenly placed in institutions for the ineducable. In *The State Boys' Rebellion* (2005), author Michael D'Antonio tells a searing story of a group of boys with average intelligence who had been placed in an institution for the mentally disabled in the 1950s mainly because the state could find nowhere else to put these neglected youth.[20] Unfortunately, it was not until the 1960s that serious challenges were made to the use of institutions as a proper venue for the treatment of delinquent and mentally disabled children.

Special education was one dimension of the social efficiency movement in education, which aimed to improve the accountability of the public school classroom (not unlike the standards-based movement today). Age grading helped to streamline the educational process, but so many children were overage for their grade—either because of immigration or migration status, poverty, or a real learning difficulty—that few urban classrooms actually complied with the ideal of children of the same age occupying the same classroom. Special education emerged as a possible solution to this problem. Discussing the development of special education in New York City, which by 1927 enrolled more than eight thousand children, a *New York Times* journalist conflated normality, age grading, and social efficiency:

> Economy has prescribed a rough classification according to age and approximate normality. But a greater differentiation of method may be employed with greater financial and social economy in the end if the "misfits" under our present system can be developed along lines that will ultimately lead them into places of usefulness in the social order as well as to their own best possibilities, for to fit the misfits is to reduce crime and inefficiency to their minimum.[21]

This passage sheds light on one aspect of the development of special education: its efforts to train so-called misfits only insofar as they would be able to find an inferior place in the social structure to which they could easily adjust. Both efficiency and the fear that abnormal youth would taint their normal peers through "social contagion" were used to justify special programs for delinquents, slower learners, and truants. This was part of the logic of Peter Mortenson, superinten-

dent of the Chicago Parental School, who argued that both truants and incorrigibles should be included under the rubric of special education in 1910:

> In administering a large system of education, there are certain abnormal types
> that cannot be made to conform to the conditions maintained for the aver-
> age, normal child . . . It has been found advantageous to segregate the blind,
> the deaf, and the sub-normal children. The Truant or the Incorrigible child
> is abnormal insofar as his moral development has been arrested, or, through
> the exercise of positively bad habits, becomes detrimental to other students."[22]

Mortenson considered both truant and deaf children to be under the rubric of
"abnormal," whose differences were structured into the very essence of their beings. Moreover, abnormal children of all types could somehow contaminate normal children, merely by virtue of their presence. Normal children needed to be
protected from the baneful influence of truant and incorrigible children, who
were distinctly different by virtue of their inferior moral characteristics.

The first step in separating normal from abnormal children was to be found in
what were first called "ungraded" classes.[23] Eventually, these classes evolved from
being a venue to prevent the contagion of unruly boys from infecting middle-
class children and working-class girls to taking on a more specialized function
within the public schools. The term *ungraded*, once used to refer to the system
employed in the one-room school, came to mean classes for children whose age
did not fit the grade to which they properly belonged. A wide range of children
came under the umbrella of ungraded classes: those with discipline problems,
those who struggled with English, or those who learned more slowly. There was
even a journal on the subject, *Ungraded*, in the early twentieth century, although
after the 1920s experts in the field largely abandoned the term for the equally
euphemistic *exceptional*. Nineteenth-century ungraded classrooms, often housed
in damp and gloomy basements and attics, had originally catered mostly to unruly boys who were apt to disrupt the regular classroom, but they became more
systematized as special education became ensconced in urban school districts.
The first ungraded classes often served as temporary way stations for boys who
would eventually find their way back to the regular classroom; in later decades
such classes, no longer termed "ungraded," would often become permanent placements for those thought to be largely incapable of serious academic learning.

The Boston School Committee opened its first ungraded classes in 1879, ostensibly for children who were overage. Historian Peter Osgood refers to these
classes as "dumping grounds" for children who were causing difficulty in the
regular classroom.[24] The ungraded classes were so synonymous with criminality

in the public mind that they were popularly called "Botany Bays," a reference to a penal colony for British convicts in Australia.[25] Detroit's ungraded classes were only for bad boys when they were set up in 1884, while classes for backward children of both genders were not opened until 1903.[26] Cleveland's first class for incorrigibles in 1876 included only boys.[27] Although some acknowledged that there were, in fact, girls who were truant, incorrigible, and backward, their existence challenged a norm that truancy and incorrigibility were, at least in the corridors of the public school, coded for masculinity.

In 1899, Chicago's newly established Department of Child Study and Pedagogic Investigation reported on the rationale for organizing special classes in the Chicago public school district. The authors of the report discovered that age and grade were not highly correlated in many of Chicago's schools and that boys outnumbered girls by four to one in special classes.[28] Backward pupils, "the extremely dull children," were the bugbear of the teachers and the greatest of all drawbacks to the normal pupils unless segregated, they believed. At the same time, the group wondered whether medical defects might be responsible, perhaps in "avenues to the brain and cord—i.e., defects in the senses and their tracts, defects in the brain itself." Questioning whether proper nutrition and medicine might offset such "brain defects," the group ultimately contended that hope for the children rested in education. They issued a fervent plea that accurate scientific research be conducted both to determine the source of children's problems and to provide remedies for their intellectual deficiencies, while still leaving to the side the question as to why boys were more likely have academic problems than girls.[29]

In Cleveland, where eugenicist Henry Goddard headed the state's Bureau of Juvenile Research, a much more pessimistic outlook prevailed. In a 1913 publication "The Treatment of Defectives: A Problem of Conservation," the superintendent of schools reported that there were at least one thousand subnormal children in the local school population, most of whom were in special classes. The number did not include "pronounced idiocy," because those students most likely already qualified for institutionalization, but instead counted those a bit more advanced on the scale of intelligence, whom they termed "high-grade Morons" and "imbeciles." Replicating Goddard's argument that the feebleminded were a "menace," the report complained that such children were "allowed to mingle freely with each other and with others" and "constitute[d] a menace to society." Although the author noted that sterilization and segregation were two solutions to this menace, he recognized that sterilization had "grave social dangers" and recommended institutionalization instead of inclusion within the public school classroom. The report warned that children who were merely backward (meaning behind in grade but not necessarily intellectually inferior) were subject to the "blighting effect" of being schooled with truly defective children without segregation. Noting that there was a high preponderance of children who were either foreign born or children of the foreign born in the Cleveland school district, the report stated that although there were "worthy and alert immigrants," they also brought with them the feebleminded, a finding that should lead to stricter immigration laws.

Yet such dire predictions about the fate of children in special classes were not pervasive. Many placed in special classes were considered redeemable, if redemption meant solely the ability to function as a law-abiding citizen engaged in some form of productive labor. Two individuals were at the forefront of the effort to transform the thinking behind the ungraded class as a quasi-penal institution for disorderly boys into a scientifically informed system of education meant to produce better-educated children: Elizabeth Farrell, a college-educated, teacher-trained educator who became New York City's first inspector of ungraded classes and went onto to be one of the founders of the Council for Exceptional Children in 1922; and Lightner Witmer, whose Psychological Clinic at the University of Pennsylvania went on to achieve some renown in psychological circles.[30]

Farrell gathered a large group of boys ranging in age from eight to sixteen, all of whom had been unsuccessful in school for one reason or another, into New York's first specialized ungraded class in 1899. The setting was a condemned school building on the Lower East Side, where newly enacted compulsory education statutes were increasingly pressuring Jewish and Italian immigrants to attend school on a regular basis.[31] For children whose attendance had been erratic because of intermittent work, language difficulties, or other poverty-related stresses, being retarded in grade level began to be defined as a social problem demanding an educational solution, which Farrell's class sought to address.

In one of Farrell's talks to special education teachers, she cast schooling as the primary engine in the quest to eradicate criminality: "if these men in jail—and the women, too—had had the kind of teachers that this government expected them to have, I question whether the jails would be full." Although aware of the difficulties presented by inferior intelligence and poverty, she remained convinced that the nation's "failures" were mainly so because of the "lack of right educational opportunity." In Farrell's case, "right educational opportunity" meant an education that was suited to the interest and capacities of the students who were doing poorly in the regular classroom.[32]

In Farrell's classroom, placement practices were driven by pragmatics. Farrell identified three types of boys who had been sent to her by principals from various schools: those who were retarded in grade level for any reason, incorrigibles, and truants. Farrell presumed that all of these boys were incapable of learning through abstract methodologies of drills and memorization currently employed in the regular public school classroom.[33] Whatever the degree of their actual mental capacities, Farrell insisted that the curriculum be individuated to meet the children's needs, which, she determined, were not necessarily academic. For those who were unfit for traditional academics, she focused on strengthening their moral abilities, especially self-control and a desire to work "so that when they go out into the world they will not join the ranks of the criminal class"— demonstrating the degree to which the aims of special education and juvenile justice overlapped.[34]

Over time, the ungraded classes in New York City expanded and included both boys and girls, with more than 250 classes in the district by 1921. In tandem with the development of psychological and educational ideas about the nature of intelligence, more discrete categories of classification of emotional and cognitive impairment evolved, as did new modes of assessment. In 1911, Henry H. Goddard was asked to assess the program and found that the ungraded class mixed so-called normal children with the abnormal, while failing to enroll what he thought to be the much larger number of truly feebleminded children in the district. Although Farrell thought that the IQ test was a limited instrument for diagnosing children's problems and disagreed with Goddard's contention that 2 percent of the city's school population should be classified as feebleminded, the test soon became widely used throughout the district not only to enroll children in special classes but also to determine their placement in regular classes.[35]

Lightner Witmer's established Philadelphia's first scientifically oriented ungraded class or clinic in 1911, which was deemed a clinic for backward children. In that first class of eighteen students, twelve of whom were boys, Witmer included several "educable mental defectives," a couple of "trainable" mental defectives, several students whose "retardation" could be attributed to physical defects, a pair of "moral delinquents," and an epileptic. The class had more class and ethnic diversity than Farrell's, mainly because it was partially dependent on referrals from parents who sought help for students who were having problems in the regular classroom.[36] This distinguished the class from most other early special education classes, where children were placed mainly on the basis of teacher and principal referral. The clinic's association with the University of Pennsylvania lent it a certain cachet that led parents to seek its help rather than see it as a quasi-penal institution for abnormal children.

The children Witmer described in his book on classes for backward children demonstrated the shifting labels and assumptions about the rationales for children's learning and behavior difficulties. For instance, nine-year-old Giovanni Arnetti was referred to Witmer's class by his principal and was described by his teacher as a "moral degenerate" and "incurably bad." The clinic's investigation into his family history did not find him to be stamped with hereditary badness. Giovanni was normally bright according to the IQ test but too consumed with mischief to pay attention to his studies. The clinic defined him as a "moral delinquent" rather than a moral degenerate. Degeneracy implied bad heredity and a reversion to a primitive past that could not be overcome, while delinquency referred to actions instead of inherent character flaws. An investigation into Giovanni's home conditions found that his parents were extremely strict and inclined to physical punishments, conditions that attracted him to the street. Giovanni's teacher's inclination to define him as "incurably bad" reflected not only prevailing eugenic assumptions but also more traditional commonsense assumptions about the nature of such degenerate classes as paupers and Italians. In the special class, however, an attempt was made to distinguish between familial and environmentally derived badness and that which was associated with a limited mental endowment.[37]

The range of problems present in Witmer's class included what might be classified under the rubric of attention deficit disorder or autism today. Consider, for instance, George Benson, a boy whose behavior was defined as "erratic," who had difficulty sitting still and was prone to explosive outbursts, or Oswald Zug, a boy of eleven who was mute but not deaf and not without intelligence, according to the clinic's observations. Henry Birch, who was described as one of the "usual Irish type" had started parochial school, where he was pronounced "dumb," eventually leading to him being sent to public school, where the principal decided that he was "impossible to teach." His parents, however, were unwilling to accept this diagnosis, claiming that their child possessed what they termed a "school disability," language suggesting that the child's learning problems were contextual, associated with the specific tasks necessary to be academically successful. They clearly believed him to be capable of remediation, even sending him to live with his aunt in another part of the city so that he could be taught properly in the special class.[38] Witmer's clinic was a harbinger of things to come: a place where parents in search of specialized teaching for their children could find teachers who were willing to focus on their children's potential rather than their difficulties.

As special education evolved, other educators also tried to move beyond the needs of social efficiency and fitting dull children to their station in life. Psychologists such as Witmer and Augusta Bronner became keenly interested in understanding how behavioral difficulties and learning problems might intersect, contributing to our contemporary understanding of classifications such as learning disabled.[39] Some of these educators demanded special, ungraded classes as a means of ensuring democratic equality in schooling, insisting that all children, whatever their degree of ability, had a right to an education. Many believed that the schools of the future would be premised on the principles espoused by special educators: an individualized and relevant education, premised on children's different ethnicities, ages, genders, and abilities. As Diane Ravitch, Jeff Mirel, and others have shown, in the long run these progressive principles could erode students' academic potential and ultimately contributed to the decline of urban schools by providing already oppressed students with an education inferior to that of their better-off counterparts, who were headed for the suburbs.[40] When reformers spoke of teaching to students' "capacities," they clearly held views about the inherent intellectual inferiority of certain groups of children. Yet it is also necessary to probe more deeply into the notions of reformers, who sought to ensure that children who avoided, disliked, or failed terribly in school had a chance at gaining some form of an education. Their justification then (as now) of differentiated teaching methods and materials was not always about fitting dull children into their slots but also about affording access to education to children who did not easily conform with the regimen of the regular classroom. The special class should "secure justice" for children and their parents, according to educator Ada M. Fitts, by providing them with an education "according to their needs."[41] In such urban settings as Chicago, Detroit, and Cleveland, which were struggling under the weight of burgeoning populations of immigrant and migrant children, special education served multiple purposes, even if the end results were dubious.

At the turn of the twentieth century, the child study movement—based on the principle that education should be premised on scientific ideas about how children learn best—also influenced the construction of public and special education. Believing that children should be treated as individuals, child study advocates argued that not all children learned in the same way or according to the same developmental timeline. Because common sense dictated that boys and girls were different and had different learning styles, proponents of child study aligned themselves with gendered approaches to schooling. To heighten the attraction of schooling, educators purposely provided subject matter customized to appeal to boys and girls. Presumably, boys were "hand-minded"; girls were interested in homemaking.[42] Specialized curricula were deemed especially appropriate for slower learners and disruptive boys who were deemed incapable of mastering the academic curriculum and more attracted to manly pursuits such as the wood shop. And because slower-learning boys and girls, as they entered adolescence, were considered less than capable of making good moral judgments about their sexuality, decorum necessitated that they be schooled in separate classes according to gender, unlike children in the regular public schools, where coeducation had become nearly universal by the twentieth century. As with assumptions about boys, assumptions about children and their needs were embedded in policies that sometimes reinforced existing prejudices and sometimes lofty ideas, each of which were essentially moral rather than technical.

Constructing Disability: Labeling and Stigma in Special Education

One of the most significant technologies in the transformation of urban schools in the twentieth century was the IQ test. Beyond keeping certain children out of school, the test also sorted children in large urban school districts by their purported intelligence, often reflecting ethnic and racial prejudices. In cities such as Chicago and New York, IQ tests were used to organize schools where a typical elementary school classroom might hold forty or fifty children of many different nationalities and levels of preparation. In several cities, such as Detroit, the tests were employed to develop elaborate tracking mechanisms that began as early as first grade. The administration of IQ tests was not without its pitfalls, however. When individual youth were tested, they might have difficulty with the English language or purposefully resist instructions. For instance, the Illinois Institute for Juvenile Research determined that Raymond, the child of Polish immigrants, was "borderline defective" in 1933. Yet the test administrator admitted to having a poor rapport with Raymond, who responded to most queries with a shrug or "I don't know."[43] Practically speaking, the IQ was only one of many factors, along with grades and teacher and social worker assessments, that went into special class placement.[44] The tracking methods designed by urban school districts reinforced social class and racial divisions, shielded by a dubious scientific veneer.

Of course, the lowest track was the special track. The main thing uniting these abnormal children was their deviation from what psychologists, educators, and others were conceptualizing as the normal child.[45] Of course, educators knew that *abnormal* was hardly a specific designation for a specialized classroom. Throughout the years, educators struggled to find more precise terminology to label the differences they observed: words such as *predelinquent, backward, subnormal, maladjusted,* and *retarded* all were common parlance at different points in time. But, however archaic these labels seem in retrospect, all were efforts to substitute moral or imprecise conventional language with terms that appeared to have a scientific meaning. They also share a euphemistic bent, avoiding the commonsense interpretations that are often applied to children who seem "odd," "slow," or "evil."

The substitution of scientific language for the vernacular was the province of experts. Most nonprofessionals continued to refer to difficult boys as "bad" and slower learners as "dumb." When they were brought to the principal's office for swearing or assaulting their teachers, or before the juvenile court for stealing from a vegetable stand, both boys and their parents could share the understanding of these actions as unlawful and bad, but they did not necessarily view their actions as reflecting an inherent state of being. For boys themselves, acts of badness could be embraced as mascots of masculinity, which demonstrated their alliance with the devious criminals who outsmarted boring straights both in cheap fiction and on the streets of their own neighborhoods.[46] But although boys were often willing to proudly proclaim themselves as bad, *dumb* carried a stigma. Boys who claimed with bravado that school subjects did not interest them in the least often became enraged when labeled as dumb or slower learning.

Whether the dumbbell with the dunce hat in the corner of the classroom benefited from being placed in a subnormal class is not a question that is easily answered, especially because there was so much variability in teachers' talents and techniques and the needs of individual students. But for those who had traditionally been labeled as bad, incorrigible, or truant, labels that appeared to question their normalcy represented a most undignified affront to boys' self-esteem. All three of the aforementioned terms imply the possibility of change, yet to be thought subnormal is to presume an inherent intellectual limitation.

Sociologist Ernest Burgess, in his pivotal essay, "The Delinquent as Person" (1923), used as a case study a boy whose troublesome behavior derived not so much from limited intelligence but from the stigma of being defined as such. Fourteen-year-old George, who was ostensibly average in reading and writing, was placed in the subnormal room because of his difficulty with mathematics, after which "he at once became truant, disobedient, and much given to fighting." He had been taunted for being feebleminded and, when asked why he continually fought with others explained, "O, you just don't understand. I've got to fight. I don't want to, but you see, these boys keep saying I'm feebleminded, and I'm going to fight 'em till they quit saying it."[47] Many boys made similar complaints, leading experts to map connections between academic difficulties, self-esteem, and delinquent behavior.[48]

Many of the boys who entered parental schools and other reformatory institu-

tions had already been placed in special classes for the dull or had been classified as retarded in grade. In reality, the threat of being placed in a special class
was used as a disciplinary tactic. A Chicago Area Project worker reported, "The
teachers call it [the ungraded room] the dummy room in the presence of the
children. They refer to it and use it as a threat the same as they use the truant
officer."[49] Boys did dread attending the parental school, but attending it did not
brand them as dumb or subnormal, an appellation that many found more terrify-
ing than bad. In 1918, even the parental school sought to exclude the subnormals
from its grounds, claiming that these children were "notoriously lacking in inhib-
itive powers . . . and constantly doing things unconsciously which are inimical to
the morale of the institution." Unlike the normal bad boy, "subnormals can never
develop a 'normal point of view.' "[50] In practice, however, the distinctions between
normal and subnormal were unclear, especially for children who moved between
special classes for subnormal children and reformatory institutions. According
to Anthony Sorrentino, once a neighborhood troublemaker himself turned reformer, the sentiment on Chicago's West Side about being sent to the subnormal
class was "you can put me in jail but I can't go back to that room. Everybody calls
me a dumbbell."[51] To be identified as mentally incapacitated by the society of one's
peers was one of the worst of all possible insults. Yet many educators recognized
that what might appear to be mental deficiency, delinquency, and truancy often
overlapped.

Because so little was known about the genesis of delinquency or learning
problems, many boys were subject to dubious and stigmatizing placements. This
problem did not receive widespread public attention until the 1960s, when social scientists and lawyers began taking note of the disproportionate numbers of
African Americans stuck in separate classes for children identified as educable
mentally retarded. Still, when lawsuits were lodged, they focused on race, not
gender, even though boys have been among the groups most likely to be identified as slow learners. When boys were clearly lacking in aptitude in academic
subject materials, they sometimes sought to make up for this gap in other ways,
such as through the use of humor, physical prowess, or mastery of other types of
masculine activities, such as shopwork, hunting, or, as in the case of delinquents,
petty thievery. There were other routes to achieving masculine status besides
school.

Augusta Bronner, a prominent delinquency researcher, attempted to differen-
tiate between learning disabilities and general intelligence, especially among the
population of delinquent boys. She complained about the tendency to polarize
normal and abnormal children, overlooking individual variations: "To classify all

persons into groups of the normal and the defective is altogether inadequate . . .
Yet, at present, this is exactly what is universally done." Instead, Bronner sought
to bring a more nuanced understanding to the many factors that might affect
school achievement. Bronner used intelligence tests as a means of differentiating
between specific learning disabilities and general intelligence, a technique that
would become commonplace in special education in the years to come. Many of
her case studies were examples of boys who had floundered in Chicago's subnormal classes and the parental school. For instance, Thomas S. had at age fifteen
been in a subnormal class for several years, where he was rendered a mental
defective. Bronner found him to have a normal IQ but difficulty with reading.
Rather than addressing Thomas' specific reading disability, administrators had
categorized him as defective and denied him an academic education. Bronner
was also critical of the widespread belief that manual education should be the
mainstay of delinquent boys' schooling. She cited the example of Melvin W.,
whose three trips to the parental school had revealed him to do poorly in manual
work but quite well with abstract thinking and language. Bronner complained
about the "dire social effects of an irrational and clumsy school system" that hap-
hazardly assigned boys with problems to programs without discerning the needs
and abilities of individual children.[52]

A sophisticated researcher, Bronner worried about the rapid expansion of
special education without a sufficient knowledge base to guide placement practices. Meant to help both the subjects of special education and their regular classroom counterparts, the slow-learner label instead often collapsed the distinctions between real and pronounced academic limitations and those more subject
to remediation and between behavior problems and learning problems. Special
education classes often stigmatized and branded as inferior the children they
served—thus contributing to their further antipathy toward school.

Day Schools for Boys

One response to the overlapping concerns of truancy, discipline, and learning
difficulties was the creation of specialized day schools for problem boys during
the 1920s and 1930s. Experts in psychology, social science, medicine, and education joined forces in creating schools where the multifaceted needs of troubled
boys could be met. Day schools for boys accommodated more children, were less
expensive, and aroused less controversy than parental schools, although they still
were widely regarded as repositories for the city's bad boys. The reformers who
championed these new institutions in such places as Chicago, Cleveland, Detroit,

Philadelphia, and Boston viewed them as laboratories and clinics, where teachers might showcase the latest developments in pedagogy and the behavioral sciences. Reflecting their multidisciplinary approach, special day schools for boys often employed nurses, social workers, psychologists, and psychiatrists. Reformers maintained that, given the right environment, boys could succeed in school and society. Hoping to make model boys out of bad boys, schools first had to make model schools out of bad boys' schools.

Three day schools for troubled boys exemplify the confluence of science and progressive pedagogy and highlight emerging concepts of learning disabilities and their relationship to juvenile delinquency. In Cleveland, Detroit, and, finally, Chicago, schools founded on the best of intentions often floundered amidst the difficulties of dealing with youngsters who were, at minimum, on the verge of delinquency. Most of these students lacked economic resources, and few could escape the inevitable stigma attached to what were also called the "bad boys' schools." Educators did not anticipate what might happen when limited resources, overcrowded classrooms, and violent or out-of-control boys were brought together in a closed environment.

Cleveland's Edison School for Boys was one of the more celebrated of such schools, although it embodied premises more traditionally progressive than therapeutic. The Cleveland boys' school had been in existence since 1876, but by the second decade of the twentieth century it looked like an anachronism. According to historian Robert Bruce Bain, the school was housed in an attic and resembled a "one-room schoolhouse for misfits." Corporal punishment, banned throughout the rest of the school district, was still in usage there, reflecting the nineteenth-century principle that some boys needed to have "the devil" beat out of them. The 1921 Bing Law, which made schooling mandatory for most youth under the age of sixteen in Ohio, provided an impetus to create a modern boys' school in Cleveland.[53]

In 1920, Chicago educator Furley Watson was hired as the principal for a new Cleveland school that was planned as an exciting experiment in progressive education, employing cutting-edge ideas about boy nature and how children should best learn.[54] Watson believed that boys needed to possess a sense of psychological well-being if they were to achieve academic success, and he advocated that educators capitalize upon boys' peer networks to reinforce desirable behavior and to foster self-esteem.[55] In order to take "his place among his fellows as a boy," young males needed to develop "certain elemental masculine qualities." Schools should foster boyishness through appropriate curricula, play, and recreation, he concluded, in order to prevent delinquency.[56]

True to its progressive intentions, the Edison School downplayed lectures and recitation in favor of group projects and permitted children to move about the room at will as they worked on their projects.[57] Educators imagined that their experimental methods might yield results that would be applicable to other school settings. Clayton Wise, who wrote about the Edison School in a column entitled "Schools as Prophecies" for the *National Education Association Journal*, hypothesized that the school's "newer ideas of discipline, moral training, ability groupings, individualized instruction, curriculum . . . should have value for other types of schools."[58] The publicity granted to places such as the Edison School demonstrates the degree to which these special classes and schools were widely viewed by professional educators as laboratories for the development of pedagogical techniques for a diverse constituency of students.

Seeking to build bridges between the school and employers, the school sought to produce productive and law-abiding young adults. Educators applauded their own success, finding in a retrospective study of a thousand graduates who were contacted in 1935 that just short of three-quarters were currently employed, surely a decent figure given the time. Still, one in three had been in a penal institution, and the survey group included only those alumni who could be easily located. The school, and most day schools for boys, did achieve higher attendance rates for its students, no doubt in part due to greater personal attention and accountability for absences.[59]

With all of its good intentions, the Edison School could not escape the stigma associated with its purpose as an institution designed to deal with the district's most troubled youngsters. Hoping to elude the bad boy label, in 1938 officials allowed any boy of junior high school age to attend, whether through choice or referral. Now termed an "occupational" junior high school, the enrollment, which had always been higher than its facilities could handle, soared to more than one thousand. Given the impact of African American migration to Cleveland, by the 1940s many of the youth attending the school were racial minorities.[60] Even with the name change, however, many of the most troubled boys in the district ended up there, and the stigma of the bad boys' school remained. As late as the 1940s, the school bus driver was reported to yell "all out for Alcatraz" when he arrived at the school.[61] *Occupational* became yet another euphemism for *problem*.

The trajectory of Detroit's special education programs for boys was somewhat similar to that of Cleveland, with exploding enrollments due to the expanding immigration and migration putting huge stresses on the school system. During the second and third decades of the twentieth century, Detroit engaged in extensive school reform focused on sorting its school population into ability groupings and systematizing its special education programs. By 1924 the school district had classified all first graders into ability groups based on intelligence tests administered by the Department of Special Education and had established ungraded classes for boys with behavior problems, as well as gender-segregated "special preparatory" and "vocational" classes for slower-learning boys and girls (but boys outnumbered girls by two to one).[62] Truants and incorrigibles, once deemed "police problems," according to the district supervisor, were now properly viewed as a "problem of special education."[63]

By 1924, 1,995 boys, or about 2 percent of the total male student population, were enrolled in classes for either backward or difficult children.[64] Later, in 1935, the program moved to the Moore Elementary School, where a wing was renovated to accommodate a new facility with its own library, auditorium, gym, and print shop. In addition to its faculty, the new Moore School employed a visiting teacher, a part-time psychologist, and a psychiatrist. Later the school would become renowned for its music program, to which Uriel Jones of Funk Brothers, among others, attributed his future success. Gone were the days of truants and incorrigibles; now, in the new psychological jargon, boys were "maladjusted"— although it is unclear to just what its largely African American population was supposed to adjust.[65]

Although eight or nine other special centers for boys were located throughout the district serving immigrant and native born boys, the Moore School served a nearly 70 percent African American constituency. School personnel were attentive to the social and economic privations their students endured. Principal Henry Obel used the language of pathology to describe behaviors that he observed as "personality deviations," which were symptomatic of the larger social and economic privations boys endured.[66] "Extreme misbehavior may be considered a disease," he said, "which grows profusely in a soil consisting largely of grave socioeconomic conditions." Detroit was a major center for medical and psychological research, and the students of the Moore School provided researchers with case material for their work on the relationships among nutritional deficiencies, glandular problems, environmental influences, intelligence, and reading disabilities.[67]

The vast majority of the boys were known to at least one social agency, and school personnel exchanged reports with the juvenile courts on a nearly daily basis.[68] In fact, by 1941, it was estimated that between 40 and 50 percent of the boys at the Moore School had been on probation.[69] Don, who was on probation for breaking and entering, thought that the teachers picked on him at Jefferson School. He was sent to the Moore School after he got "mouthy" with a teacher who had "bawled him out" for failing to take his jacket off, according to his own version of the story.[70] Detroit's intensive efforts to deal with juvenile delinquency through its crime prevention bureau and neighborhood community councils, which sought to keep youth out of institutions, may have meant that public school teachers encountered disciplinary problems beyond their capacity to address. However, there is also significant evidence that teachers and students in many of the racially mixed areas of the city mistreated African American students, exacerbating disciplinary problems. Drawing the lines between the school, child welfare, and the juvenile justice system proved nearly impossible as educators sought to address the many needs of the Moore School boys.

As concerns about juvenile delinquency escalated during World War II, the Moore's School's attendance rolls swelled to 1,194, with continual waiting lists. The war also offered educators the opportunity to recycle the rhetoric of equal opportunity in justifying their program: "the ungraded department recognizes the fact that boys who are not interested in academic pursuits, or who are unable to profit adequately from 'book learning' do not have equal opportunity when compared with normal boys, unless special forms of education are provided for them."[71] These special forms of education were to be suited to the native abilities—assumed to be limited in many cases—of the maladjusted boys who attended these ungraded classes. Because, in the terminology of the times, social maladjustment was derived from a frustration of basic instincts, schooling aimed at instilling feelings of success rather than frustration was deemed most appropriate, leading to a limited academic curriculum. Yet by the 1940s there were some perceptions among members of the African American community that special schools such as the Moore School were "sometimes used by the principals to get rid of their problem children. It was felt that this was not the function of the schools."[72] This was a theme that would recur in Chicago's special schools for boys, where parents thought that their children were being given short shrift in the regular public schools and sent to languish in special schools.

The curriculum at the Moore School was deemed to be especially suited to maladjusted boys. Education for adjustment, including classes in family relations, sex education, and budget management—which were becoming increasingly prevalent in the high school curriculum at midcentury—was deemed especially relevant for problem boys, who were disenchanted with algebra and English literature. It was this watered-down educational curriculum that would fuel decades of complaints, protests, and lawsuits, starting in the 1950s, about the inferior education offered African Americans in cities such as Chicago and Detroit.[73]

Chicago's efforts to rehabilitate delinquent and maladjusted male youth were some of the most comprehensive in the nation. As with Detroit, individualized classes for boys were somewhat consolidated when reformers opened the centralized Montefiore and Moseley Social Adjustment Schools for Boys. The Montefiore School opened with great fanfare in 1929 in the Northwest immigrant section of the city, where large numbers of European immigrant children and smaller numbers of African Americans resided. Its principal was Edward Stullken, a prominent researcher who would end up playing national leadership roles in special education, child welfare, and criminology.[74] The following year, Chicago also opened the Moseley School on the South Side for the city's African American population. This decision was apparently based on the need to provide a school in the South Side neighborhood for African American youth, since the Montefiore School from its origins contained a significant population of African American boys who lived closer to the school. However, the Moseley School never garnered the resources or attention that the Montefiore School did, no doubt in part because of the neglect of African American children and child welfare in the South Side more generally. In addition, the famous immigrants of the West Side had already acquired substantial resources and researchers intent on studying this population. The Montefiore School generated a substantial body of published research, but this was not the case with the Moseley School, which probably did not employ educators with the same credentials as those at Montefiore, making its story harder to tell.

As with the other day schools for boys, the aim of the first administration was to fit the school to the boys' needs, recognizing that both truancy and delinquency were but symptoms of larger problems. The idea of individual differences was utilized here, but these differences, Stullken observed, were not always inherent, but instead rooted in "the environment and economic condition of home and neighborhood, the influence of the many personalities with which the child comes in contact, the effect of cheap movies and the places of recreation which he attends."[75] In his first annual report, Stullken stated that he hoped that the school would "fit the school work and the school activities to the special needs of its problem pupils."[76] Yet administrators used the newer scientific methods in addition to progressive education techniques, subjecting the students to a battery of psychological and intelligence tests upon their arrival. Maybe it was true that the average IQ was a low 80, but Stullken argued that the written tests employed were inadequate for measuring the intelligence of boys who spoke different languages and had learning difficulties.[77] The school was pioneering in its approach to boys' language and reading disabilities and sought to discover any neurological deficits that might explain gaps between ability as measured by IQ and performance.[78]

Stullken explained that "when there is a wide discrepancy between a boy's mental age and reading age a reading disability is suspected." In addition, the school also examined the differences between boys' skills in arithmetic and reading, hoping to discern clues to the nature of the academic impairment.[79] Given that most of the literature on learning disabilities places the understanding of such issues in medical terms in the late 1940s and 1950s, it is striking that practitioners rather than scientists paved the way for seeking scientific explanations for these academic deficits.

The Montefiore School served multiple purposes: as a school, as an arm of the juvenile justice system, and as a therapeutic center that sought to remediate children's social and intellectual disabilities. From the beginning it enrolled not only ethnic children but African American children, a figure that would rise from 12 percent of the population to almost 50 percent in the 1950s. The classes would be ungraded, with boys attending twelve months a year for a longer day to "extend the influence of the school." At the same time, however, the school described its pupils in medicalized language, with reference to a significant portion of boys as having "severe reading disabilities" and "psycho-educational" problems.[80] Yet it was also clear that the school would function as an arm of the juvenile justice system, and from its outset it was intended to steer boys away from penal institutions. In fact, when Chicago boys were brought before the juvenile court for petty offenses such as truancy or disorderly conduct, many were remanded to the Montefiore School instead of either a juvenile detention center or the parental school, meaning that most boys associated attendance with punishment.[81]

A glance through the case files of typical Chicago delinquents reveals a variety of placements from Montefiore to the parental school and—for the more egregious offenders—on to the reformatory.[82] Although the reformatory was clearly outside of the bailiwick of the public school system, the first two demonstrate the linkages between the court system and the public school. For the most part, students with lesser infractions were sent to day schools, once they had been established, but these placements hinged on such variables as number of spaces available at particular schools and the ability of parents or guardians to supervise errant youth. Still, it was not uncommon for a student to be released from the parental school to the Montefiore School, or if a boy was found to be intractable at Montefiore, to be sent to the parental school. And in some cases, it was pure luck, the temperament of a particular judge, or the boy's attitude at court, along with the extent of his record, that made the difference between being sent to a day school, the parental school, or even the juvenile reformatory.

Most of the boys attending Montefiore experienced the profound environmental disadvantages wrought by poverty: poor housing, inadequate nutrition, and shabby clothing, to name just a few. In a study of 438 boys, 115 had lost a parent to death, 39 had parents who had separated or divorced, and 360 were either poor or very poor.[83] The school provided free hot lunches when they could, offered appropriate medical care, and furnished clothing and shoes when it was determined that the lack of such items was a contributing factor in truancy.[84] During the height of the Depression, some even termed the entrance to the school "welfare alley" because of the assistance school personnel provided students in dealing with eviction notices, relief checks, and court summonses.[85] Thus, the school served as a social services center as well as a school.

Many implicit ideas about boys were embedded in the nature of the curriculum at Montefiore. As with other day schools, the curriculum featured a hands-on approach to learning, and the school was outfitted with extensive facilities: electrical and metal shops, a woodshop, a science lab with an aquarium, and a reed and rug-weaving workshop. But, over the years, the school began to reject the idea that training troubled youth for only industrial labor was an equitable solution to their mandate of educating troubled youth. This issue likely came to light through the debates about democracy and racial equality that emerged in the context of World War II. In the annual report for 1946–1947, Stullken appeared to be responding to the trend in Chicago toward expelling difficult-to-handle children, arguing that "socially maladjusted children are entitled to an education. State constitutions and legislative enactment call upon all school districts to provide a thorough and efficient system of free schools for 'all' children of the state—none should be excluded." At the same time, he argued against the trend of substituting manual for academic education. He recommended early diagnosis and identification of disabilities and emotional and intellectual handicaps as a way to address and remediate delinquency. The school notably embodied a growing trend toward the identification of specific disability categories that are still in play: educational retardation, emotional disturbances, and reading and learning disabilities.

Schools such as Montefiore would now be described as therapeutic. Like other such language, the term masks the more turbulent and punitive aspects of schools that were meant for troublemakers. Among the student inhabitants the Montefiore School held a dubious distinction, at least for those boys for whom the setting was merely a stepping-stone to more serious delinquency. One youth was quite scathing in his indictment of the Montefiore School: "The school isn't worth a dime . . . You went into the place and there seemed to be a lack of help . . . You found that when you went in there if a guy felt like reaching over the desk and punching you in the jaw, well, dammit, he just did it."[86] Other students claimed that the "tough teachers" were a deterrent for truancy but that the peer group of tough boys was an equally strong pull. Apparently, boys were not the only ones to find the school a tough place. When teacher Catherine Fitzgibbons tried to put an end to a game of dice in the hallway, two of the players drew pistols and threatened her before finally surrendering their weapons to another teacher.[87]

It was, indeed, the case that many of the city's most aggressive and violent youth attended the schools, and there were recurrent scandals involving Montefiore youth in criminal actions. Some of the most notable occurrences happened in the 1950s, as documented in various newspaper articles. From the period of 1954 to 1957, Montefiore "rowdies" were involved in several incidents on the city buses they took to get to the school. The first time, after Montefiore youth knocked a roll of coins out of the reach of the bus driver, who reacted to the unruly youth by driving to the police station, charges were dropped. Stullken refused to discipline the youth, insisting, "These boys aren't hoodlums."[88] By 1957, however, the incidents were numerous and increasingly menacing. In one of the more egregious violations, eighteen youth were charged with assaulting, molesting, and robbing a woman at the back of the bus, tearing her clothes and underwear, and taking two dollars from her purse. In the wake of this incident the Chicago Transit Authority hired private detectives to ride on the bus that took the youth to school and paid for police vehicles to trail the buses.[89]

Clearly, Montefiore had become a place where youth in trouble with the law were sent as a last resort before placement in a residential institution, such as the parental school or the reformatory at St. Charles. But amassing some of the district's most troubled youth in public day schools was causing more problems than Stullken confessed in his annual reports. He firmly believed that the delinquents who came through his doors had a "social handicap" and begged the public to show more sympathy toward these troubled youth. In a speech, which was quoted in the *Chicago Tribune*, Stullken explained his position: "A crippled or a blind child gets sympathy at a glance . . . But let a child steal a hubcap and the owner generally is interested in having something done to, rather than for, that child. Sometimes a child like this is more to be pitied than the one with a gross physical handicap."[90] Stullken's compassionate response to the delinquents attending his school was no doubt well meaning, but it is unclear whether attaching a disability label to children "in trouble" is apt to engender the help they most need.

After the initial years of the experiment, when the excitement of the reform years had faded, it seemed that the Montefiore School only made the news when its students were apprehended for a violent crime. Yet in succeeding years the school managed to reinvent itself in response to changing needs. Though often on the chopping block, it has responded to community demands to educate youth who have difficulty not only with school but with the juvenile justice system.[91]

As special education evolved, it used the medicalized language of disease, handicap, and disability to describe the young boys who were placed into sub-normal classes and special schools. With growing sophistication, special educators interviewed young people about their individual traumas, tested not only their IQ's but also their reading and mathematical abilities, and even employed strategies such as small-group therapy to attempt to remediate boys' difficulties. Rarely, however, did they interrogate their own assumptions about what was best for boys and delinquents, nor did they grapple systematically with the structural forces that contributed to boys' embracing of marginal masculinities that put them at odds with school and society.

Still, educators such as Stullken advocated for the youngsters they served, arguing that troubled youth had a right to some form of an education, even if that right meant segregating them from their peers in the regular public schools. At the same time, their techniques continued to employ a number of the gendered premises that guided the direction of reform schools, juxtaposing therapeutic and punitive approaches. Amassed in single-gender schools, many boys continued to propagate peer-based cultures of masculinity that were resistant to adult intervention.

The types of schools that special educators developed morphed in succeeding decades into schools not too dissimilar from the earlier versions, given such titles as opportunity or alternative schools. They also paved the way for contemporary special education classifications, rationales for compensatory education for the disadvantaged, and the establishment of the Education for All Handicapped Children Act in 1975, which guarantees a free and appropriate education for children with disabilities. Yet the medicalization of disabilities that are difficult to define or measure provided another venue for disproportionate segregation in terms of race and gender and made the granting of certain educational rights and benefits contingent on the authority of experts.

CHAPTER 5

"The Boys' Own Story"
Masculinity, Peer Culture, and Delinquency

By the age of seventeen Barney already had a distinguished "delinquent career." It started at the age of eight, when he tried to snatch a purse at a Chicago department store. His immigrant father, a day laborer and a bootlegger, accompanied him to court. When the judge asked him how the boy should be punished, his father responded, "Take him away. Maybe you can teach him a lesson." The residential St. Mary's Training School for "semi-delinquents" with its whippings and harsh punishments, proved to be too much for the young boy, who ran away before his father dragged him back. After a few stints in and out of the institution, Barney's mother was fatally injured when she fell from the second story of their tenement flat. He was twelve years old at the time; at that point, his father went to court requesting that institutional care—whether orphanages or training schools—be found for his four children. Barney was returned to the dreaded St. Mary's, but after he was released his crimes escalated from stealing to armed robbery. Between the ages of twelve and seventeen, he was placed in no less than four different institutions, ending up at the Pontiac statewide penitentiary for adult males. Barney was finally released from jail in 1921 and completed his parole in 1923, whereupon his record ceases. Whether Barney weathered the storm of adolescence and youth and moved onto a more respectable existence or came to a less fortunate end is unknown.[1]

Barney's story—that of a delinquent whose offenses escalated from petty theft, truancy, and vagrancy to more serious crimes throughout his young life, with a poignant story of poverty, a mother's death, an Oliver Twist–like "training school," and a father whom his children deemed neglectful and uncaring—was unexceptional among the stories that Clifford Shaw and his team of researchers collected from criminals and juvenile offenders in the 1920s and 1930s. The documents that Shaw and other researchers like him amassed, including "life stories" of individual boys who ended up in the penitentiary, render a disturbing glimpse of delinquents living in urban Chicago. Stories of neglect, abuse, poverty, and time spent in institutions abound. Many boys seemed to caper about the city with minimal adult supervision, their values shaped more by the peer society of other boys than adults or social institutions. Although it is tempting to vaunt the agency of marginalized social groups such as this subculture of children—and there are certainly times when one wants to applaud youthful inventiveness and adventure—it is problematic to romanticize youth who challenged the powers that be by harming themselves and others. There is no romance in the penitentiary, nor is robbing and assaulting a drunken homeless person a sign of agency.

Social scientists such as Shaw, in contrast to many psychologists or special educators, understood delinquency as a normal response to pathological social environments. In so doing, they implicitly rejected the disability-based approach to special education for delinquency that was taking hold in the 1920s. Instead of identifying such youth as abnormal, with inherent mental or emotional defects, Chicago school sociologists were more interested in the social processes that led boys to find meaning and sustenance outside of mainstream culture. Yet, like special educators, they drew on long-standing biases in their approaches to working with boys. They did not so much reject delinquents' value systems in regard to masculinity as seek to work within the parameters of boys' peer cultures. Documenting an era when poverty was unmitigated by such government policies as social security, public housing, health care for the very poor, food stamps, and workers' compensation, these stories of boys and the reform efforts meant to help them illuminate the realities of the era's urban "underclass" of white first- and second-generation immigrant boys.

Poverty, immigration, nativism, urbanization, and familial suffering were not boy problems; they were social problems. But responses to social distress and suffering were gendered. From the juvenile court, meant to rehabilitate delinquent boys and girls, to the Chicago Area Project, which centered its efforts on preventing delinquency, these institutions operated according to traditional and emerging notions about the characteristics associated with boys. Indeed, the code of masculinity operating in delinquent peer groups—which celebrated physical prowess, the mastery of public space, the acquisition of wealth, risk-taking, autonomy, and physical and sexual aggression—was in many ways mainstream. The killer Clyde Barrow and gangster Al Capone were cultural icons, while talented boxers such as Jack Johnson were being catapulted into national stardom. In fact, the working-class masculinity exemplified by these glamorized figures was increasingly becoming an ideal to which less muscled and physically adventurous men would aspire.[2] It was outside of the boundaries of public discourse to crack the code of masculinity; programs for delinquent youth instead sought to allow for the expression of these masculine ideals in a more respectable fashion.

In imagining boyhood, reformers at first drew upon the nineteenth-century ideal of children as essentially innocent, tarnished only by environmental forces. This presented a paradox for street-level boy workers, who encountered boys who seemed far from innocent, who appeared to treat armed robbery as casually as truancy, and whose predatory behaviors displayed a degree of cynicism and remorselessness that seemed completely out of keeping with any existing notions of childhood. Yet even boys' assaults and sexual transgressions, whether they were directed at girls or boys, were sometimes conceptualized as impulsive behaviors that were unchecked by adequate social mechanisms. Reformers as a group—educators, social workers, and others—were moving away from moralistic responses to boys' antisocial behaviors. Boy workers who conceived of boys' behaviors as only variations on the norm predicated primarily on environmental conditions had difficulty differentiating between normal boyish antics and the more troublesome behaviors that led down to the perilous path to the penitentiary.

The Juvenile Court

The juvenile court, established in 1899 in Chicago as a special venue for adjudicating cases involving youth, vacillated between the extremes of viewing boys as innocent pranksters or as dangerous monsters. Founded on the principle that youth were inherently more innocent than their adult counterparts and required specific forms of justice, the courts also transformed many of today's status offenses into criminal activities. A symbol of either a new reverence for childhood or the increasing oppressiveness of the state, depending on one's perspective, the institution of the juvenile court embodied the sentiments of early twentieth-century child savers who fervently believed that state intervention was required to give children the protections and "rights" they deserved. Perhaps it is true, as some scholars attest, that the court merely perpetuated principles about the role of the state in child saving that were generated during the first wave of the reformatory movement in the early 1800s. But what made this new court so distinctive was the widespread and nearly universal acclaim accorded to it. With such acceptance, the courts would play a central role in adjudicating the competing claims of children, parents, schools, neighbors, and law enforcement agencies.

The Chicago Juvenile Court was initiated in response to the Illinois Juvenile

Court Act, and was one of a platform of reforms—including compulsory education and child labor laws—meant to empower the state to intervene in the lives of children who were not being properly parented.[3] Whether children were dependent or delinquent, the intention was to keep them out of adult courts and to bring flexibility and hopefully sensitivity to their judicial treatment. The courts also removed due process from the children's courtroom, a deficiency that would not be corrected until the *In re Gault* case in 1967, when the Supreme Court ruled that even children were entitled the legal rights of adult defendants. But the removal of due process was fully in keeping with the intentions of the court's defenders, who wished to make the process of adjudication less formal and more "familial," an ideal that would ultimately prove wanting.

The rapidity of the juvenile court's adoption is astonishing and suggestive of evolving attitudes toward youth: as of 1915, a total of forty-six states, three territories, and the District of Columbia had mandated juvenile courts.[4] By the 1920s every city with a population over a hundred thousand had created such a court.[5] Its genesis was heavily influenced by concerns about boys, who greatly overrepresented girls: between 1904 and 1906, five times as many boys as girls appeared before the juvenile court for delinquency in Chicago.[6]

The juvenile court was built on two major premises, both of which expanded upon the English common law principle of *parens patrie*, or "the state as parent." Ironically, these premises balanced both rehabilitative and punitive ideals: children were in need of protection because of their age and society required protection from children who were likely to endanger the public good.[7] By separating juvenile offenders from adults, advocates hoped to shield youth from contamination by more hardened criminals and dispense justice that was in keeping with children's age, crime, and particular circumstances. Advocates of Chicago's juvenile court demonstrated that, just prior to the passage of the Juvenile Court Act, 1,983 boys (under sixteen) were incarcerated in adult prisons, a quarter of them for only truancy.[8] Although some complained about children languishing in these prisons, others contended that many youth brought to the criminal court evaded trial because they were of "tender age," leading to suspicions that judicial inaction was contributing to more pronounced offenses down the road.[9] United States Children's Bureau chief Julia Lathrop, for instance, claimed that judges would neither send "children to the bridewell nor bear to be themselves guilty of the harsh folly of compelling poverty-stricken parents to pay fines." As a result, children were burrowing ever more deeply into criminality as they escaped the consequences of their actions.[10] Juvenile court advocates thus drew on two major arguments: some youth were getting off scot free for their crimes while others were thrown into jail for minor offenses only to be further schooled in crime by truly hardened criminals.

The juvenile court, prison reformers such as Miriam Van Waters believed, offered new "rights" for children, particularly the right to grow up as properly parented law-abiding citizens. She envisioned the court as determining whether the delinquent "is in such condition that he has lost or has never known the fundamental rights of childhood to parental shelter, guidance, and control."[11] In fact, juvenile courts typically dealt with cases of both dependency and delinquency, with the lines between the two often being hard to draw. The rights of childhood in this sense, then, had nothing to do with legal protections or youthful autonomy but with the right of a child to be properly raised, either by the parents or the state.

Even though progressive women such as Van Waters, Lathrop, and Jane Addams had been at the forefront of efforts to establish the juvenile court, the court itself was heavily masculine. The masculinity of the juvenile court judges seemed critical, insofar as they were able to model respectable manhood, stand in for missing or inept fathers, and empathize with the inherent waywardness of boys.[12] Judge Robert Tuthill of Chicago insisted that he would treat each boy before him as "his own son," while the charismatic Judge Ben Lindsey of Denver was known as the kids' judge.[13] Where boys might have sought to escape poverty-stricken homes and boring and punitive schools by fleeing to the streets or the railroads, their search for autonomy was countered by the juvenile court, where the judge, ideally a fatherly looking man, who was both friendly but firm, issued warnings, offered advice, and had the power to determine the fate of a dependent or delinquent youngster.[14]

Part of the problem with establishing a court with unlimited jurisdiction over youth, however, comes with defining delinquency. *Delinquency* is a legal term that is not in young children's vocabulary, and its definition is wholly contextual. The term *juvenile delinquent* itself did not originate until the early nineteenth century, when separate reformatory institutions for young offenders were established. Not only are understandings of delinquency historical, they also are constructed by adults to identify certain actions performed by youth as antisocial and detrimental to the normal course of healthy child development. Many so-called crimes, those known as status offenses, are violations only when committed by youth: examples include truancy, running away from home, or drinking alcohol. Still other illegal activities, such as stealing a bit of coal for the fire at home, were considered to be essential family functions in some poor and immigrant communities. When boys skipped school on a lark, stole an apple from a fruit cart, or loitered around pool halls or other presumably adult venues, they were participating in activities that were sanctioned by their peers and even members of the adult community. The juvenile court transformed many of these somewhat normal behaviors into acts of transgression that could potentially lead to incarceration without due process. Instead of mixing up innocent youth with hardened adults, juvenile courts often conflated youth who had committed only status offenses with those who had committed armed robbery (or worse).

For youth who had engaged in serious crimes, reformatories and even parental schools were the options of choice. But the flexible sentencing that was the hallmark of the court also furthered the use of probation, whereby boys could be afforded state supervision while living at home. Judges could also send children to live with a relative, commit them to a residential institution, or collaborate with the school district to send them to a special class. There were close ties between school districts and the courts in many cities, with truant officers petitioning both children and their parents to appear. In Philadelphia's juvenile court, white children who had committed only mild delinquencies often encountered a fairly desirable outcome whereby they were assigned a mentor, usually an upstanding businessman who supplied not only moral support but also trips to baseball games, camp scholarships, and access to jobs through the Big Brothers organization.[15]

As the court's jurisdiction over status offenses expanded, the potential to be branded with the label "delinquent" increased. Pauline Goldmark critiqued the broad hand of New York's juvenile court, which brought boys in for vagrancy, selling newspapers without a badge, sleeping outside, pitching pennies, and building fires. Of the 463 offenses that landed boys in court in 1909, only 119 were offenses against property, and 13 were assaults. Believing that most of these so-called crimes "are more or less excusable in boys," she complained, "almost every one of their offenses is due to one of four causes: neglect on the part of the parent, the pressure of poverty, the expression of pure boyish spirits, or the attempt to play."[16] Goldmark highlighted the tension between seeing boys' offenses as ordinary and excusable or as signposts along the way to a delinquent career. As the court increased its reach over juveniles, the rates of status offenses escalated. In 1911, after four years of the establishment of the juvenile court in Detroit, status offenders were nearly double what they had been in 1907, and the numbers of juveniles tried in courts of law spiked dramatically.[17]

The use of the court for minor offenses was disturbing to sociologist Henry Winfred Thurston, who wrote about the Cleveland Juvenile Court in the early 1900s. Thurston wondered whether the court had not been arbitrarily apprehending young boys whose misdeeds were on the spectrum of normal boyish behavior. When ten to fifteen young boys scoured a local railroad yard for copper, only one was accosted and brought to the police station; Thurston worried that the lone youngster would distrust the justice system as a result. In the Cleveland of 1918, stealing a bit of something from the railroad yard was common enough among the children of the poor to preclude its being viewed as a sign of serious delinquency, at least among immigrant communities. Thurston speculated, "They had not planned delinquency. They were merely coltish young Polish boys, some of them with Paderewski brows and hair. Their attitude toward the waste ribbons of copper was very much like that of city boys and girls everywhere toward the bits of ice they seize from the ice wagon." Noting that the number of youth brought before the juvenile court was escalating at a rate two to five times higher than Cleveland's population growth, Thurston ruminated about the impact on children of encountering police and courts for everyday misdeeds.[18]

Social worker Helen Cody Baker, upon visiting the courtroom of Judge Bicek in early 1930s Chicago, was similarly appalled by the minor offenses that children were called to account for in a court of law: "with four exceptions, these juvenile offenders had committed no crime that had not, at one time or another, been perpetrated by one of my own children." The infractions she named included "violations of the speed law, throwing stones at a freight train, stealing a fountain pen, or 'annoying the director of the Red, White, and Blue Club.'"[19] Baker appeared to be reflecting on the differences in the treatment of "other people's children"—that is, the children of the middle class—whose misdeeds were typically dealt with in a more informal and less punitive fashion than those of the children of the poor.[20] These reflections also put the juvenile court squarely in the center of the community as a venue for neighbors, reformers, business owners, and others to settle disputes with disorderly boys.

Mischief was an example of a status offense that differed remarkably depending on its social context. Social worker Mabel Rhoades noted in 1907 that the cities of Syracuse and Chicago defined the juvenile offense of mischief very differently. She discovered that playing ball and swimming naked were deemed mischief in Syracuse, while in Chicago most youth charged with mischief had committed offenses against the railroad.[21] Beyond mischief were the common acts of theft of trinkets from the tempting department stores or of items from local stores that might otherwise embellish meager incomes and feed hungry stomachs. Of course, there was a difference between petty thievery, vandalism, and other youthful indiscretions and more serious and sometimes planned offenses such as armed robbery and violent assault, generally performed by older boys and usually subject to more severe consequences. Thurston was concerned that criminalizing more commonplace boyish behaviors as truancy and petty thievery could have negative consequences by causing boys to develop an antagonistic relationship to law enforcement.

Once at court, it was not only the child who was on trial but the family, as historian Steven Schlossman attests.[22] There were probing inquiries into children's home lives, their physical environments, and their parents' personal characteristics. Case notes depict delinquent homes as dirty, dark, crowded, cluttered, and unheated, while parents often appear as drunk, immoral, slatternly, feebleminded, violent, or seemingly unconcerned about their children's well-being.[23] Reformers also took note of the seemingly concerned parent who made an effort to keep a clean house even in the most destitute of circumstances. Yet many social workers' judgments of parents and their living situations were clearly shaped by their own middle-class backgrounds and values; from their perspective any home, even an institution, was better than the living situations that many children endured.

Yet juvenile courts also served a constituency of parents who were either unable or unwilling to provide for or control their children. In his study of the Milwaukee court, Schlossman discovered that between the years 1914 and 1916, a full third of the petitions brought against youth were initiated by their parents, who were "hoping to shore up their waning parental authority in the domicile."[24] Similarly, New York reformer Pauline Goldmark commented that uneasy working mothers in New York were apt to ask the judge to "put him away until school begins to keep him off the streets."[25] Residential placements for male youth could serve not only as punishment but also as a form of child care in an era where there was virtually none available and as a way for parents to secure what they hoped would be a disciplined and safe environment for wayward boys.

Ultimately, the ideals of the juvenile court were in conflict with the practical exigencies of the legal process, especially in larger cities. Chicago's juvenile court judges often presided over twenty-five cases in a single morning, leaving little time for reflection and counsel. And, in reality, timeworn methods for dealing with bad boys often won out over the progressive treatment reformers had envisioned. The courtroom became a place where disciplinary "lessons" were given by both the police and the judges. In New York's juvenile court, police routinely arrested young delinquents, committed them to detention for a day, and then gave them a "licking" in court.[26] Chicago reformers complained that truants were often held without being charged in the detention home, so that the boys would "learn their lesson."[27] Parents in the Milwaukee Juvenile Court were instructed not to bail their children out too early, so that detained children would have time to mull over their misbehavior and confront the potential consequences of future offenses.[28] Was the court like a parent? Maybe, but perhaps not the type of parent that the more idealistic social reformers had envisioned.[29]

The "right to childhood" that some reformers envisioned in the premise of the juvenile court was also undermined by indiscriminate sentencing. Disorderly children were turned into criminals when they walked into the halls of the juvenile court or detention home. What is more, even the smallest offenses, such as truancy, loomed as predictors of children's future lives as adults.[30] Were children truly being treated as children if their every action was evaluated on the basis of their potential as adults? Many contemporary scholars have found that although the new correctional apparatus promised to be "benevolent" in its dispensation of juvenile justice, it instead strengthened and expanded the state's role in the surveillance of youth.[31]

Doling out lessons in incarceration and confinement may even have undermined the imagined innocence of youth that reformers sought to protect. A Chicago clubwoman, philanthropist, and reformer who had fought to establish both the juvenile court and detention home, Louise de Koven Bowen, was optimistic about the fate of the seemingly innocent youth who were schooled at the detention home. She applauded the home and its management, yet the stories she shared about some of the boys' actions seem harrowing. During the course of one visit, she met up with the harried-looking elderly female superintendent, who muttered that the boys had been "bad" that particular day. The supervisor had encountered a throng of boys in the yard sitting atop a guard they had bound; the inmates were striking the guard in the head with his revolver. Instead of calling the police, the woman simply asked the boys to unbind the guard and apologize, which they apparently did: a resolution that Bowen believed demonstrated both the supervisor's competence and the ability to manage boys' misbehavior through humane methods. Bowen's tales also included that of an angelic-looking seven-year-old who took a can of kerosene, poured it over the beds in the dormitory, and set fire to the place.[32] Bowen's depictions normalized boys' transgressions, portraying boyhood as a time when departures from civilized norms, including violence, were to be expected. To her, the boys of the city slums were no different from innocent country kids, except that they had been deprived of good wholesome influences, clean houses, respectable parents, and orderly neighborhoods. Yet it is worth questioning whether the detention center itself fostered the kind of behavior it sought to correct by grouping boys charged with varying levels of crimes together, even if they had not yet been proven guilty.

Delinquency, Gender, and Gangs

Bowen's sanguine assessment of boys' misbehaviors was not matched by juvenile court reformers' attitudes toward girls, whose sexual escapades or autonomous actions were not so often seen as innocent. The charges that boys and girls faced when encountering the juvenile court diverged considerably. Boys were most likely to be apprehended on charges of thievery, truancy, and vagrancy, whereas girls were often charged and committed to institutions for sexual immorality, a crime that was sometimes thinly disguised as incorrigibility.[33] The sexual activity of girls and young women was construed as not only unlawful but also psychologically abnormal. Yet much of what reformers were seeing was a result of changing norms of behavior for working-class young women, who were more likely to live outside of their parents' home for a period of time before marriage and who were taking advantage of city pleasures, some of which involved engaging in sexual activity.[34] Some reformers imagined that delinquent girls were also acting out of their adolescent instincts when they engaged in sexual activity thought to be beyond their years and outside of the parameters of legitimate marriage. Despite the fact that girls were tempted by commercial amusements such as movies and dance halls, bored by limited recreational activities, denied access to athletics, and raised by families that did not conform to conventional standards of morality, many female reformers believed that girls who were provided suitable recreational pursuits would be able to sublimate their sexual drives.[35] Despite the overrepresentation of boys brought before the juvenile court, girls who appeared were much more likely to be institutionalized. In the first ten years of Chicago's juvenile court, only 21 percent of the boys charged with crimes were institutionalized, while 59 percent of girls were sent to training schools and reformatories.[36] Conversely, the sexual activity of young boys, even if it involved coercion and violence, was barely acknowledged, let alone adjudicated.[37]

Most publications about delinquency treated it as a male phenomenon, wholly separate and different from the misbehavior or unlawfulness of girls. Unlike girl delinquents, who were thought to break the law as individuals, delinquency theorists contended that most young males committed their crimes in groups or gangs. The gangs of the 1920s and 1930s were distinct in many ways from the gangs of the post–World War II years. Many gangs were less formally organized, lacking the extensive paraphernalia and rituals of membership that would come to be associated with the ethnic and racially defined gangs of later years. They were also more heterogeneous in age, often spanning from eight to twenty-one, including younger siblings and cousins along with older youth.[38] The elasticity of age in boys' peer networks would change in succeeding years, as more youth became stratified in school by the age-grading system and entered high school. And once boys were able to leave school at fourteen or sixteen, they also more clearly differentiated themselves from their younger brothers and cousins, as they entered a world of more formal labor and adult pleasures.[39] Historian Eric Schneider, in his study of postwar gangs in New York, *Vampires, Dragons, and Egyptian Kings*, depicts early twentieth-century gangs as relatively unproblematic. He concludes that such gangs "were hardly innocent, but their conflicts were generally nonlethal and so commonplace as to arouse little concern."[40] And it is indeed true that earlier gangs featured less organized violence between rival racial and ethnic groups than in the later period, and juvenile homicide rates were relatively low (in part because of the relative difficulty of securing firearms). At the same time, it must be said that rampant law-breaking, which could range from truancy to petty thievery, armed robbery, assault, group violence against racial minorities, and rape, was not uncommon among the more vicious gangs of the early twentieth century.

One contemporary sociologist who shared Schneider's assessment was Frederic Thrasher, who built his career studying gangs, including a landmark study of 1,313 Chicago gangs published in 1927. In the introduction, Thrasher's mentor, the influential sociologist Robert Park, described the gang as a perennial problem: "every village has at least its boy gang, and in the village, as in the city, it is composed of those same foot-loose, prowling, and predacious elements adolescents who herd and hang together, after the manner of the undomesticated male elsewhere." He continued, "Gangs are gangs, wherever they are found."[41] Thrasher invested the gang with a gendered sense of universality, an unchangeable male essence. That adolescent boys were innately "predacious" and "undomesticated" was taken as a given. The problem was not so much how to get rid of the gang, which would be impossible because it was based on primeval impulses, but how to control its more negative features. Thrasher found gangs to be picturesque, and he seemed rather enthralled with the "comedy, tragedy," and "melodrama" associated with their comings and goings.[42] Simultaneously repelled and entranced by the habitat of the boy gang, he observed, "The buzzing chatter and constant motion reminds one of insects which hover in a swarm, yet ceaselessly dart hither and thither. This endless activity has a tremendous fascination . . . and it would be a marvel indeed if any healthy boy could himself aloof from it."[43] In other words, the same habitat that produced delinquency, vice, and social disorganization constituted an irresistible draw for boys whose very natures demanded sociability and excitement. In the primeval gang, boys were unfettered by the traditional constraints placed on them by parents and schools.

Thrasher's relatively sympathetic gloss notwithstanding, it was during this period that gangs captured the imagination of the American public and were seen to be the source of much juvenile and adult crime. By the 1920s the infatuation with the notion that boys must recapitulate the primitive past was diminishing, and nostalgia for a rowdy boyishness was waning as professional social workers and sociologists began confronting the harsh texture of life for impoverished boys. Delinquent boys' street culture, although often exuberant and playful, normalized violence, theft, assault, sexual coercion, and even rape.[44] Unlike earlier theorists, some of today's social scientists are beginning to consider the role that gender plays in boys' criminality. Criminologist James W. Messerschmidt claims that in the process of "doing gender," today's boys may embrace delinquency because it confirms masculine status and differentiates boys from girls, especially when there are few respectable pathways for normative masculinity.[45] This is somewhat similar to the theory of the "cool pose" that Richard Majors and Janet Mancini Billson write about, arguing that contemporary black male youth do not have access to "traditional white manhood" and thus embody a form of "cool masculinity" to "ward off the anxiety of second-class status." Cool masculinity is not only a pose but also a dynamic performance that, in addition to exemplifying coolness, style, and toughness may also include physical and sexual violence.[46] By warding off second-class status as marginal men, however, boys enhanced their own status at the expense of all girls and boys who were unable or unwilling to embody the ideals of masculinity they upheld.

The unrestrained boy culture of the streets put a premium on demonstrations of masculinity as manifested in a disregard for social conventions, the police, schools, church, girls and young women, and even parents at times.[47] Boys claimed the streets as their own, but boys also had to earn the right to the streets, mainly by proving their physical prowess through fights with other boys. Boys vigilantly patrolled the boundaries of appropriate masculine behavior, accepting only those who met their standards and punishing or expelling those who strayed. Girls, effeminate boys, unwitting adults, and boys from different racial and ethnic groups could become the victims of boys who were also often victimized by poverty, racial and ethnic antagonism, other youth, and even their own families. Victims and victimizers, innocent and knowing, normal and deviant: sociologists wrestled with these dichotomies as they sought to understand delinquent boys who lived on the margins of mainstream culture yet within cultures where their actions conferred status and masculinity.

Interventions to deter potential delinquents from crime and to rehabilitate those who had already been found guilty of offenses abounded during the first half of the twentieth century. Some programs clearly enabled youthful trouble-makers to stay out of prison, find jobs, and achieve a respectable existence, yet the obstacles reformers encountered were formidable. These impediments were not only the deeply rooted behaviors of boys themselves caught up in devastating social, economic, and political environments that did not nourish their humanity, but also in the interventions that capitalized on pre-existing peer networks, delinquent cultures of masculinity, and the punishment and segregation of delinquent males. Taken as a whole, these actions could potentially exacerbate boys' negative attitudes to mainstream social institutions.

The Chicago Area Project

Although criminology was not yet a distinct academic discipline in the early 1900s, behavioral and social sciences were central to the development of many children's legal reforms. The science of child psychology was built, beginning in the second decade of the century, on the study of delinquency, with such pioneering scientists as William Healy researching its sources in children's school adjustments, intellectual abilities, mental conflicts, family pathologies, and social milieus.[48] The Juvenile Psychopathic Institute was created in 1909, with Healy as its leader, and was as a counterpart to the Chicago Juvenile Court. The institute worked with both schools and the juvenile justice system to assess troubled youth. Although many psychological clinics of the period, such as the Ohio Bureau of Juvenile Research, continued to cleave to the notion that delinquents were primarily of low intelligence, Healy compiled evidence revealing the intrinsic intellectual and psychological normality of delinquents, asserting that each delinquent was responding to specific circumstances.[49] Because he viewed delinquents as individuals with their own stories to tell, Healy advocated counseling for youth and their parents. Ultimately, this approach would lead to the development of the child guidance movement.[50]

Chicago sociologists such as Clifford Shaw were sympathetic to Healy's conception of the individuality of each delinquent, but they sought to extend the purview of their research to include the boys' habitat, including the city, the neighborhood, and the peer group.[51] In 1927 Shaw, who had started a delinquency intervention project on the North Side of Chicago, was put in charge of the sociological department of the Juvenile Psychopathic Institute. With the assistance of sociologist and coauthor Henry McKay, Shaw began to develop the program that would become known as the Chicago Area Project (CAP). This initiative was so sweeping in its vision—involving various delinquency-prone communities in the remediation of their own problems—that it would be copied in various cities and continues to operate in Chicago today.[52]

Shaw and his colleagues with CAP also left considerable documentation of the lives and cultures of delinquent boys in Chicago for the years spanning from the 1920s through the 1950s. In addition to "life stories," they included more "objective" data such as school reports, psychological testing, ethnographic accounts of boys' gangs, and social casework records in the files of the delinquents they studied. These gritty accounts, which include reports of boys' street life, groupings, activities, and delinquent escapades, reveal a world where violence, conflict, and abuse were intermingled with affection, camaraderie, and adventure. In his defense of recording the delinquent "boys' own story"—a concept he borrowed from psychologist William Healy—Shaw pointed out the utility of representing the delinquents' perceptions of their own reality.[53] Shaw's collection also reflects his interest in second-generation immigrants, especially Poles, Eastern European Jews, and Italians. These groups are overrepresented in the collection in part because they were the most recent newcomers among the immigrants in Chicago and therefore of particular interest to Shaw. African Americans, in contrast, already constituted a significant number of youth appearing before the juvenile court by the 1910s but barely appear in the study.

Before conducting his research on individual delinquents and their peer groups, Shaw and his colleagues investigated and mapped the city of Chicago to determine not only where the majority of delinquents lived but also the common characteristics of what they termed "delinquency areas." In a groundbreaking book of the same title, *Delinquency Areas* (1929), Shaw identified five neighborhoods in Chicago where delinquency rates were exorbitantly high—where approximately one in five of the boys had already had contact with the police.[54] Another intriguing aspect of several of these neighborhoods was that, despite generational changes in their ethnic composition, the rates of delinquency remained high. Some of these areas had once been home to older immigrant populations, such as the Irish and Germans, but had now housed Poles, Italians, Eastern European Jews, and, increasingly, blacks and Mexicans; still, delinquency statistics remained essentially the same. This led Shaw and his colleagues to attribute delinquency to the nature of the geographical spaces in which boys lived rather than individual temperaments or socioeconomic, ethnic, or racial characteristics.[55]

Shaw identified poverty, overcrowding, low rents, high geographic mobility, unemployment, and heterogeneous and transitional ethnic populations as characteristic of delinquency areas. Taverns, poolrooms, dance halls, factories, coal yards, and other industrial enterprises littered the cityscape, providing multiple arenas for both witnessing and participating in illicit activities. The social ecologists of delinquency believed that the competing purposes of these neighborhoods, along with transiency and ethnic transitions, contributed to the inability of the local community to effectively exert social control over its youthful residents.

Because of the heterogeneity of youth's habitat, Shaw and his colleagues believed that delinquency areas were socially disorganized, lacking in the community institutions and neighborhood coherence that would support the socialization of youth. The heterogeneous habitat of a delinquency area was echoed in a CAP report on a neighborhood in Chicago's North Side, which was described as "one square mile of factories, taverns, rummage shops, and aging, red-brick cottages." Yet the area also housed an active intergenerational street life. The old people sat on benches along the curbstone, while teenagers played craps on the sidewalk and young boys pitched pennies and hung out in the ubiquitous candy stores. Youngsters intermingled petty crime and fun, according to one of the workers: they "carried on their sidewalk crap games, penny-tossing, junking expeditions, rides in hot cars; anything to make a bit of extra change."[56] These minor illicit activities, which were intrinsic to neighborhood life, were portents of potentially more dangerous delinquent activities in the future, according to Shaw and the reformers.

CAP sent out male indigenous street workers, also known as "curbstone counselors" and later as "detached street workers," whose headquarters would be the streets and meeting places where boys and members of the community convened. Shaw championed the detached worker idea in part because he believed that most delinquents were already alienated from more traditional institutions such as schools, settlement houses, formal boys' clubs, and religious organizations.[57] By seeking to recruit workers with ethnic backgrounds similar to those of the youth with whom they worked, CAP sought to disassociate itself from those reforms that had involved middle-class Protestants imposing their cultural norms on resistant Catholic and Jewish immigrants. Ultimately, the detached street worker concept would be employed in numerous juvenile delinquency efforts throughout the country, including community-building strategies adopted by the War on Poverty in the late twentieth century.[58]

One of the unanticipated consequences of this approach, especially in an ethnically and racially divided city like Chicago, was its potential to further reinforce pre-existing ethnic and racial boundaries and hostilities, as workers were urged to rely on the "natural groupings" of the gang. In a proposal to integrate the work of CAP with that of the supervision of parolees, this strategy was justified: "By this means the natural relations and controls in the group are preserved. In the case of the delinquent groups, the task becomes one of introducing into the life and structure of the group, values of a constructive character."[59] The use of the word *natural* to refer to groupings and leaders implicitly suggested that not only maleness but also ethnicity and race were hardwired for the organization of society. Street workers became a part of these natural groupings, all the while recording their interactions in hopes of cracking the delinquent code and providing insight into the meaning behind illegal activities. But these indigenous street workers straddled a perilous divide. They were expected to ally themselves with and follow the group in its meanderings while also intervening to prevent delinquency. In practice, this meant that some street workers spent their time in recording and gaining the confidence of delinquent kids rather than deterring unlawful activities, putting them in the difficult position of choosing whether to report illegal activities and thus lose their connection with the gang.[60]

But using detached street workers was only one of CAP's innovations. When Shaw started his first initiative in the Polish working-class neighborhood known as Russell Square, or the Bush, he not only sent an individual to work with groups of boys but also instructed him to begin organizing a community council meant to galvanize neighborhood residents to put in place strategies to solve their own problems.[61] CAP set up community committees in all five of the neighborhoods in which they worked, inviting local preachers, principals, park officers, concerned residents, and even tavern owners to brainstorm about how best to advocate for better conditions and to reduce delinquency. Committee members lobbied the city for more playgrounds and community centers and sought to control boys' access to poolrooms and taverns. The Russell Square Community Committee ended up recruiting up to 80 percent of the children in the community to take part in its activities, which included offering boys their own billiard room to substitute for the deleterious pool halls, forming athletic teams, and providing camping experiences and dances.[62] The Russell Square initiative was also part of a larger effort to integrate delinquency programs with school-based initiatives. In 1939, CAP persuaded the Chicago Board of Education to hire truant officers who were culturally and linguistically familiar with the local community to work in tandem with the juvenile delinquency program.[63]

Although CAP dealt with some of the most confirmed delinquents, they also reported some success at keeping youth on parole out of jail. As with all such programs, however, it is difficult to discern the true cause for the drop in recidivism. One of CAP's reports noted that delinquencies had dropped in some of the areas where the group worked in 1939 but also observed that one reason may have been that boys who might have been "booked" for their misdoings were instead turned over to the group for supervision.[64] Individual workers such as Stephen Bubacz exercised vigilant advocacy on behalf of boys in their program. He helped one youngster who had been indicted with truancy obtain a transfer from the Montefiore School to a vocational school. He also helped the young man, who was later charged with auto theft, to get an after-school job at the Republic Steel plant.[65] Building on their networks with the criminal justice system, the schools, and local businesspeople, CAP staff endeavored to use the system to keep kids out of jail and in school or at work.

But the program was far from a cure-all, and there were many accounts of delinquents who seemed impervious to program efforts. In such cases, as in that of the Kelly Rats, who were "proud of being a notorious gang" (the group had successfully stolen tens of thousands of dollars in products from a beverage truck), program workers went over the ethical edge. After previous leaders had failed to rein them in, new leaders decided that to "hamstring a Kelly by restrictions and edicts was to put a chip on his shoulder . . . They would be given complete trust and latitude." Apparently, the Rats were enthusiastic about camping, but, even after two of the members were accused of attempted rape at the camp and "scurried into hiding at the last minute," they were allowed to continue unpunished so as to not deter the leader from his "experimental undertaking." One must wonder, then, at the complicity of the leader in taking what he termed a "tolerating attitude toward their behavior and unconventional activities."[66] Surely this tolerant approach served the purpose not only of normalizing crime but also of perpetuating the ethos of an aggressive gang that engaged in sexual violence.

It is unlikely, of course, that reformers sought to sanction rape or other harmful actions, although they likely harbored sexist ideas about the instinctual basis of male sexual aggression. They presumably believed that tolerance of some of the gang's actions might enable them to intervene more effectively at a different time. Their tolerance was rooted in the notion that boys' behaviors—including those that sought to subordinate those who were different from them—were natural responses to their situation. For instance, Shaw hypothesized that ethnic and racial diversity promoted delinquency.[67] Critiquing communities comprised of shifting racial and ethnic populations, Shaw declared, "The delinquency areas lack the homogeneity and continuity of cultural traditions which are essential to social solidarity." Shaw betrayed his small-town origins and his longing for places where the church and family could exert greater control when he waxed nostalgic about the "village form of community organization."[68] Because immigrants, migrants, and Native Americans with different cultural traditions coexisted in these spaces, families and the community were thwarted in their efforts to raise youth according to their own ethical values.

Shaw's declamations about the importance of racial and ethnic homogeneity in reducing delinquency were repeated by many other delinquency researchers. Chicago-trained sociologist Walter Reckless explained a youngster's theft on the basis of his heterogeneous neighborhood:

> The family was marooned in a neighborhood that was changing in its racial complexion. And just such half-and-half areas, in which one race or nationality is encroaching and the other one retreating, are breeding spots for delinquency; for the interpenetration of races, classes or nationalities is usually accompanied by a decline in the efficiency of the neighborhood to control its members.[69]

Rather than situating delinquency in the context of poverty, the culture of working-class masculinity, and ethnic and racial oppression, many boy workers of this era chose to view racial integration as responsible for social disorganization.

Sidney, the child of Jewish immigrants and a convicted robber and rapist, wrote his life history for Shaw, who then published an edited and supplemented version of the manuscript as the *Natural History of a Delinquent Career* (1931).[70] Sidney's neighborhood fit Shaw's thesis of a delinquency area: Shaw described it as "deteriorated" and changing from a neighborhood mostly composed of Jews and Italians to one which witnessed the arrival of blacks and Mexicans. Because ethnic traditions could not be maintained in this new heterogeneous environment, the breakdown of social control had resulted in delinquency being "a more or less permanent aspect of the social activity of the boys living in the neighborhood."[71]

Sidney described his neighbors as living in poverty, like his own family: "Many of them supported by charity societys [sic] like my people were. Others that found it hard to make a living and sent their children out to earn and steal whenever they could, just to bring home the bacon as we say."[72] The population changes in the neighborhood gave rise to racial conflict, in which male youth played a prominent role. Sidney said that his father attributed negative changes in the neighborhood to the arrival of "Mexicans and 'Niggers,'" which "changed everything." Black and Indian families lived in his building, and he and his friends would "break their windows, holler in their doors, and throw tin cans onto their house."[73] Whether Sidney and his friends were merely acting as agents for their families in their harassment of their neighbors, the white male youth of European immigrants were an increasingly visible force in the effort to maintain racial boundaries. In suggesting that racial diversity caused delinquency, reformers ignored the boundary-making activities—around gender, race, and other points of difference—that were often at the center of delinquent boys' behaviors.

Shaw and his colleagues confirmed the universality of the boys' neighborhood play group, a group that Thrasher termed the "gang in embryo."[74] Healthy boys, regular boys, and real boys were said to demonstrate an affinity for their peers and an opposition to all that was not boy-like—a hypothesis that continues to have its advocates today. Boys were not only swept away by the powerful pull of the peer group but their physical well-being required its protection.[75]

The stories that Shaw and his colleagues collected about individual delinquents both helped to produce and confirmed many of their predictions about boys and their natures. In these stories, boys frequently referred to the excitement and adventure of petty crime, as they sometimes risked their lives to snatch a bit of coal or even engage in a planned robbery. Joseph, a Polish American Chicagoan, started stealing at age nine, more for the excitement than for the money, which he often used for candy. And even stealing coal off a railroad train for use at home was thrilling: "Take a train that is in motion. You're on top of a car heaving coal onto the ground. You don't know if you're going to fall off and break your neck, or fall under the wheels, or what."[76] Boys' use of words such as *adventurous* and *exciting* to associate delinquency with pleasure led researchers to presume that legitimate substitutions for these types of activities would inhibit delinquency. Scouting and camping offered outdoor adventures on precisely this premise; however, both reforms appealed more to middle-class than to working-class boys.

Reformers also struggled with the thrill that young boys found in associating themselves with older boys' illicit behavior. Interviewee Andy Patrone remembered hanging out on the West Side of Chicago and being impressed by the big boys who played dice and laughed when they lost a few hundred dollars. If the small boys were lucky, they would be asked to play watch guards and receive a sandwich and a pop as a reward. "We thought we were really good, we felt pretty big to be watching for the coppers," Patrone recalled. Another delinquent remembered his first job "in the racket" as the "biggest thrill of his life." He hung around with his older brother and teenage friends, who decided to break into a butcher shop. Because he was so little, he was able to crawl through a small space where he could unlock the doors from the inside. His success, he claimed, was "the kick of my whole life." Jack, age twelve, said that he admired the gang members who were "swell dressers and had big cars and carried 'gats [guns]."[77] In marginalized communities, where bootlegging and other illegal activities helped keep some families afloat, Al Capone and other leaders of organized crime were revered for their financial success and their ability to outsmart law enforcement. In comparison, slaving away at the factory with little to show for it seemed the unmanly thing.[78]

Peer groups propelled boys into actions that they might otherwise have avoided. The gang, reformers claimed, gave its members a "'we' feeling for dealing with conflict," but that "we" feeling could often come at the expense of others outside of the group. Yet, CAP and other urban boys' programs did not seek to disrupt the gang but rather to work with it from within, accepting its basic structure in hopes of turning the group's attention from delinquency to other more respectable activities, such as athletics and supervised dances. Lewis Larkin, the director of the Detroit Area Project, critiqued the YMCA for trying to mix boys from different neighborhoods, believing that only conflict and divisiveness would result if reformers ignored the intractable ethnic, racial, and neighborhood antagonisms that plagued male youth.[79] But others objected that, by keeping the gang together, reformers might actually have contributed to its cohesion, leading to further delinquencies.[80]

Delinquency, Parents, and the Neighborhood

Not only the peer group but neighborhood norms and family values and practices often contributed to identifying youth as delinquent. A longtime resident of Chicago's Northwest Side admitted that, because of both the proximity of the coal yard and the poverty of the population, "stealing coal is a daily habit and accepted as part of juvenile life." A youngster from the area, Louie, agreed with this assessment: "It ain't a sin to steal coal if it's for da house. If ya need it in de house, it ain't a sin."[81] Louie differentiated between stealing for the family's needs versus stealing for the fun of it, a distinction that not all youth ascribed to. Of course, when parents appeared before the juvenile court or in front of caseworkers, they had to deny that they were complicit in their sons' activities, but, as in the case of truancy, they may have been less stringent than the judges in their expectations of their sons.

Many families undoubtedly experienced extreme stress that made them less able to be the kind of parents they longed to be. Social workers surely overestimated the degree of family pathology in the inner city insofar as they were unable to overcome their own cultural biases about appropriate family life. The fact that many immigrant homes featured lodgers, stepparents, boyfriends, or other kinship arrangements outside of the nuclear family led many social workers to view these families as unworthy and illegitimate.[82] They depicted single mothers as pitiable, incompetent, or immoral, believing that the male breadwinner family was the only viable model of child rearing.[83]

Social workers and sociologists were partially correct, though, in their conceptualization of the weakening of parental controls in some neighborhoods. Throughout the first part of the twentieth century, many new ethnic families in urban areas were able to successfully Americanize while still maintaining their community traditions, especially when children attended parochial or bilingual schools and their families participated in cultural institutions and made a living wage. Others, however, experienced not only cultural differences but also poverty, poor health, unstable housing, unemployment, alcoholism, parental separations, and work outside the home that undermined parents' ability to maintain control over their offspring.[84] Additionally, these factors impinged on parental competence and added stress, further inhibiting parents' ability to effectively guide their children.[85]

Among the immigrants who filled the ranks of juvenile court, some children held their non-English-speaking parents in disdain, assuming adult roles as translators and negotiating with physicians and even school personnel, thereby mitigating the ability of parents to take the lead in matters outside of the home. At the same time, the distance between increasingly Americanized youngsters and their immigrant parents enabled youth to fashion unique peer cultures, blending elements from their ethnic upbringings, mainstream American culture, and the particularities of the neighborhoods in which they resided. Historian Sarah Chinn describes the urban children of immigrants as the first real teenagers, who most fiercely differentiated themselves from their families as an age group. She speculates about these youth: "united with each other and often against their parents, by their familiarity with the English language and their experience with city kids, the immigrant young people constructed an identity—most commonly referred to as 'youth.'"[86] As youth, peer groups were sometimes more essential than parents in helping to construct their identities as delinquent boys.

Immigrant males were freer of adult interference than were girls—whom caretakers saw as in greater need of protection. A daughter whose sexuality was in question was far more stigmatizing than a son who was known to get into fights and pitch pennies. It was not just that parents were unable to supervise their sons—although this was often the case—but that many families believed that male youth should have greater autonomy and access to public space. Historian

Linda Gordon finds that Progressive Era immigrant parents in Boston were less than stringent about their boys' time away from home once they reached the age of ten. These boys' activities might even include "bunking out" in doorways and alleys—activities that would never have been tolerated in girls.[87] Yet many boys still felt hemmed in by parental restrictions. The gang enabled them to establish themselves as autonomous beings, free from the strictures of family rules. One need only look at parents' complaints (and boys' accounts) of boys' staying out all hours, running away from home, and jumping freight trains to see that establishing personal autonomy and, more specifically, determining where one will be at any particular time, was central to delinquent boy cultures.

With the diminishment of child labor in the 1920s and 1930s and increasing high school enrollments, a distinctive adolescent youth culture emerged.[88] During the late nineteenth and early twentieth centuries, many immigrant children viewed labor and financial contributions to the family wage economy as central to their family role. But with the idea of the child having distinct rights apart from his or her family, boys, even more so than girls, began to wince at turning their wages over to their parents. Stanley, Shaw's famous "jack-roller," got a job at a pharmaceutical company after getting out of jail. Upon receiving his wages, he thought to himself, "Why should I work hard, without any encouragement except to take all the money to the old lady [his stepmother]?"[89] It was not just that boys were hostile to their parents, although that was certainly the case with Stanley, but that the emerging consumer society beckoned young people to partake of its many pleasures, including recreation, candy, sports paraphernalia, clothing, and the other new accouterments of youth.

Many second-generation ethnic boys shared with their parents the idea that growing up should not have to wait until adulthood, but their version of growing up differed from that of their parents and the reformers. Growing up meant that they should have more autonomy from their parents' injunctions, as well as the freedom to play, explore, and even exploit their environments without the intrusions of police and truant officers. Insofar as they were bound to the collective, it was often the peer group rather than the family that had the greater pull as boys aged.[90]

As the century progressed, some youth went further to question why they should be laboring when their friends were playing. Nick, a fourteen-year-old Greek American delinquent, was hauled before the juvenile court in 1931, where his father told the judge:

Nick no wanta work. He big man, 14, and wants to play ball all day. Father say, "You go to-day and work in restaurant and work with uncle, for he pay you and you learn the business." What does he say? He makes faces, cusses, and runs out to play ball . . . He very bad boy . . . He like nothing but ball. He gets very mad and breaks the chairs, smashes the house, and falls on the floor kicking saying bad names to me.[91]

Nick's right to play ball was reinforced by his peers and his neighbors, who thought his parents' behavior was unacceptable. Nick's mother would publicly whip him for playing ball, eliciting snide comments from his peers: "You've got a heck of a mother. Our mothers don't make us stop playin' ball." The neighbors in general were hostile to the parents' disciplinary techniques, claiming that they "beat the life out of him." Some of the neighbors attributed the family's "meanness" to their son to their foreignness. According to one neighbor, "I don't blame the kid. I told him he didn't have to work that it was against the law for him to work yet. These foreigners want their kids to work before they're out of the cradle." But apparently Nick's father was not too foreign to refrain from using the American justice system when the boy stole from his parents to buy athletic equipment. Nick's father asked the court, "Won't you scare him hard, maybe have him arrested and put in jail to scare him and make him work and not fight and steal anymore?" Both Nick and his parents attempted to use American institutions and ideas to solve what was essentially an ethnic and generational conflict. Shaw and McKay contended that the youngster's main problem was that his behavior was accepted by the neighborhood but not his family.[92]

What might be termed "child neglect," or lack of supervision by child savers, could lead to mixed feelings on the part of boys who may have missed their parents while still relishing the freedom that their absence afforded them. Among delinquents, families where a mother was working, a father was missing, or a parent was dead were common, while long hours and the lack of day care left many children to fend for themselves. When fathers left the home, mothers often had to labor for long hours to compensate for lost income. Yet, when his mother got up early to go to work, one youngster found a thrill in skipping school with his pals: "Every morning the bunch would come past my home about school time. We left home this time to make our parents think we were going to school. It was easy for me, my mother working and didn't know much about me."[93] Rather than viewing his parents' absence as a disadvantage, this youth found it a plus when it came to having the freedom to escape school and scamper about with his peers.

Some parents felt guilty and defensive about their inability to keep their children in check. This Polish immigrant mother tried to explain to a CAP worker why her boys were "running wild": "It's not their fault. Since they were four-years old, they have been left alone to play, while I went to work." Since then, she had "licked them, put them to bed without supper etc. for doing these bad things, but they still do them."[94] This mother believed she needed to explain her children's misdeeds to the worker by showing that, although her children had not had adequate supervision while she worked, she was doing her best to exert control now that they were older.

When delinquent youth did remain at home, they often reported excessive drinking, spousal abuse, and frequent physical punishments.[95] Mothers, too, were capable of physical punishments, which in one case put stitches into the head of a confirmed delinquent, although the child in this case continued to love and even mourn his mother when she died.[96] At their wits' end when dealing with wayward boys, families often resorted to stern whippings, believing that such strong remedies were the only solution to arresting misbehavior.[97] Physical punishment was seen not as a measure of last resort but as a legitimate disciplinary practice: a sign of a parent who took his or her son's infractions seriously. When confronted by a street worker about her son's truancy in the late 1930s, one parent complained, "You know Mr. Brown I get so mad at him I could kill him. I beat him terrible and it doesn't seem to do any good."[98] It is difficult to know whether this mother was merely reciting what she thought the worker wanted to hear or whether she was more ambivalent about her son's truancy. But although such comments were commonplace, some youth were (understandably) bitter about the punishments they had received as children and attributed their delinquent actions to these early experiences. An Irish reformatory inhabitant vividly remembered his father's harsh punishments, to which he attributed his lack of parental respect:

His method of whipping my brother and I was to have us take all of our clothes off, that is we were stripped naked, then we were taken into the bedroom and given a lashing with an ordinary rubber belt . . . If during the whipping proceedings, I became a too elusive target for my dad's well aimed lashing he would lay me on the floor, turn my head to the side, put his foot firmly enough upon my neck and jawbone to hold me and continue the whipping.

According to this delinquent, "If the old adage 'spare the rod and spoil the child' were true I would have passed through my childhood with a halo about my head."[99] In reviewing his life stories of delinquents, Shaw noted the pervasiveness of corporal punishment among his subjects and sought to disabuse readers of that notion: "It is a common notion that delinquents become such because there is a tendency on the part of parents to spare the rod and spoil the child. As a matter of fact, corporal punishment is administered in these homes if anything to the extreme. How little effect it has on the behavior of these youngsters, these stories attest."[100] Of course, Shaw's statement lays open the question as to whether the expected effects were in the opposite direction of what was hoped. For boys, corporal punishment delivered a strong lesson: those in power had the ability to physically harm the weak and vulnerable, a dynamic that was integral to the boys' peer culture.

Masculinity, Sexuality, and the Peer Group

For boys, embodying masculinity was part of growing up—on this, reformers, parents, and boys could agree.[101] Masculinity is particularly important to many adolescent boys, who often seek to appropriate the qualities of manhood that seem best to embody what it means to be a gendered human being. Much of the literature for "regular boys" during the early twentieth century confirms that certain aspects of delinquent boy culture coincided with conventional notions about the characteristics of boys. Angelo Patri, the principal of an immigrant high school and an advice writer, viewed young boys who did not fight back when challenged or bullied as abnormal: "I have always noticed that if the boy is a normal healthy young one, the day comes when his wrath rises and he takes his own part."[102] Yet the assumption was that such regular boys would outgrow their pugilistic tendencies to become solid citizens. Regular boys might display their masculinity by proving their mettle camping in the wild, wielding a baseball bat, being sexually assertive with girls, or even standing up to a fist fight. The delinquent boys described in this chapter, even more so than other boys, exerted their ability to subdue, overpower, and outsmart those outside of the group: girls, younger children, effeminate boys, and racially and ethnically different youth. Although they could not subvert the power structure that relegated them to inferiority, they used their masculinity to enhance their status and prove themselves worthy exemplars of their gender in their own realm.

Proving one's masculinity was central to a boy's status in the peer group or gang. In fact, it was through bonding with the peer group and rejecting so-called feminine influences that many boys claimed a masculine identity. Peer groups and gangs used denigrating language, mockery, physical domination, and expulsion from the group to patrol the boundaries of masculinity. As with the word *fag* today, which is used to denigrate boys—both homosexual and heterosexual—who do not embody masculinity, they used the word *sissy* to exemplify all that was antithetical to their culture, and this word was picked up by sociologists and psychologists who also used it to define boys who were "abnormal." Sissies, psychologists were beginning to believe, were homosexuals in the making, and thus the condemnatory word signified deviance both in gender identity and sexuality.[103] Other types of name calling also helped define the boundaries of masculinity. Using words such as *sissy-girl* and *molly-coddle*, boys taunted less aggressive youth with labels that were meant to besmirch their masculinity.[104]

Delinquent boys associated rule following and school attendance with effeminacy: childlike, subservient, and girlish. In gangs of younger adolescents, Thrasher observed, the attitude toward girls was one of "indifference, scorn, or open hostility." He claimed it was considered a "disgrace" to play with girls: any boy caught talking to a girl other than his sister was subject to derision.[105] Although acknowledging that not all boys partook in delinquent activities, Dan O. clearly valued the ethos that his gang represented: "Of course there were boys in the community that weren't in on this at all. A lot of boys were good. We called them sissies, they didn't have the guts to take a chance."[106]

CAP workers who recorded the voices of the gangs they followed found that the use of the word *sissy* was ubiquitous among delinquent youth. One youngster was recruited by a local gang called the Rough Stars, who lodged the *sissy* insult at him to get him to join. As he recalled, "They were all bumming from school, and they started throwing things at me and calling me a sissy, until I joined them," at which point an autonomous boy-centered life began: smoking, playing cards, flipping freight trains, and fishing. Being called a sissy served dual purposes: it was not only meant to demean kids who violated delinquent norms but also to provoke sissies into complying with the mandates of masculinity. This type of derision was not limited to delinquents, encompassing a wider range of institutions, persons, and places.[107]

The word *sissy* was not used to refer only to boys but also to clothing, spaces, and institutions that boys thought signified a type of deportment that was out of keeping with their version of masculinity. According to one delinquent who was outraged by his parents' treatment of him, "I was tired of a lot of things. One of the things I hated were those sissified clothes. The buster brown collar, and the red bow tie . . . they were my most hateful clothes. I wasn't that type of a person. I wasn't a sissified person."[108] These clothes not only signified effeminacy but a certain class status that was differentiated from working-class masculinity. By definition, boys who failed to partake in the activities valued by delinquent boys were sissies.

Delinquent boys viewed schools, churches, and settlement houses as inhospitable spaces. Settlement house workers tried their best to incorporate urban boys into their programs, but they found that many were not particularly fond of the activities or ideals they sought to propagate. The Burley Lions were asked why they did not attend the local settlement house, to which one replied, "That ain't no club, it's a Sunday School!" The term *Sunday school* had become a description of all that was goody-goody, girlish, and unduly subservient. No one wanted to be a "Sunday school boy," and by describing the club in this way they were calling attention to the club's overly moralistic approach and its attempt to refine tough working-class kids into middle-class genteel boys.[109]

An account of Detroit's Forest Tigers gang, written in 1938–1939, demonstrates the ways that *sissy* was used both to control members' behaviors and to describe different types of organized activities foisted upon them by adults. The group's field worker characterized the boys as "wild and wooly," showing little respect for the community center where they gathered. The worker, not yet acclimated to the delinquent code, complained that the boys "seem to favor a program of the lowest order of physical activity, i.e., wrestling . . . Games that demand intellectual curiosity and interest are strictly taboo." When the worker tried to engage the boys in a game of "numbers," some called it a "sissy game," and they rejected his moralistic lecturing. Boys who cried or were unwilling to fight were deemed sissies and teased and taunted by the other boys. The worker also had a tough time keeping the kids from responding with violence to gangs that threatened them. He tried to restrain them when they suggested that they "get their own clubs and slug some of those guys" who had beaten up one of their members. His message of self-restraint was ultimately unsatisfying for boys whose own self-esteem and identity depended on their ability to physically defend themselves. The word *sissy* proved useful for boys who did not want to have to bow to the dictums of middle-class decorum and morality. It was the ultimate slur.[110]

In demonstrating that they were invulnerable, delinquent boys sometimes took advantage of those who were vulnerable. Unwitting or unsuspecting adults—who might be drunk, disabled, or homosexual—were frequently chosen as objects of abuse. According to one Jewish immigrant boy who belonged to a gang with ages spanning twelve to fifteen, "when the boys want money and sport . . . their most common resort is the drunken man or the blind beggar . . . To knock off the man's hat and stoop to pick it up 'like a regular guy,' incidentally picking his pockets; or to borrow a knife and return it to his pocket rather than the man." In this instance, the lure of obtaining money or objects is mingled with the "sport" of abusing a less-than-competent adult.[111] The jack-roller learned how to roll drunks from another buddy on the streets: "we sometimes stunned the drunks by 'giving them the club' in a dark place near a lonely alley." It was "bloody work," he acknowledged, but by then his own need not only for sustenance but a flashy life "demanded it."[112] "Fairies" who were interested in sex with boys were another common target who, after enticing boys they thought might have sex with them back to their homes, were sometimes assaulted or robbed.

There is also considerable evidence of sexual activity, both homosexual and heterosexual, as a common component of delinquent boy culture. Many of the younger boys, prior to the age of fourteen or so, seemed to limit their sexual experimentation to mutual masturbation and same-sex sexual playfulness and experimentation, but such play could also veer into abuse. John Brown, whose field diary of the Russell Square neighborhood was particularly graphic, observed many frank discussions of sex among the boys, including sex with girls and boys. According to one of the kids, "Last night Barney stuck his prick in Pug's mouth while he was asleep"—an example of what might be termed nonconsensual sex.[113] When Brown took the group to the supposedly wholesome environment of an outdoor camp, he overheard one boy say to the other, "I'll fuck you in the ass and you suck me off"—an example of what might have been consensual sex.[114]

But sex with other boys could also clearly involve forms of domination, abuse, and assault. In yet another gang, composed of boys who were no older than fourteen, Cat and his friend Jimmy routinely "banged" a child they called their "moon boy," promising him that they would let him join the group if he complied. After the youngster was injured by a much older boy who tried to penetrate him, he stopped coming around to the group's abode. Reform and industrial schools also often featured abusive same-sex sexuality, including rape. An inhabitant of St. Mary's Training School noted the ubiquity of homosexuality there, which he termed one of the most "cruel places in civilization," particularly because of the older boys who would "obtain a number of boys of various ages."[115] In the case of older boys who coerced or forced younger boys into having sex with them, it was not homosexuality but masculinity that was being practiced: using aggression, physical prowess, and manipulation, they demonstrated their ability to subdue those younger and inferior in status to satisfy their manly desires.

Observing the ubiquity of same-sex sexuality among delinquent boys, Clifford Shaw attributed it to a lack of adequate social controls: "Such incidents involving homo-sexual behavior are a matter of common practice among delinquent gangs. They reflect the experimentation in all the different kinds of sexual experience that goes on in a group of boys who are completely free of the controls that the adult world exerts over the conventional youngsters' sexual development."[116]

Framing these acts as sexual activity rather than as demonstrations of a specific sexual identity, Shaw viewed such actions as natural behaviors that would occur if society did not intervene.

Although homosexuality among youth was beginning to be investigated, analyzed, pathologized, and punished through institutionalization and treatment during this time, most such youthful behavior, especially when it did not involve adults, escaped the gaze of legal authorities. The attitude toward sexual activity among boys was as yet not codified to any significant degree. Boys were almost never punished for consensual sex with females, and when apprehended it was typically for male-on-male sex practices. Boys' sexual offenses, which were rarely prosecuted or discussed, were often treated as examples of their "badness" rather than pathology.[117]

Psychologists and others who worked with youth charged with sodomy focused on the "psychopathy" that lay behind the same-sex behavior, but streetworker sociologists took a different approach. They viewed boys' same-sex activities as part and parcel of the delinquent culture of the neighborhoods in which they lived, places that spawned immorality and vice of all types. Boys seemed to have harbored conflicting feelings about their same-sex activities, with most seeming to regard sexual activity of all types as a demonstration of masculine toughness that treated sex as merely another appetite to be indulged. Although some seemed to have uncritically participated in these activities, viewing them more as sexual than homosexual, others were more conscious of the increasing tendency to equate same-sex activity with the stigma of homosexuality. In any case, boys clearly made a distinction between homosexual practices, such as oral and anal sex with other boys, and homosexual identities—which most did not subscribe to.

Some delinquent boys actively engaged in sex work as a means of acquiring a quick dollar. As historian Don Romesburg shows, even social investigators who observed sex work and same-sex sexual behaviors among adolescent male youth barely knew what to make of it and rarely alluded to it in their reports.[118] Newsboys were apparently quite casual about discussing the sex work that some used to supplement their paltry earnings. It is sometimes difficult, however, to establish the lines between abuse and sex work. For instance, B.D., an Irish reformatory inhabitant, was asked to help out a farmer who turned out to be what he now called a "sex pervert." However, he used the situation to his advantage, as he described it, and took the ten dollars he received to try to escape from the institution.[119]

Whether boys exhibited homosexual or heterosexual behaviors, some reformers viewed all such activities as a product of learning from or association with those engaged in similar practices. Marjorie Bell, the field secretary for the National Probation Association, put a remarkably benign spin on boys' heterosexual offenses as a consequence of exposure to unsavory associates. A fifteen-year-old boy had been charged with the attempted rape of a much younger girl. As Bell described the boy, however, he did not fit her image of a potential rapist, having a "sensitive, intelligent face" and being still in knickers. Further investigation found him to be entirely normal psychologically, but he had been hanging about with older boys more sexually experienced than he was. His curiosity was aroused and "he was too immature to realize either the gravity of his act with its criminal implications or the injury to the other child involved." Instead of being charged and committed, the two fathers of the girl and the boy discussed the situation amicably, with the only outcome being the expulsion of the youth from his current school. Bell found this situation untenable, because an entire clique of "sex experimenters" remained in the school, which she saw as an institutional, rather than an individual, problem. Failing to distinguish between consensual and nonconsensual sex, Bell categorized the attempted rapist and the sex experimenters into one group of boys who were "learning to be 'bad' " at school, in the street, and "even in the home." Bell preserved childhood innocence even for male youth who had not only participated in early sexual activity but who had coercively attempted to have sex with an unwilling and much younger child.[120]

Not all reformers were as apt to consider boys' sexual behaviors in such an innocent light. Observing a group of racially mixed boys who were playing on the streets of Detroit in 1939, one worker was appalled to see that one of the boys flashed some pennies and "held them out in his hand in a knowing manner" to a local prostitute. This same group was as apt to recite obscene poetry as they were to try to start a fight with the Mexicans who moved into the neighborhood, displaying sexual knowingness as a marker of masculinity.[121] The ethnic boys who populated the CAP programs obviously found explicit talk about sexuality as a bonding experience. Those who did not participate in the sexual culture they promoted were denigrated. In one of the CAP diaries, a youngster reported that after he told his friend that he did not want to see a film where "guys and girls stripped, sucking each other off," his friend "began to razz me, saying that I'm a big fuckin' sissy."[122] Unlike some reformers, Shaw and his field workers found sexual knowingness to be part of the delinquent context, *normal* in its particular cultural milieu.

Were these the children that Thurston had in mind when he pictured Polish youth with their "Paderewski brows" searching the coal yard for waste that they could sell or take home? Were all delinquents really as innocent as the early child savers had intimated? Perhaps, as many scholars have theorized, it is spurious to try to ascribe middle-class ideas of childhood innocence onto children and families whose lives stood in contrast to those of middle-class reformers. Innocence is a luxury purchased by affluence; the ability to "protect" children through extensive parental supervision and safe neighborhoods requires time and resources. And innocence was certainly antithetical to the kinds of delinquent boy cultures that populated cities such as Chicago. These cultures, where what Elijah Anderson has termed the "code of the streets" displaced the code of schools and mainstream American society, embraced experience rather than innocence.[123]

As European ethnic boys increasingly moved to the better-off sections of the city and the suburbs, where they started to attend school regularly and their parents achieved solid working-class status, they swapped the code of the streets for the American teenage code that often featured a period of experimentation and minor risk-taking before entering into respectable adulthood. Their newly acquired whiteness, with its social and economic potential, protected them in ways inaccessible to black and Latino boys. Succeeding decades witnessed white flight from the inner city, intensified segregation of racial minorities, continued economic impoverishment, and an increasing sense of desperation that fueled black males' resistance to school and participation in peer groups, where they manifested their frustration at school and in lawlessness and violence.

CHAPTER 6

Black Boys and Native Sons
Race, Delinquency, and Schooling in the Urban North

In his memoir *Black Boy* (1945), Richard Wright recounts the experience of growing up in the South during the 1910s, as well as his subsequent migration to Chicago in the 1920s. The book, originally titled *American Hunger*, echoed some of the experiences of other marginalized and disempowered boys; yet the unremitting racism endured by migrating blacks made their saga utterly exceptional. Whatever racial antipathies Poles, Italians, Germans, Czechs, and Jews had to contend with when they first entered America were later eclipsed by the consolidation of whiteness among European ethnics and the radical redrawing of the color line in the North. Yet the young black boy's emerging understanding of manhood and masculinity did not depart substantially from European or white American sensibilities: in fact, it was the denial of mainstream avenues to manhood that furthered alienation, despair, and anger at school and white society.

Wright first began to understand the expected masculine role when his father left his mother and an empty pantry, when the young child experienced an excruciating hunger. When he asked his mother why there was no food in the house, she said: "Who brings food into this house?" and Richard answered, "Papa, I said, he always brought food." The loss of a father meant the loss of a breadwinner and deepening hunger, both spiritual and physical. Just because African Americans often occupied family structures at odds with mainstream American ideals did not mean that children and their mothers did not bemoan the loss of a father, spouse, and breadwinner. Once his mother found a job, she left the not-yet-school-age boy to fend for himself during the day and asked him to help with her daily household chores. Sending him to the grocery store in Memphis with money to buy some groceries, Richard was attacked and beaten up by a gang of boys who stole his money. His mother refused to take him in or comfort him, sending him back to the streets with a large stick: "I'm going to teach you this night to stand up for yourself." This time, when attacked by the young hoodlums,

Richard beat the boys until they ran away. "That night," he claimed, "I won the right to the streets of Memphis."[1]

The street life that Richard mastered would be one that he would write about through the ignominious character of Bigger Thomas, who, in the novel *Native Son* (1940), was both brutalized and brutalizer on the South Side of Chicago. Wright believed that American racism distorted the personalities of African Americans and, in particular, those of boys and young men—there is a reason why Wright's memoir is named *Black Boy* and his novel *Native Son*. In a prologue to a later edition of *Native Son*, Wright acknowledged that he had known several Bigger Thomases in his lifetime, including in the South, but in Chicago Bigger's rage was exacerbated by the discrepancy between the "taunting sense of opportunities" and the realities of life in the Black Belt. In the end, Wright wondered whether there had ever been a more "corroding and devastating attack upon the personalities of men than the idea of racial discrimination."[2]

One could argue that Wright's use of the word *men* is meant to be universal for blacks, but the type of personal devastation that Wright describes is in keeping with societal definitions of manhood. Unable to feed their families, surrounded by the bodies of other men who sought to keep them "in their place" through lynching and other forms of terror, and enduring daily humiliations and slights, black males had only a "precarious sense of manhood," according to historian Martin Summers.[3] But if marginalized black youth were not afforded opportunities to live up to the societal standards of manhood, they also learned that they could adopt alternative versions of masculinity with which to express their sense of themselves as gendered subjects. Being a man involved standing up for oneself in the face of indignity; defending territory, the neighborhood, and loved ones; and rejecting the passive amiability of Uncle Tom. In this sense, then, the responses to racism on the part of black male and female youth were heavily gendered. Insofar as the black experience has been represented in memoirs and other literature of the period, it is generally *Native Son*, Ralph Ellison's *Invisible Man* (1952), and later Claude Brown's *Manchild in the Promised Land* (1965)—all of which signify manhood in the title—to which we refer, despite the attempts of scholars to bring the literary contributions of African American women to the fore.[4] Both writers and social theorists alike defined the roadblocks to securing the conventional masculine role for African American men as a defining characteristic of twentieth-century racism.

Having published *Black Boy* in 1945, a period when theories about the impact of racism on personality and the American social structure were percolating, Wright embodied the critiques of black social scientists such as Allison Davis,

Edward Frazier, and Mamie and Kenneth Clark in his interpretation of his own saga.[5] Wright blamed his own maladies not only on a white supremacist society but also on the resulting family dysfunctions that made his own hard-fought-for masculinity such an important aspect of his adolescent development. But, as Wright was well aware, it was not only the "same old story" of weak or absent males and strong matriarchal figures that made the plight of both male and female African Americans so dire.[6] Although nonstandard family structures were present in both ethnic and African American communities who lived in poverty, they were not the sole or even main explanatory factor for juvenile delinquency and academic difficulties. Discrimination embodied in educational policies, juvenile justice, housing, employment, and in social reform efforts thwarted urban black boys' prospects at every turn.

Moving up North

Although small black populations existed in most Northern cities at the turn of the century, during the first decades of the twentieth century blacks began migrating en masse from the South. The large numbers made possible the creation of identifiable black communities in such places as Harlem and the Black Belt of Chicago. Between the years 1900 and 1940, the percentage of black inhabitants increased from 1.9 to 8.2 in Chicago, a city of nearly 3.5 million residents in 1940. In New York, a city with nearly 7.5 million residents in 1940, the percentages increased over the same period from 1.8 to 6.1.[7] Some participants framed these migrations as a matter of manhood. When one African American minister was asked what drew the migrants, he replied, "Well, they're treated more like men up here in the North," he said, "That's the secret of it. There's prejudice here, too, but the colour line isn't drawn in their faces at every turn as it is in the South. It all gets back to a question of manhood."[8] The latent promise that males could have unencumbered access to public space remained a central component of masculinity, one with particular salience to black Americans who were encumbered at every step in the South.

The prospect of housing all the migrants who either chose or were forced to live within their borders stretched both the South Side and Harlem to the limits.[9] At first, migrants tended to be young single men, then women, and few children. But over time the numbers of children and especially adolescents grew, a phenomenon documented in the rising numbers of black students in the public schools and in the juvenile court.

With the family wage virtually inaccessible to black males and retail and office jobs severely circumscribed, adult women often resorted to domestic labor or service, where they might be kept from their families for long hours. Jobs were irregular, income uncertain, the costs of living high, and intimate partnerships fragile, making poverty always a possibility, even when times were good.[10]

Because of overcrowding, high rents, and red-lining policies that excluded them from more prosperous areas, migrant families often squeezed into small and decrepit living quarters. They were frequently accompanied by lodgers, friends, or kin who helped with the rent. Their family structures were at odds with Anglo-American norms, with substantial numbers of children living in homes with single parents, unmarried adult partners, relatives, friends, and boarders residing in a single residence.[11] At the same time, city zoning officials found it convenient to locate gambling houses, saloons, and brothels in African American sections of the city, providing profitable, if illicit, ways to make a living—but also making neighborhoods less safe for young children.

With rampant poverty, illegal enterprises, and inadequate supervision for youth, both dependency and delinquency rose rapidly in the Black Belt, Harlem, and other African American districts. By 1910, black children represented 6.2 percent of all delinquencies in Chicago, even though they constituted only 2.0 percent of the entire population. The figures continued to rise as the migration escalated, with blacks representing 21.2 percent of all delinquencies in 1930 but only 6.9 percent of the population.[12] In the Black Belt itself, between the years of 1927 and 1933, one out of every five boys aged ten to sixteen was brought into the juvenile court on a delinquency charge.[13] Black males made up a disproportionate share of delinquency petitions in New York; although white youth were most often accused of stealing, African American boys were more often charged with the more amorphous crime of "disorderly conduct."[14] It seems very likely the case then, as it is now, that African American children were more likely to be apprehended their white counterparts, especially when they veered into predominantly white areas.[15] In most of these cities, boys in the juvenile system greatly outnumbered girls, but the extent of girl delinquency was far greater among African Americans than among whites.[16] In Cleveland, African Americans were only 6 percent of the population between 1920 and 1926 but made up a whopping 38 percent of those committed to the Cleveland Industrial School for Girls, most of them on incorrigibility and "sex offenses."[17]

Throughout the urban North, child welfare advocates complained that there were inadequate foster care placements for dependent and delinquent African American youngsters and few private institutions that were willing to take in black youth. Even with the strong extrafamilial bonds that enabled sisters, grandmothers, and even non-kin to take in a straggling or errant youngster, the system struggled to accommodate those youth for whom no family-like situation presented itself.[18] Boys may have been seen as less desirable for families who were willing to harbor an extra child; girls had the advantage of often taking on needed child-care and domestic responsibilities.

The result of this institutionalized racism was that boys whose only crime was having nowhere to live were often sent to places like Illinois' statewide reformatory at St. Charles—widely known for the abuses perpetrated among its inhabitants by both the staff and the young criminals—where they were incarcerated along with youth who had committed serious crimes. By the 1920s, about 25 percent of the reformatory's inhabitants were African American (about three times their percentage in the state), and they tended to have longer placements than white males because release was contingent on the availability of a suitable home placement.[19] Thus incarceration, with hardly a nod to rehabilitation, became one of the most common placements for youth who were homeless, vagrant, or guilty of the minor crimes of disorderly conduct or petty thievery.

The harsh poverty inflicted on African Americans during the Depression was reflected in higher crime rates, although many complained that police seemed to ignore black-on-black crime. Homicide rates were high in the Black Belt, in part because Southern migrants had taken to carrying guns and knives in the South out of fear of racial violence—leaving black youth with more access to lethal weapons in comparison to white ethnic youth.[20] This was similar to the situation in Cleveland, where there were commonly reports of "fist fights, shooting, and robberies" in the black section of the city. By 1930, the black homicide rate in Cleveland was several times higher than the white rate.[21]

Keen to make sense of the experiences of Southern black migrants, sociologists spun theories about the similarities of blacks to European immigrants who had previously lived in ethnic and racial ghettos. Yet no immigrant group encountered the rampant hostility and violence that accompanied a rising population of African Americans, particularly when they tried to buy or rent homes on presumably white turf. From 1917 to 1921, the homes of fifty-eight Chicagoans, including both blacks moving into white neighborhoods and those who had sold to them, were bombed.[22] Bombings and riots surely altered the cityscape in ways that made moving across white and integrated spaces a treacherous endeavor. Increasingly violent clashes between gangs of white, black, and Mexican youth occurred, especially when youth of color attempted to transgress the unwritten color line and ventured into a neighborhood, playground, or pool that had been claimed by whites. Yet, when youth of color and white youth fought, it was always on an uneven playing field, with whites having a whole institutional apparatus on their side—from police to schools, realtors, courts, and even mentors in delinquency prevention programs—that kept many of them from having to suffer the consequences of their actions.

Uniting diverse groups of ethnic kids into gangs furthered the process of racial formation by assimilating various ethnic groups of boys into the category of "white" as they jointly protected white neighborhoods. On a daily basis young black boys encountered assaults, harassment, and humiliation as they traversed city space, leaving them bereft of many of the so-called rights of childhood: a good education, a comfortable home, a safe neighborhood, and wholesome recreational outlets.

These rights were denied many children, including those who were white native born and those who were children of immigrants. Yet immigrant children who were barred from these rights were commonly cast as victims of either depraved parents or an uncaring society that had failed to recognize their innocence. Their innocence is what impelled reformers to build playgrounds, pass child labor laws, and steer children away from delinquency (although not always successfully). The assumed innocence of white ethnic boys, whose quest for adventure led them to delinquency, spurred reform. In the mass media, stories about immigrant children, including boys, generally expressed sympathy for their struggles, celebrated their cultural differences, and reported on the work of agencies designed to assist them.[23]

The presumption of innocence was the province of white children, with black males rendered as implicitly violent and sexually aggressive. When black male youth made their rare appearances in the media during this time, they almost always did so as violent criminals. Headlines of newspaper articles such as "Negro Boy Arrested for Assaulting Child," "Child Victim of Negro," and "Negro Attacks Four-Year-Old Child" pack a powerful punch by suggesting that whites were primarily the victims of black males.[24] If innocence was the dominant trope for understanding childhood and even youth, the fact that black male youth, regardless of age, were not associated with innocence may tell us much about why reformers did not direct much energy toward them.[25] Innocence is what emboldened reformers, who cared much more about children than their parents. Francis Kellor, a nativist, whose anti-immigrant sentiments were profound, was even more scathing in her treatment of black Americans. In *The Criminal Negro* (1901), she claimed, "There is no race outside of barbarism where there is so low a grade of domestic life and where the child receives so little training, as among the Negroes."[26] With Northerners primarily seeing themselves as victimized by blacks—parents and youth alike—they were unlikely to engage in the same sort-ing process they did with immigrant youth, for whom they envisioned an inno-cence separate from their parents.

In his report *The Negro Migrant in Pittsburgh* (1918), Abraham Epstein ob-served the rampant media attention given to black violent crime—reports that were in conflict with evidence that most blacks were actually arrested on charges of drunkenness and disorderly conduct. Pittsburgh blacks also were far more likely to be incarcerated for minor crimes than whites. The "colored migrant," he said, sounding like Michel Foucault, had become "an object of surveillance" and inherently suspicious, and this was especially the case for black men.[27] The popularity in the North of the film *Birth of a Nation* (1915), featuring a black male would-be rapist chasing after an innocent young Southern girl, certainly did nothing to assuage the perceptions of black males as inherently threatening and dangerous. Young black males were no less suspect and soon found themselves disproportionately arrested and incarcerated for the most minimal of charges, fueling their suspicion and hatred of the American justice system.

Even if reformers did not see black youth as dangerous, they considered it harmful to mix black and white youth and denied black children entry into their neighborhood centers and programs, claiming that they there were worried about the violence that might ensue when the races mixed together in the same space. Perhaps because they construed black children as potentially dangerous, some reformers tried to duplicate in segregated areas of the city the institutions for youth that had been built in ethnic communities. The Rockefeller Founda-tion and the Julius Rosenwald Foundation lent their support to such institutions for racial uplift in black communities as the YMCA during the early twentieth century. Some blacks took pride in their glittering new YMCAs, such as Chicago's Wabash facility, although others derided them as elitist institutions with high dues that kept them out of reach of the youth who needed them most.[28] Even with this criticism, YMCAs became important venues for some black youth who sought secure recreational sites and opportunities to learn new skills, helping to launch the careers of numerous African American athletes. Still, these facilities were limited in what they could accomplish to prevent delinquency among the masses.[29]

As a result of segregationist attitudes, most boy work with black youth trans-pired within black communities, while black youth living in integrated neighbor-hoods were refused admittance to local facilities. The Boys' Club Federation of America began doing work with "colored negroes" in the 1920s, opening segre-gated chapters for black youth in New York, Philadelphia, Columbus, and Toledo.

African American boys' club leader William T. Coleman led the charge to spread boys' clubs nationwide. A "race man," as historian Carter Julian Savage calls him, Coleman drew on ideologies of racial uplift but also implored a middle-class constituency of black Americans to help the lower classes as a means of protecting their own class privileges:

> Thoughtful colored citizens who are successful must think seriously of [their] so-called undesirable brother. They may succeed in building up wonderful enterprises, but it is possible that their worldly goods may be put in jeopardy if an illiterate Negro commits a crime that kindles racial strife. Therefore, if only for self-preservation, it behooves those who have made the mark to reach down and lend a hand to a weaker brother.[30]

Coleman appealed to a black bourgeois audience by stressing that their "worldly goods" might be endangered by black crime, but the advocate was also onto something in his perception that black wealth and progress were fragile in the contemporary social order. Coleman envisioned boy work as a central tool for rehabilitating the image of the black male and preventing riots, lynching, and terror.[31]

Perhaps it was this vision of boy work that was disturbing to Richard Wright, a one-time Marxist who for a short time worked with the white philanthropist-sponsored Southside Boys' Club. Although the ostensible purpose of the club, organized in 1924, was to instruct "needy colored boys" to respect the law, Wright believed that the group's real purpose was to divert "Negro Dead End Kids" from damaging white property. As evidence, Wright contended that two of the trustees for the club were realtors involved in protecting white neighborhoods from black incursions through restrictive covenants. Wright was depressingly negative about the seven- to seventeen-year-old youngsters with whom he worked, describing them as a "wild and homeless lot, candidates for the clinic, morgues, prisons, reformatories, and the electric chair." His experience with the Southside Boys Club was reflected in a passage from *Native Son*, when a millionaire, who had profited from the outrageous rents that Black Belt residents paid, donated ping-pong balls to the club. One of the characters indignantly responded: "My God man! . . . Will ping pong keep men from murdering?"[32]

Whether one agrees with Wright about recreation as a solution to delinquency, the resources available to children on the South Side were minimal in comparison to those available to children on the immigrant West Side. Although outside reformers worked aggressively to prevent delinquency among white ethnics, they neglected black children, who were tainted by assumptions about their inherent immorality, criminality, and inferior intellectual abilities. Many African Americans in Chicago attended the same schools for behavior problems as did white children, including the Montefiore, Mosely, and parental schools, but they were far more likely to be placed in the most hardened of institutions for boys, such as the state reformatory, than white ethnics, who were more often placed on probation or put into less punitive institutions. Thus punishment and incarceration, rather than rehabilitation, remained the de facto strategies for staving off lawlessness among African American male youth.

Opportunity and Achievement in the Public Schools

When Chicago's Juvenile Protective Association reported on child welfare in the black community in 1913, the writers attributed delinquency to entrenched racism and perceptions about the lack of opportunity, particularly in the public schools. Observing that immigrant children who had gotten through even eighth grade in the public schools could get decent jobs and move out of slum neighborhoods, ostensibly erasing their "tenement-house experiences," the reformers noted that this was not the case for blacks, who "continually find the door of opportunity shut in their faces."[33] Journalist Ray Stannard Baker, in his book *Following the Color Line* (1908), observed that many unemployed blacks who completed high school rejected the demoralizing work opportunities available to them: "They don't want to dig ditches or become porters or valets any more than intelligent white boys. They are human."[34] Yet these were the jobs that awaited many black youth, even if they had accomplished their parents' dreams of completing a high school education.

When Southern black migrants entered Northern schools between 1910 and 1930, many social scientists equated their status to that of Eastern European immigrants, who were also experiencing difficulties adjusting to the demands of urban compulsory education systems. But comparing the descendants of native-born ex-slaves to new immigrants was at best inept. As early as 1895, in his acclaimed *The Philadelphia Negro*, W. E. B. DuBois observed presciently that the obstacles facing black Americans differed dramatically from those confronted by even the most stigmatized European immigrants:

> Here is a large group of people—perhaps forty-five thousand, a city within a city—who do not form an integral part of the larger social group. This in itself is not altogether unusual; there are other unassimilated groups: Jews, Italians, even Americans; and yet in the case of the Negroes the segregation is more

conspicuous, more patent to the eye, and so intertwined with a long historic evolution, with peculiarly pressing social problems of poverty, ignorance, crime and labor, that the Negro problem far surpasses in scientific interest and social gravity most of the other race or class questions.[35]

African Americans and some of the more recent immigrants had distinctly different attitudes toward education. Some immigrant groups, such as Poles and Italians, had come from regions that had only very weak education mandates, where higher learning was not associated with the ability to earn a living and where children's labor was accorded a higher value than education. Although many blacks had also come from regions where there were barriers to schooling and weak compulsory education statutes, they tended to believe in education as the doorway to a better life in American society. Historian James Anderson explains that ex-slaves developed a "shared belief in universal education as a necessary basis for freedom and citizenship," a belief that was not as commonplace among some immigrant groups.[36] As a Chicago truancy officer reported, teachers found it difficult to understand "the Polish parent who feels that the school is robbing him of the services of his children, or the Negro who is typically suspicious of vocational education."[37] White ethnic youth could reasonably expect that with an eighth-grade education they could find decent working-class jobs—contributing to their avoidance of secondary schooling—and were more open to the concept of vocational education, in keeping with their future prospects. Blacks, on the other hand, were often suspicious of vocational education, fearing that this type of education was meant to keep their aspirations low and that unions would bar their access to good working-class jobs in any case.[38] Black parents, for their part, thought that they had already done their time serving in menial labor and hoped that a solid education would secure a better life for their children.

In Philadelphia, scholar Philip Albert Boyer wondered how, given the difficulties that poor black youth faced in their communities, they were able to prosper in school at all. Living in tiny tenements in parts of the city where gambling, prostitution, and even drug dealing were some of the more prosperous occupations (a situation that had been true for many earlier immigrants as well), many city youth were more preoccupied with survival than studies. With little space at home, many family members appeared to spend much of their time on the street, with its "baneful influences," according to Boyer, making it unreasonable to expect the kind of concentration that school necessitated: "It is folly to expect children under such conditions to have the incentive, the repose or the seclusion necessary to adequate preparation of school work. They live in the streets late into the night and some indeed spend the whole night there."[39]

In spite of these and other barriers to adequate schooling, there is evidence that, in the earlier part of the century, black youth were more likely than immigrants to stay in school past the age of sixteen, no doubt in part because they found it more difficult to find work. Black mothers were also more apt than their immigrant counterparts to work and often sacrificed their children's potential earnings to allow them to attend school. But, even while many African American families displayed a greater commitment to schooling than did immigrants, the institutionalized racism their children encountered in school meant that most of them were blocked from the doors of economic opportunity.[40]

Chicago officially had a desegregated school system, but there were many ways to impose segregation despite its theoretical commitment to equity (it would later become known as one of the most segregated school systems in the North). Doors began shutting as soon as black children entered public schools, when—if they were behind in grade for any reason—they were identified as retarded and incapable of learning. As we have seen, boys in general bore the brunt of the label, but the phenomenon was even greater in the black community. School districts also used IQ and ability tests to track black youth into lower ability or subnormal classes. All black students suffered from assumptions of intellectual inferiority, as supposedly demonstrated by numerous tests that found them to be deficient. In one such test of the all-black Chicago DuSable High School, a full 49 percent of the students were judged to be of dull or defective intelligence.[41] In majority black schools, teachers in Chicago identified up to nearly three-quarters of the children as retarded, in comparison to just under half of the children in mostly immigrant schools.[42] Many black children had migrated from the South at older ages and were behind in grade level, thus labeled as retarded or overage and placed in special classes for children who were behind. When black children found themselves in integrated schools but in all-black classrooms, they justly wondered whether they were not being subjected to segregation once again.[43] Blacks were also disproportionately placed in schools for difficult boys, which some defined as "terminal" education, meaning that students often remained in these semicustodial classes and schools until they reached the age of fourteen (later sixteen), the age at which they no longer were legally required to attend school.[44]

From the earliest days of the Great Migration, some educators acknowledged a gender gap in the education of African American youth. In New York, principals judged girls to be the superior students, possibly even more "intellectually capable" than boys. Another principal attributed girls' superior scholarship to the fact that boys were more likely to be gainfully employed while in school.[45] This proved to be true in a predominantly black school near Center City Philadelphia in 1920, where it was found that approximately 20 percent of schoolboys were employed after school and on weekends in street trades and in stores, while the girls were more often caring for children in the home.[46] By 1920, there was already a significant gap between the numbers of black males and black females attending school in their teens throughout the country, according to the U.S. Census. In Illinois, by the ages of sixteen and seventeen, 43.5 percent of girls were still in school, but only 34.5 percent of boys; in Michigan, at the same age girls clearly outstripped boys, with 40.4 percent of them continuing to attend school compared to only 29.9 percent of boys. It is likely that the educational requirements of some of the professions open to black women, such as teaching and nursing, partially accounted for this trend. Beyond this, however, boys may have had reasons for resisting school that would be familiar to boy workers in immigrant neighborhoods: threats to the ethos of masculinity at the heart of boys' peer culture, including submission to authority and a willingness to endure without complaint insults, harassment, and assumptions about their inherent inferiority.[47]

Only a minority of girls or boys could expect that a high school degree would lead them to jobs better than their parents'. Belief in the intellectual inferiority of blacks was profound and widespread, with educators often commenting that bright and lively youngsters' intellectual talents faded as they progressed in the grades. We now know far more about the impact of poverty and discrimination on children's academics, but at the time the most accepted explanation was genetic inferiority. As had been the case with troublesome boys, some educators theorized that black boys needed a curriculum that "would emphasize the practical and industrial side," a sentiment that Booker T. Washington would have endorsed, albeit for different reasons. Blacks, it was said, were more "motor-minded" than whites—except, that is, for the troublesome boys we discussed earlier.[48]

But even if blacks lowered their sights and sought technical or vocational schooling, there were only a few high-quality schools that provided youth decent training opportunities leading to apprenticeships in the skilled trades. When blacks had the rare opportunity to attend such schools, they found yet more obstacles. A Chicago principal of a technical school who took boys to visit potential employers was plainly informed by the bosses that they would not be hiring "niggers"—that black boys were fit only to be "laborers."[49] Many labor unions had clear stipulations excluding blacks or relied on nepotism to fill existing slots; when blacks entered into workplaces as strikebreakers they furthered the animosity of working-class laborers. At the Illinois state reformatory, a supervisor complained that it was worthless to teach trades to black youth because "is it so very difficult for a skilled colored man to secure employment."[50] At the conclusion of *The Negro in Chicago* (1916), Junius B. Wood ominously predicted that, unless the city offered equality of opportunity to black youth, it "shall suffer for our indifference by an ever increasing number of idle and criminal youth, which must eventually vitiate both the black and white citizenship of Chicago."[51]

The lack of opportunity posed a clear threat to African American boys in school, particularly in the light of their ascription to social norms that associated manhood with the ability to earn a decent wage. The large gap between the idea of opportunity and the realities that awaited them in school and employment sparked adolescent attitudes toward schooling that contributed to black youth being viewed as "socially maladjusted," "aggressive," and "indifferent" to their schooling. A perceptive New York schoolteacher spoke to this problem:

> They become acutely conscious, not of some individual who is unfair, but of an impassive society that is shutting them out. In the discussion of which courses they should pursue in school or which work they should take up on leaving at the age of fifteen or sixteen, they hear the word "race" coming up constantly . . . It seems quite probable that the indifference and resentment, the dullness which may really be timidity, the self-assertiveness and impudence, with which the teachers are constantly contending with in these adolescents, may be the direct result of the first shocks they have received on the race question.[52]

Apparently, this "first shock" that black children received would be repeated for successive generations, leaving a legacy with which we still have to contend.

The active hostility many black children encountered at the schoolhouse doors was another serious barrier to academic achievement. Black youth from the South had to endure animosity not only from whites but also from other blacks who looked down on the "greenhorns," leading one teacher to say of the black boy of the South, "No wonder he meets the world with a blow."[53] The teacher's empathic response to young males from the South embodies the assumption that violence was an understandable response among males to discrimination. Girls' responses to discrimination were equally gendered. Perhaps they did not meet the world with a "blow" but with a sneer or more passive or covert forms of violence.

The degree of violence and racial animosity that accompanied integrated schooling had a much larger role in establishing black antipathy toward education than it did for white ethnics. Boys and girls both suffered from antagonism and violence, but boys were more readily schooled in aggressive retaliation, and white ethnic boys who viewed black boys as rivals for their turf usually directed their vitriol at them. As early as 1905, New York spring weather would bring out "junior race riots" among black and white boys, according to Helena Titus Emerson of the Charity Organization Society. She also noted that even little kindergarten children had been "shamefully abused" on their way to school and that many parents had to walk their boy (her wording) there, "lest he be attacked by several white boys and unable to reach school."[54]

In keeping with the common observation that younger children were more tolerant than older ones, things typically got "hotter" at local high schools when integration was attempted. For instance, the white male youth at the highly regarded Tilden Technical High School were proud of their ability to keep black males out of their school, reported the Chicago Race Commission in 1922. When thirty to sixty black youth registered to attend the school "they [white youth] made it so hot for the colored boys that they had to withdraw." The white youth explained their strategies: "we didn't give them any peace in the locker room, basement, at noon hours, or between classes." They hadn't wasted their time harassing the few blacks who had attended earlier and "know where they belong," but when the numbers rose, it became clear that there would be a war to claim the building.[55] As a result of this type of violence and harassment, a number of black parents sent their children to majority black schools instead of their own integrated neighborhood schools.[56]

Overt racial discrimination on the part of teachers and principals was commonplace in the North. Some New York principals quite frankly admitted that they did not want black children in their schools and were likely to use the epithet "nigger" when chastising their young charges.[57] Many of the identified incidents of harshness and discrimination were directed at black males. The black newspaper *The Pittsburgh Courier*, in the sarcastically titled article, "White Teacher Says, 'I Love Negro Pupils,'" reported on the son of a well-known black citizen who was apparently assaulted by his teacher to the point of having his mouth bloodied, after he refused to apologize for hitting a girl who had hit him first. Perhaps even worse from the point of view of the black American community, however, was the teacher's statement that "black people should not put their hands on white people" and that white girls and colored boys should not become overly friendly.[58] Yet she claimed to "love" her black pupils individually, as long as they did not transgress racial boundaries, a statement that drew the ire of black citizens.

The image of the black male as potentially polluting white females was at the root of some of the most blatant discrimination, as the above example suggests. Boys who threatened racial boundaries by appearing to favor the mixing of black boys and white girls were vulnerable to punitive action. A New York schoolboy of fifteen was brought before the juvenile court and charged with disorderly conduct in the early 1920s. His offense: he had "annoyed" his classmates by boasting that he had given blood for a transfusion to a white girl. Although his story was a lie, the court viewed this infraction—which involved a disruption of racial boundaries by insinuating that the blood of a black boy might mix with that of a white girl—as serious enough that he was put on probation and transferred to another school.[59]

Black males were also singled out for severe disciplinary penalties, including corporal punishment. Parents and children at Northern schools complained vociferously of discrimination in how the school handled disciplinary problems.[60] Philadelphia's Education Equity League kept records of parents' complaints about their children's mistreatment at school beginning in the 1930s. Most of the complaints involved sons, and Principal J. W. Foote of the Barry School received so many complaints that he was ultimately brought to court, but the grand jury declined to bring an indictment. One complaint involved a youth whose mother had died in the morning. When Mr. Foote found the boy in his front yard, he "manhandled" him and asked whether he was "celebrating" before bringing the boy to school and putting him in the boiler room in the basement. Other parents testified that the principal had punched, hit, and kicked their sons to the point that they required medical treatment. In their complaint, the league protested "Mr. Foote's persistent mistreatment of colored children and parents" and argued that no teacher should be employed who "is prejudiced against any racial group to the extent of inflicting brutal punishment on a defenseless child." But their calls for justice for black children apparently went unheeded.[61] The daily assaults on their humanity and their bodies by school officials and youths from other racial backgrounds posed a challenge to boys, who were trained to "stand up for themselves" and fight back, an ideal manifested not only in poor communities but in the highest halls of leadership.

The Great Depression imposed new hardships on blacks, who were the first to be fired when plants laid off workers. They often suffered evictions, with many scrounging just to stay warm through the harsh winters in the North. On top of this, the financial pressures on the schools resulted in the practice of using "double shifts" in some of the most crowded districts, which were almost entirely in black sections of the cities. All of these factors took a toll on black youth and their ability to attend school, leading to an exacerbation of truancy, enrollment in "truant schools," dependency, and juvenile delinquency.

Race, Ethnicity, and Delinquency

Although staff with the Chicago Area Project program had been well aware that black youth had high rates of delinquency, dependency, and truancy from the earliest days of the migration, it was not until the 1940s, as blacks became a more significant presence in Northern cities, that the agency began to devote resources to black youth welfare.[62] Given CAP's prior experiences working in ethnic and immigrant neighborhoods, it is perhaps not surprising that its researchers continually compared the situations of African Americans with those of their earlier subjects. Despite the fact that CAP reformers had originally described immigrant communities as "socially disorganized," destitute, and lawless, by the 1950s, they contrasted them favorably with what they perceived to be the dysfunction of African American neighborhoods. In 1959, Anthony Sorrentino, a CAP organizer, detailed the origins of the organization as follows:

> For example, twenty-five years ago when the Chicago Area Project program was launched, inner-city areas were inhabited primarily by European groups which brought with them strong institutions such as the family, the church, and governmental agencies. These institutions gave stability during the assimilative process and helped these groups to make the transition from the old world to the new.[63]

Sorrentino offered a more pessimistic assessment of black newcomers:

> The newcomers to the city today are migrants from the rural South where isolation, racial barriers, and limited opportunities have militated against the development of strong basic institutions adequate for city life. As a result the development of neighborhood programs among migrant groups will be more difficult because these groups are faced with more serious problems than their predecessors.[64]

Sorrentino's 1950s-era comments stand in marked distinction from earlier CAP analyses that characterized the original delinquency areas as home to socially disorganized neighborhoods and communities, featuring intense poverty, vice, and delinquency. What is more, he seemed oblivious to the social institutions—such as black churches, black workers' organizations, business associations, the Urban League, the National Association for the Advancement of Colored People, and the extended black family—that had developed in areas like the Black Belt to counter the racial barriers and limited opportunities citizens faced.[65] Though it might have appeared chaotic, Chicago's black community was hardly disorganized.

By 1941, Clifford Shaw acknowledged that earlier theories of ethnic succession were flawed in light of the recent experience of black migrants. Shaw admitted that although older immigrant groups had entered into city life at the economic bottom, they "experienced a subsequent rise in status as they acquired the knowledge, skills, and capital necessary for successful competition in the broader arena of the city," which inevitably led to reduced levels of delinquency. Even so, Shaw identified continuities between rural black migrants and European immigrants, both of whom, he theorized, experienced family disruptions and a lack of parental and social controls in their new environments.[66] Both groups, for example, had to contend with hostile outsiders who considered many of their traditional folkways—including styles of clothing, recreation, worship, and domestic practices—as out of sync with city living.[67] Having worked more closely with these populations, Shaw was now ready to conclude that there were stark differences in the openness of the environment facing immigrants and migrants, with immigrants finding greater chances for economic progress and mobility. Black Americans had been "excluded from participation in the life of the wider community so systematically and completely that [their] problems are virtually different in kind from those of other minority groups." Moreover, he argued that their exposure to the individualistic ethos of America, with its promise of freedom and prosperity, "create[d] psychological strains and burdens which no other segment of the national community is called upon to bear."[68]

For all that could go wrong with immigrant and poor white delinquent males, their fortunes could take a turn for the better. Some white delinquents were able to acquire decent working-class jobs, even after the most difficult of upbringings and without the advantages of exceptional talent or skill. Many had the opportunity to participate in the Civilian Conservation Corps, where white males, in particular, received training that allowed them to find skilled work during World War II, join unions, and access the social policies associated with the New Deal and the G.I. Bill.[69] European ethnics' newly assumed whiteness gave them access to the privileges that allowed safe access to jobs, housing, and schools, many of which were off limits to black Americans.

As counterexample of what could happen to white delinquents, consider the role of Philadelphia's Big Brothers Association, founded during the very early twentieth century to help primarily Jewish and Catholic immigrant delinquent males. The Big Brothers organization, established in 1904 by Ernest Coulter, clerk of New York's juvenile court, did not accept black youth.[70] When the Philadelphia association was started shortly thereafter by the assistant district attorney, it also excluded blacks. The organization provided one-on-one mentoring, an employment bureau, and a large, well-equipped boys' club, even for boys who found themselves in the juvenile court. The Philadelphia organization refused to assist blacks until the 1950s, even though the center—which included numerous recreational facilities—was located in the middle of a neighborhood that was largely black by the 1940s and despite the fact that community residents had asked to use its services.[71]

The experiences of Joseph, born in 1923, show how troubled youth could be helped by boy worker organizations. The son of Russian Jewish immigrant parents, Joseph was a habitual truant. When tracked down by a school counselor, Joseph's father inquired about sending his son to an institution but settled for in-home services. In 1938, a member of the Philadelphia School Board recommended that Joseph be assigned a big brother. This proved to be a stroke of luck, as the big brother vouched for Joseph's character when he was called into court once again for truancy. After dropping out of high school, Joseph found a temporary job with his uncle. After passing through a series of jobs where he "did not make the grade," the Big Brothers Association stepped in to find a job for him as a shipping clerk, where Joseph did well, and the case was closed in 1941.[72] Joseph's case was not unusual, and it highlights the organization's ability to attract respectable businessmen who were willing to invest their time in diverting youth, especially youth from their own ethnic and religious groups, from the juvenile justice system. In a period when nepotism was a widely accepted practice and when delinquent youth were thought to be redeemable, contacts could make all the difference in acquiring employment.

In contrast, consider CAP's hands-off approach to dealing with delinquency on the South Side. In 1938, John Miller wrote to Shaw that the group should hire the services of a worker in the "main negro area of Chicago." The area had dire problems, he wrote, especially because it lacked parks and blacks were "going farther and farther into the large parks around the district that are used by whites only." But Miller was not actually suggesting that CAP invest in the black neighborhood for its own sake. Instead, the problem was that black youth were encroaching onto white turf, making it difficult for CAP to restrain white delinquents from retaliating. Miller explained, "Even if we have to hire Atwell for a year or two it will still be a better investment than going into any sort of activity program in the negro community."[73]

Why Miller thought that it would be a bad "investment" to go into an activity program in the South Side is an unanswered question, but the fact is that CAP largely opted to leave the community to fend for itself. Reformer-driven programs such as CAP were not a panacea for troubled neighborhoods, but their arrival at least signaled an investment in the future, and their expertise in navigating municipal social services often made all the difference in delinquent boys' encounters with the courts. When CAP finally did support the Southside Committee, one of its prerequisites was that the community do most of the work for itself with little help from "outsiders." CAP firmly believed in the "natural" form of organization, seeking to corral indigenous members of the community, but they had always hired representatives from the agency to work with boys and help to organize the community. In any case, even CAP, one of the more progressive programs of delinquency prevention, neglected the South Side until late in the game.

Black Chicago sociologists who studied the problem of delinquency on the South Side, such as E. Franklin Frazier and Earl R. Moses, also frequently appropriated the social theories that had been developed in response to the white ethnic boy problem. In his highly touted *The Negro Family in Chicago* (1932), Frazier discerned the causes of crime, delinquency, illegitimacy, and vice to be not so much a "matter of race as of geography." This statement was reiterated by an early black criminologist, Earl Moses, who pointed out that delinquency was not distributed evenly throughout the community but was concentrated in areas that were "deteriorated" and "disorganized." Both Frazier and Moses adamantly opposed the theory of innate criminality among blacks. Moses observed that 77.2 percent of the black boys appearing before the juvenile court had been born in the South, supporting his theory that cultural dislocation was key to delinquency.[74]

But there is one significant difference in the accounts of the causation of delinquency in the African American community. Settlement workers and educators had noted that many immigrant homes had been disrupted by the death or absence of a parental figure. This issue, in addition to that of "debauched" and "depraved" families, had constituted one of the explanations for the problem of delinquency among problem boys. But among boy workers, so-called pathological family formations were only one indication of a pathological community. Most delinquency workers focused far more on the social influence of the community itself and on deleterious peer influences. Frazier, in contrast, identified the disorganized family as the "chief handicap from which the Negro suffers"—a framing narrative that would reverberate throughout the twentieth century, most famously in Daniel Patrick Moynihan's *The Negro Family: The Case for National Action* in 1965.[75] Frazier was careful to acknowledge that the disorganized family was so because of the disorganized community in which such families existed. In fact, he found that when stable black families moved into areas where "vicious and delinquent patterns of behavior" had become established, their children learned the patterns of delinquency from the neighborhood peers.[76]

In spite of this caveat, however, Frazier envisioned "broken" families and working parents as key factors in producing delinquency. His thesis's framing suggests how deeply Frazier, and other black theorists, felt about the impact of nonstandard family formations on African Americans. In a depiction of the prototypical delinquent child, Frazier described a boy who had migrated to Chicago from Jackson, Mississippi, at the age of eleven. Both parents labored outside of the home, beginning work at six in the morning, making it difficult to keep track of their son's whereabouts. Even if he made it to school, when he heard the gang "whistle" he quickly absconded from the building. On one of her days off, his mother found him capering about with his friends under the trestle. The child often went outside to play at night, but when he failed to return until morning, his whippings were so severe that the neighbors intervened, telling the family that the beatings had gone too far.[77] Although Frazier used the example to show the inadequacies of the family, it also inadvertently showed the power of the community to enforce appropriate norms of parenting behavior.

Although the above boy's father clearly believed that whippings would help to stop his son's truancies and misbehavior, some black families, particularly single parents, turned to the court for assistance with delinquent boys and girls. One exasperated mother brought her twelve-year-old son Carl, who had broken into a fish market, burglarized a flat, and stolen a car, to the juvenile court and asked that he be put in a detention home. A widow who was peddling narcotics for a living, finding it more profitable than domestic servitude, brought her ten-year-old son before the court in 1924 with the complaint that he was "beyond her control." Banished to Chicago's parental school, when he was thirteen he was arrested for burglary; thereafter, he was in and out of reformatories for the rest of his youth.[78] But, as Frazier attempted to show, the worst rates of delinquency were in the most poverty-stricken neighborhoods. Stable, middle-class African American families tended to reside in areas less ridden by poverty, vice, and congestion. Class, for Frazier, was more salient than race in predicting family disorganization.

The Southside Committee, an offshoot of CAP, was formed in 1941 and shared Frazier and Moses' concerns about the black family structure and its contribution to delinquency. Because boys caused more overt chaos and were more visible in the black community, they were at the forefront of the group's agenda, but committee members also expressed many concerns about disorderly girls. Some black girls diverged considerably from middle-class norms of respectability, thereby threatening reformers' desires for African Americans to conform to white middle-class gender roles. Black girls could be loud, confrontational, and sexually adventurous, all qualities that were deemed unladylike by middle-class reformers. They were more visible in public spaces than many white girls, making their presence known on city sidewalks and engaging in truancy and the kind of petty thievery commonly practiced by boys. The fact that sex work flourished in the district also worried reformers, who feared that young girls would be drawn to this profession by its potential for wages higher than those provided by domestic service. Rates of pregnancy among young unmarried women also alarmed reformers. According to one South Side resident, "It's hard to keep girls straight here."[79] Unlike their colleagues working in white ethnic delinquency prevention programs, then, it was not long before South Side reformers began to address delinquency among girls.

The Southside Committee, which published an account of its work in the book *Bright Shadows in Bronzetown*, shared the staunch conservatism of reformers in its approach to gender roles and racial uplift. At the same time, its members were also direct in attacking the social structures that produced delinquency. When announcing the startling finding that 18 percent of boys on the South Side had been brought before the court in 1939 and 1940, they attributed the statistic to three main issues: economics, discrimination, and inadequate relief.[80] All of these problems, they claimed, contributed to the inadequate black family structure and the dearth of black men whom male youth could use as models for manhood. Quoting from the groundbreaking work *Black Metropolis* (1945), a study of the South Side by black social scientists St. Clair Drake and Horace Clayton, they contended that black men had never been able to provide adequately for their families, leading to "a peculiar pattern of restless wandering on the part of Negro men."[81] Once again, deprived of access to traditional gender roles, absent black men were theorized as major explanatory factor for delinquency.

The members of the Southside Committee ranged from tailors to the head of a trade union to ministers of small churches. In fact, every member of the fifty-nine-person executive board was a community resident. Their president, perhaps honorary, was an exceptionally successful black migrant entrepreneur, Samuel B.

Fuller, who was also head of Chicago's NAACP. The members believed that the two-parent nuclear family with a stay-at-home mother was the optimal structure for raising children. They used the social studies of Drake and Crayton, along with Frazier's work, to call attention to the problematic nature of black family life. They contended, "The customary organization of the family in our society calls for the father to be the breadwinner, and for the mother to be the housekeeper." They maintained the need for mothers to remain at home "to maintain a constant surveillance of the children, ministering to their physical and emotional needs, disciplining, training, and educating them." Without this maternal surveillance, they implied, black children lost their bearings and took their cues from negative peer influences and crime-ridden and decrepit neighborhoods.[82] Their promotion of more adequate relief for black families was predicated on the view that it was best for mothers to remain in the home whenever possible. Increased Assistance to Dependent Families, committee members argued, would mitigate black males' incarceration levels.[83] And in their emphasis on maintaining motherhood as a full-time job, they were also advancing a right to childhood that many members believed had been denied to the children of the South Side.

The Southside Committee was also highly critical of the many dangers and invitations to delinquent behavior found throughout the Black Belt. As soon as a black youth left his home, they claimed, he entered a "social jungle," surrounded by young people and adults who had been in and out of the criminal justice system. Children were exposed to drunkenness, gambling, stealing, the "flash of the knife and explosion of the revolver." Prostitution, homemakers complained, was ubiquitous, and children were exposed to illicit sexuality at an early age—phenomena that made it difficult to raise youth who would adopt middle-class mores in regard to sexuality and marriage.

Schooling was also compromised on the South Side. Instead of being in school, children, both boys and girls, flocked to local movie houses as early as 9 a.m., freed of suspicions of truancy by the double and triple shifts at local schools. Often the centers of juvenile social life, the movies functioned as places where children talked and shouted, fought, and engaged in sex play, oblivious to the action on the screen and free of adult surveillance. Taverns, pool houses, and dance halls flourished in the community, offering opportunities for recreation that could easily turn into delinquency. Young boys were on the streets selling newspapers, shining shoes, and combing through debris to find something of value, all actions that, in the words of CAP reformers, inculcated that "combination of enterprise, intelligence, toughness, and sophistication which makes them particularly vulnerable to prevailing attitudes of lawlessness."[84] Even strong families found that their children could easily be led astray by these neighborhood influences.[85]

Members of the committee were particularly enraged by the state of education in the community. Double shifts were so ubiquitous that it had become a "wry joke among Southsiders to say that children of this community must be twice as bright as other children since they seem to require only half-day schooling."[86] By 1941 all of the fourteen schools in Chicago listed as having double shifts were on the South Side.[87] This was hugely problematic, insofar as it made it almost impossible for the few truant officers employed on the South Side to determine which youth roaming about the street were playing truant and which were out of school for the day. And, because such a large population of South Side parents worked starting very early in the day, supervising and ensuring that their kids went to school was a difficult task.

As had been the practice throughout urban schools since the turn of the twentieth century, many of the difficult children were placed in special education classes. Committee members were enraged at this practice, which disproportionately affected black boys. They complained about the "the wholesale shipping off of the boys to the special school for delinquents," that is, the Moseley School for Boys, and challenged the "unbridled prejudice" of many of the city's teachers who sent boys to the special school to "learn the techniques of delinquency from their new associates." Questioning the disciplinary techniques of public school teachers, as well as their tendency to prejudge black boys, the committee asked that "problem boys" be referred to them for counseling and intervention rather than be the recipients of stigmatizing placements in special education.

But the most damaging problem, the committee asserted, was segregation and discrimination in housing and employment. "The world of the growing youth," they said, "becomes shrunken to the small compass of Negro society." Clearly integrationist, the committee was not so much damning black society as it was the social structures that restricted movement out of the compact region of the Black Belt. Using the language of social handicap that would later become common currency in describing black youth, they argued that racism "acts as an irremovable scar blurring the social vision of young men emerging into adulthood," producing a sense of "discouragement and defeat." Delinquency was an understandable response, they hypothesized, to facing "imprisonment in a racial ghetto."[88]

The committee worked in spite of these difficulties to reverse the delinquency statistics. They counseled youth referred to them by the public schools, worked with St. Charles parolees and those who had been referred to them by the juvenile courts, and organized clubs and recreational activities. Although severely lacking in resources and funds for the type of facilities enjoyed by the mass boys' clubs founded for white ethnics, the committee set up several "neighborhood centers" for recreation, community meetings, and counseling. As did reformers throughout the entire delinquency-prevention movement, the committee's members believed that supplying adequate recreation was central to keeping youth off the streets and engaged in legitimate activities. Yet, as time wore on, committee members seemed to become desperate about the state of delinquency on the South Side, as gangs, narcotics, and violence became increasingly prevalent.

Community Programs for Hard-to-Reach Youth

Almost 1.5 million blacks traveled north during World War II, finding work in such major industrial centers as Detroit, Chicago, and Philadelphia. Their arrival led to a new era of racial tension, as Southern white and black migrants rubbed elbows in crowded neighborhoods and Poles and Italians—the lowest on the totem pole of white immigrants—felt increasingly threatened by the movements of blacks across white space. One young child complained that blacks were invading "his" playgrounds in areas that had been lily white before the war.[89] Racial tensions reached a new height in 1942, when 242 racial battles occurred in forty-seven different cities, including New York, Detroit, and Philadelphia, with male youth—both white and black—at the forefront of the riots, fights, and brawls.[90] Black youth were brutally treated by the police, and the brunt of subsequent arrests and sentencing almost always fell on African Americans, exacerbating their distrust of the justice system. Schools increasingly hired policemen to keep order in the schools; some these officers, residents of Chicago's South Side complained, were excessively brutal and prejudiced in their treatment of black youth.[91] Events such as these inspired both a heightened sense of racial consciousness in youth and the formation of gangs as a means of community protection.

Child welfare reformers in Northern cities raised concerns about rising juvenile delinquency due to wartime pressures: absent fathers, working mothers, and child labor. Whether the increase in delinquency was real is debated by modern historians. In any case, these wartime explanations in regard to causation did not appear to hold water, given that delinquency and gang activity intensified in the late 1940s and the 1950s. Much gang activity was directed toward resisting black incursions into white spaces, but there were also significant incidents of black-on-black fights and violence. Gang activity was not just the province of older youth but of younger children as well. Exasperated that their efforts to constrain delinquency had had no palpable effect, the South Side Committee sounded defeated in describing the youth situation in 1947: "More preadolescent gangs of a destructive nature are marauding the streets than at any period during the life of the operation of this committee. Open gang-warfare is a common weekly affair. Police do little or nothing."[92]

But even if police were not to be counted on, community leaders still sought to initiate new programs to arrest delinquency. What would come to be termed "hard-to-reach" youth were the subjects of many of these programs that attempted to recruit youth who would not typically make use of "supervised leisure."[93] Working with youth in their own "backyards" and neighborhoods, these programs shared with CAP the idea that workers must enter the programs as allies rather than authority figures to gain the cooperation and respect of local gangs.

Chicago's Dunbar Community Center opened in 1945 as an attempt to reach out to youth whom organizers construed as destructive and disrespectful of positive community influences. Purposely seeking to entice the boys who were least likely to use the recreational facility, the reformers were nonplussed by the difficulty of securing compliant behavior from area youth. Boys smoked, swore, and even drank beer on the baseball diamond. Although many of the youth were teenagers, even younger children ran "helter skelter," wildly upturning furniture, and ransacking the center. Austin Johnson, who worked with these youngsters, reported gang fights and "incredible" public conduct. One gang in particular seemed determined to undermine the reformers' efforts to bring them under their influence. Led by a twelve-year-old boy, gang members would "climb upon the roof of the center, throw rocks at the center and make overbearing remarks."[94]

Workers approached the boys' parents in hopes of getting them onboard with their attempts to control the disorderly behavior. After a short-term improvement, more reckless behavior followed. Clearly out of their element, workers resorted to corporal punishment to wrestle the youth into compliance, giving one youngster a "severe shaking up," "knuckling" another on his head, and employing the "belt line." Although some parents complained about these techniques of managing children, they learned that if they did not endorse them, the center would be off limits to their kids. Parents themselves were not averse to corporal discipline, but they often saw it as their own prerogative; they were less happy about investing others with the authority to inflict physical pain on their children. As well meaning as the punishers might have been, their disciplinary actions taught the boys something about how to get people to do what you wanted: violence was necessary to keep violent boys in line.

The recreational opportunities offered to youth were undoubtedly a blessing for many, especially for those who had previously been excluded. But getting the most difficult gangs on board—the Dunbar Center's ultimate aim—was a more urgent and difficult goal to attain. Center workers borrowed earlier reformers' idea that organized recreation would transform youth who had nothing else to do. But they underestimated the power of youths' own peer networks, pleasures, and antipathy to authority. In light of the few respectable avenues to manhood— for manhood and all its associated powers was central to midcentury society— gang youth especially seized onto alternative forms of masculinity that posited autonomy and violent demonstrations of mastery as central to their own sense of self-identification. Many youth would not allow reformers to rob them, as historian Eric Schneider, terms it, of "their one token of agency: their ability to cause trouble." Still, that does not mean that the organization and its workers did not touch individual lives by offering kids a chance to play on a baseball team, to learn to make a chair, or to confide in an adult about their problems. But it was often the case that the easiest to reach were the easiest to reform.[95]

This dynamic was particularly evident in Operation Street Corner, a program for delinquent youth founded in 1945. The program was contained within Phila- delphia's Wharton Centre, a settlement house that had been working with the black community since the turn of the century. The center had been sponsor- ing programs for boys that were typical of the settlement house model: offering classes in aircraft building and woodworking.

But the youth who used the center were not the worst of the neighborhood troublemakers. With community members feeling besieged by gangs, Operation Street Corner attempted to reach those youth who were unlikely to utilize center- based activities. Crime, particularly violent crime, had risen dramatically in the region, spurring the local citizens to demand that something be done about the gangs, especially after a local shoot-out at a poolroom resulted in the death of a thirteen-year-old girl.[96] Determined to tackle the gang problem, Operation Street Corner's organizers conducted research before initiating their endeavors, finding twenty gangs in the area and eight nearby, all of which were engaged in violent skirmishes with each other and white outsiders.[97]

Borrowing from the CAP philosophy that boy workers must meet youth on their own turf, the Wharton Centre used indigenous workers to seek out gang youth and work with them on street corners and in pool halls and other local haunts. The group also worked with the city's crime prevention bureau, which referred boys from ages seven to sixteen (including a seven-year-old who had been arrested for attempted highway robbery) to them for supervision and organization into clubs. Many of the ten-year-olds referred had been charged with disorderly conduct or malicious mischief, but the center also received referrals for assault and battery and larceny, even for preteenagers.[98]

Publicly, the group touted its success in reducing local gang-related crime. Stories about redeemed gang members spurred nationwide interest in the group's work. The most repeated story was that of a local druggist who had previously been tormented by gang members. That all changed when he decided to sponsor the same group as a baseball team, paying for their uniforms and equipment: lo and behold, the vandalism and petty thievery vanished. These public stories notwithstanding, the private reports of field workers reveal more tenuous findings. Field workers complained that even their young members smoked, drank, gambled, and engaged in crimes both minor and serious. One gang of fourteen- to seventeen-year-olds let their worker know that they planned to "shoot down on sight" members of another local gang who had threatened them. One worker counseled two fourteen-year-old boys who had returned to the corner after having been incarcerated for rape, telling them that "crime does not pay," before moving onto more mundane conversations about the day's activities.[99]

The level of violence that some gang workers tolerated, one even going so far as trying to keep a youngster from going to jail for shooting a rival gang member, is reminiscent of the ways that a previous generation of boy workers tried to protect white ethnic children from the clutches of the juvenile justice system. Did the ethos "boys will be boys" also guide their efforts, or did they sincerely regard the redemption of youth as a possibility? Were they willing to overlook violence among youth, assuming it as a given? Whatever the explanation, early and mid-twentieth century boy workers clearly displayed more patience than is currently at work in zero tolerance policies and tough penalties for criminal infractions such as assault and rape.

Such moral ambiguities caused some to reflect upon the guiding premise of the work: "Although it is considered good technique to begin where the group is, there are times when it is not easy . . . I found it impossible to accept certain of their standards—such would have been encouraging them in delinquent pursuits."[100] And a social worker who had been engaged in street-level work with delinquent gangs wondered whether an empirical investigation of the group's work would yield the kind of optimism that was reflected in their anecdotal accounts of gang transformation. Workers' comments increasingly displayed cynicism, such as when one noted that workers were "deluded" if they thought that one to two hours of club work a week was likely to ignite gang transformation.[101] In 1958, Operation Street Corner closed its doors not only because its funding had been exhausted but also because advocates thought that they would be better off directing attention to larger community problems.

Perhaps they shared the sentiment of Kenneth Bancroft Clark, the famed psychologist noted for his penetrating analyses of black child psychology. In *Dark Ghetto* (1956), Clark observed that Harlem had more recreational services than it needed. These resources surely brought "gratification and pleasure" to some, he admitted, but the "fundamental predicament of ghetto youth remains unchanged." "Recreation," he went on to say, "cannot compensate for the depressive reality of their lives."[102] The depressive realities of their lives involved inadequate education; ongoing discrimination in housing, employment, and social services; and an incapacity to imagine a brighter future for themselves. Given these realities, Clark wondered not that so many fell prey to crime and truancy but that so many managed to avoid the treacherous territory of gangs and delinquency.

Although much would change in succeeding decades, the structures of inequality and the disempowerment of the black community had already been laid in schooling and in juvenile justice. By the time that blacks finally did dismantle some barriers to success in the working-class job market in the 1960s through antidiscrimination laws, deindustrialization had already begun, and those jobs that remained increasingly moved to the suburbs, leaving inner-city blacks isolated and unable to attain work.[103] Racial profiling of black males, discrimination in school and work, and the deprivation many youth faced in inadequate housing and in neighborhoods with crumbling infrastructures contributed to the development of boys' alternative peer cultures. As special education evolved, it increasingly became a dumping ground for these lost boys, many of whom were identified as educable mentally retarded or emotionally impaired.[104] They spent their time in special education classes or "alternative" or "opportunity" schools, or they were expelled from school entirely, spending their time on the streets before ending up in prison. Expressing their discontent with white American institutions, including schools and law enforcement, these boys engaged in peer cultures of masculinity where violence, sexual prowess, and law breaking were the norm—in ways similar to those of their previously marginalized ethnic counterparts.

Epilogue

In 1965, Assistant Secretary of Labor Daniel Patrick Moynihan released his unforgettable report, *The Negro Family: The Case for National Action*.[1] Moynihan's claim that the distorted structure of the black family was at the root of racial inequality was not new. Yet the drama the report exuded, as reflected in its use of language and call to action, made for sensational news. For decades, social theorists had characterized black families as deficient, in analyses that veered from biological to cultural to environmental explanations. For Moynihan, the forecast for social change was grim: "all efforts to end discrimination are worthless if they do not address family damage."[2] In a society where the heterosexual married family was both normalized and valorized, Moynihan's statistical data was damning. He claimed that 20 percent of black fathers were either divorced or "absent" from their children's lives. Even more problematic, from his point of view, was the large number of births to unwed mothers, a proportion that had risen to almost one out of every four children during this time.[3]

Moynihan deemed the "matriarchal structure" of the African American family as not only "out of keeping with American life" but also as generating a "social pathology" that kept African American males from securing dominant roles in keeping with their white counterparts. The story Moynihan tells is well known, constituting a kind of antifeminist parable that identifies strong black females as responsible for the black community's privations, welfare dependence, and encounters with the criminal justice system. This oft-told narrative stands in contrast to the commonly told story from successful black males about the powerfully positive impact their mothers had on their lives. This is not to discount the fact that it can be difficult for boys to be separated from their fathers and for their mothers to raise their children alone; rather, what was most problematic was that the discourse shifted attention away from the racist social structure and limited opportunities afforded African Americans in housing, schools, and employment.

What is not the usual takeaway from the Moynihan Report is its attention to the comparative prospects of black boys and black girls. Even if all blacks were disadvantaged at every step by their family pathology, males seemed to suffer greater consequences than girls, according to Moynihan. Using statistics from 1964, Moynihan showed that although all blacks dropped out of high school at high rates, girls had an 11 percent advantage over boys, with 55 percent of girls apt to drop out versus 66.3 percent of boys. Both black and white boys attended college in greater numbers than girls; what appeared troubling was that although only a small number of white males attended college (12 percent compared to their female counterparts at 7 percent), black girls were *almost* as likely to attend college as their male counter parts, at 4.1 percent versus 5.2 percent. In other words, blacks did not sustain the same record of male dominance in college as their white counterparts. But even if African American boys entered campus life in greater numbers, girls stayed on and completed higher education in greater numbers.

Moynihan cited other data, both empirical and anecdotal, that suggested that black girls were stronger academically than boys. Girls dominated in the small numbers of Advanced Placement classes for blacks. Approximately 70 percent of the black applications for Academic Achievement Scholarships funded by the Ford Foundation were from girls. A young black male, he claimed, was "disempowered" in the family and found other avenues to "compensate for his low social status" in delinquency. In the midst of the debate that followed about whether black families were really "tangles of pathology," Moynihan's treatment of the gender gap in education was largely ignored.[4] In an era when both black and women's civil rights were in question, it was hardly politic to call attention to the inequities in black males' educational treatment.

Moynihan's report was the first to bring the black family to the fore as a national public policy issue. But, as we have seen, the structure of the black family had worried both white and black social theorists for decades. Black sociologist Allison Davis described African American families as "relatively ineffective" at training persons to "take on the normal sexual and familial behavior of American society" and cited statistical data similar to Moynihan's, but in 1939.[5] At the 1940 White House Conference on Children in a Democracy, attendees reported that minority children suffered "damage" and "deprivation" and described racism and poverty as social "handicaps."[6]

Social problems were increasingly viewed through the lens of psychological health in the 1950s. In the report *A Healthy Personality for Every Child*, speakers at the Mid-Century White House Conference on Children and Youth (1951) decried the impact of racial discrimination on the self-esteem of minority youth, lead-ing them to "defy middle-class standards and expectations, and to compensate by overly aggressive behavior" and delinquency.[7] Psychologists such as Gordon Allport examined the concept of prejudice and the personality damage that oc-curred as a result of racism.[8] The damage argument resurfaced in the *Brown v. Board of Education* case in 1954, which established that integrated schooling was inherently superior to segregated schools, in part because of the damage of segregation to black children's self-esteem. When James Coleman published his famous report on equality and education in 1966, one of his major findings was that integrated schooling was central to educational equality, mainly because it mixed black students with those whose social situations had better prepared them for school.[9] According to Coleman, no matter how good the school, black children in black schools were more likely to fail mainly because of their social and familial characteristics.

Coleman's report was one of the legacies of both the civil rights movement and the War on Poverty, both of which made education a weathervane for assess-ing racial equality. Such legislative victories as Head Start and the Elementary and Secondary Education Act of the 1960s promised enriched educational op-portunities and government funding for low-income children. In tandem with these legislative triumphs, a welter of new terminology circulated to describe black children, such as *culturally deprived, culturally disadvantaged*, and *under-privileged*. Though this terminology sought to undermine biological explana-tions for educational outcomes, it contributed to what has been termed a "deficit approach" to black children's families and cultures.[10] A new approach to black children's academic deficits called "compensatory education" arose to fill the gaps left by homes that lacked the social and cultural capital that would facilitate aca-demic success among black children.[11] In compensatory programs it was hoped that black and impoverished youth could be brought up to speed with their white middle-class counterparts through extensive interventions, such as Head Start, after school programs, and tutoring. Advocates of compensatory education put the environmental factors that contributed to academic problems first and did not put the onus on children's intelligence, as was the case with special education. Compensatory education, however, continued to promote the idea that such chil-dren were deficient and in need of educational compensation for their familial and social backgrounds.

Although initially white and black educators had embraced concepts like cultural deprivation, critics of the terms, such as Frank Riessman, soon began launching assaults on the idea that children who were different from the white middle-class norm were somehow deficient. But Riessman's book on the topic, which was widely read, still stereotyped low-income children and the learning styles best suited to them. The prototypical "culturally deprived" child, so he said, was uninterested in "knowledge for its own sake" and more apt to learn in a "physical or motoric" fashion—language that we have heard and continue to hear in debates about the boy problem. Later he made the gender implications of his argument more explicit: the culture of the school was overly feminized and needed "increased masculinization" to attract boys from the underclass.[12]

At a major research conference on compensatory education for cultural deprivation in 1965, the speakers sounded as if they were talking about males, even though the issues were not meant to be gender specific. Arguing that culturally deprived children were victims of a "handicap" based on the fact that their families "do not transmit the cultural patterns necessary for school," the imaginary culturally deprived child whom speakers described was a delinquent male youth "frustrated by the school's demands and by its repeated punishment (and lack of rewards)." As a result "he" finds more meaning in the peer group, where he enjoys an exciting life "relatively independent of adult control" and has the opportunity to be and follow countercultural leaders.[13] Such an analysis could have equally been applied to a delinquent member of an ethnic gang in the 1920s who found meaning and sustenance in autonomous peer networks outside of social institutions such as schools and families.

Even while educators were debating the pros and cons of different terms and of different approaches to dealing with unequal educational outcomes among African Americans, long-standing practices of relegating blacks to lower ability tracks and to special education became a significant civil rights issue. According to historians David Connor and Beth Ferri, special education had emerged as a new venue for the segregation of African American minorities in the wake of *Brown v. Board of Education*'s integration mandate. Forced into putting blacks into schools with whites, the District of Columbia placed 24 percent of "newly admitted" blacks into special education classes in light of the integration mandate.[14] The existence of so-called soft disability labels open to interpretation, including educable mentally retarded, learning disability, and emotional impairment, made it more possible to provide a diagnostic label for students who were slower learners or troublemakers. In *Hobson v. Hansen*, decided in 1967, parents challenged the use of ability testing to place African Americans in the basic track while reserving the honors track for whites. The court decision asserted that the tests were normed on white children, thus inadequately measuring the capabilities of black children and shunting them off to an academic path to nowhere.[15]

Hobson v. Hansen was followed by other cases, such as *Larry P. v. Riles* (1972), which determined that the administration of IQ tests in San Francisco was inherently discriminatory. As evidence, plaintiffs noted that the test relegated twice as many African Americans as whites to classes for the educable mentally retarded.[16]

As education stakes grew higher and special education expanded, white students during this era were more likely to be identified with the less stigmatizing label of learning disability (LD). In eleven Missouri school districts, LD programs were filled with white upper-class children (97 percent), while 34 percent of classes for the educable mentally retarded were composed of blacks.[17] The LD label was perceived by many as less stigmatizing because it implied a normal or superior level of intelligence, while mentally retarded implies basic intellectual inferiority. Even today, urban middle-class parents may seek to have their children labeled as having a learning disability, because it provides their children with greater services and presumes that learning difficulties are not tied to inherent intelligence.

Many districts harbored long histories of relegating black males to the margins of the education system, either in classes for the intellectually deficient or in disciplinary classes and schools. A Philadelphia report challenging the special education system in 1968 found that blacks—mostly boys—represented 86 percent of the kids in remedial disciplinary classes. The report concluded that evidence is "overwhelming that the great majority of children separated out of regular classes into special ones—hence stigmatized—are poor non-whites who already bear the stigma of caste and color."[18] In the wake of such findings, many districts sought complete overhauls of the systems of disciplinary classes and schools during this era; in many cities, however, especially Philadelphia, special disciplinary classes abounded through the 1990s.

An important development for children with disabilities was the passage of the Education for All Handicapped Children Act in 1975. The legislation had the effect of ensuring that children would not be denied placement in school because of a disability, and successive versions of the law gave parents more rights to determine where their children were placed and what services they received.[19] In the past, blacks had often been excluded from schools on the basis of disabilities, and this legislation gave children new rights to an education.[20] The nature of the legislation, however, made it easier for white middle-class parents to use these services and keep their children in inclusive settings, while children of color were more often assigned these labels by their teachers and more likely to be educated in segregated settings.[21]

Because special education both at its outset and in the more contemporary era offered substantial leeway in its placement categories, it allowed for differential placement of boys. The fluidity of some of these categories can be seen in rising numbers of children receiving special education services, especially in inner-city schools. In all except the more easily defined medical categories (for instance, hearing impairment), boys, some racial minorities, and low-income children are overrepresented among children receiving special education services. Using medicalized, supposedly accurate technical terms, such as *emotionally impaired*, *attention deficit disorder*, and *learning disability* to describe children who are difficult to teach helps to shield us from addressing the larger social contexts that lead to the labeling of these children. Yet the inherently messy process of trying to establish nomenclature for boys who are troublesome, difficult, or slower learners suggests the fluidity of these labels.[22]

The new field of disability studies has led us to more questions about the ideology of normalcy that has dominated American education, medicine, and society since the twentieth century, and it has raised more questions about boys.[23] Disability studies theorists suggest that we place more emphasis on the social factors that make certain conditions disabling, rather than putting the onus on individuals who are branded with stigmatizing labels that imply inferiority. In other words, instead of focusing on fixing kids who are difficult or having difficulty learning, we need to fix the society and schools that are not serving them well.[24]

Boys were not the main story in attempts to address education inequality prior to the 1990s; race and gender were. In 1972, the passage of Title IX ensured that girls would not be excluded from any of the educational benefits accorded males. The legislation did not define the gender that was to be protected from discrimination, but those who agitated for the law were women, and the law is mostly widely known for affording girls access to high school and collegiate athletics.

However, as juvenile delinquency continued to rise, new delinquency programs sprouted, many of which focused on black males. The passage of the Juvenile Justice and Delinquency Prevention Act of 1974 promised to stem the institutionalization of youth who had committed only status offenses —crimes such as drinking that are dependent on the age of the offender—and to seek rehabilitation instead of incarceration of youth whenever possible. However, rising rates of serious juvenile crimes, the emergence of "get tough" sentencing policies in the 1980s in response to the War on Drugs, and the portrayals of menacing "superpredators" stemmed the efficacy of the act. In 2008, black youth represented only 16 percent of the population but accounted for 52 percent of violent crime arrests for youth between ten and seventeen, and 33 percent of those who were charged with property crimes.[25] These same youth are more likely than their white peers to be incarcerated for their crimes, and for longer periods of time.

Contemporary research also demonstrates that black youth have been especially negatively affected by the growth in zero tolerance policies in schools and are more likely to be the victims of school suspensions and expulsions. Black youth routinely receive more severe punishments than their white peers for the same misdeeds and are more often the recipients of corporal punishment. These differentials in punishment reinforce the idea that black males are inherently bad and further serve to distance them from the education they need so badly. How can we help without diagnosing or punishing young males, such as ten-year-old Lamar whom Anne Ferguson describes in her book *Bad Boys*? Watching the young boy shuffle down the hall toward the school's "punishing room," a black adult said to her, "That one has a jail cell with his name on it."[26]

Such attitudes toward boys who exhibit "trouble" in their clothing, attitudes, posture, and behavior lead to expectations of further failure that can only detract from young males' sense of possibility. Quite unexpectedly, I chanced upon an example of this same phenomenon in a project I have been coleading with students in an urban middle school in the Midwest. This inner-city school has recently been reorganized because of declining enrollments in the district, resulting in nearly eight hundred youngsters crowding a K–8 building originally built for middle-schoolers. The school has several rooms for autistic children, and the population includes many African Americans, children who are English language learners, and refugees, and a majority of the students are on free and reduced lunch. The school relies on suspension as a major disciplinary action to keep classrooms running as smoothly as possible.

The leadership club at this school is coed and serves sixth through eighth graders through mentoring, team-building activities, and field trips and is meant to enhance positive attitudes toward college through the use of college student volunteers. Some of the boys in the club have contributed to an atmosphere that is sometimes chaotic. Boys more often than girls make offensive remarks, disrupt activities in the room, and sulk in the corner. Sometimes, however, their actions spill beyond the confines of our designated room. For instance, one boy set off the school fire alarm on the way to the bathroom, and another walked home from the club to his friend's house, much to the chagrin of his non-English speaking mother who came, distraught, to school looking for him. One of the administrators at the school encouraged us to kick out the kids who caused trouble: leadership club was a privilege. But these are the boys we most want to nurture, for if we leave leadership only to those who are easiest to reach, we lose the possibility of inspiring youth whose potential no one else has recognized. We praised one such youth's improved behavior to his mother one day as she arrived to pick him up, and she was ecstatic, responding, "No one has ever said anything good about Thomas!"

My coleader and I identify with the administrator who feels that the only way to have an orderly club is to eliminate the troublemakers—or even to include only girls. We would certainly have a more orderly club if we kept only the nontrouble-making kids, and we would probably serve our more motivated older girls better. But we would negate the chance to inspire a positive sense of self among boys, some of whom have never heard a good word about themselves at school.

Boys who make trouble have been a cause for concern since the origins of compulsory education. The problem has resurfaced with a vengeance during a time when high school completion and college attendance are becoming mandates for all youth. The fact is, more youth of all races, classes, and genders are finishing high school and going to college, which further enhances our awareness of existing racial and gender gaps in educational performance.[27]

Barriers to women's equality that are currently being dismantled in education may have masked our awareness of gender disparities in the past and minimized the extent of the gap between boys and girls. It is not the expansion of women's equality that has minimized boys' chances in school and society, as some hyperbolic commentators have warned; women's growing equality reveals pre-existing issues in the education of boys that have been disguised by socially constructed barriers to women's advancement.

It is a travesty that so many boys are lost to school and will instead populate incarceration facilities, as Michelle Alexander pointedly observes in *The New Jim Crow*, and Pedro Noguera in *The Trouble with Black Boys*.[28] But, in addition to addressing issues such as discrimination and disproportionality in special education, expulsions, and incarceration, we might consider investigating some of the protective factors that allow some girls from even the most difficult backgrounds to have greater success in school and in life than do some of their male counterparts. In the past, we have encouraged girls to develop characteristics that will further their own advancement in school and society: speaking up, being assertive, and stepping out of confining gender-normative ideas about what professions they can occupy. Why not do the same with boys? In other words, perhaps it is not tapping into boyishness that will best serve our boys but encouraging the development of human qualities—such as courage, strength, perseverance, kindness, and empathy—that enable personal and social development.

Boys are first and foremost human and individuals, as are girls, and our goal should to be to nourish boys' their humanity as full of potential, giving even the most difficult boys chances for success and public engagement. It is imperative that teachers be given accurate data about the issues facing marginalized boys and engage in classroom practices designed to encourage inclusiveness for children whose cultural backgrounds and learning styles may be different from that of the instructor. Strengthening awareness of the ways in which some boys may manifest gender differences in their learning styles and the ways peer cultures of masculinity may thwart boys' potential in school should be on our educational agenda.

It is foolhardy, however, to expect overstressed and underresourced teachers to bear the full brunt of the responsibility for addressing the boy problem. Teachers can have all of the cultural competency training in the world and a wide array of teaching strategies for children with cultural differences, but if they have too many kids to teach, too many tests for their students to prepare for, and a limited range of disciplinary strategies to resort to, boys who pose trouble are doomed to suspensions and segregation in special education settings. In other words, we cannot address the boy problem without addressing educational policies that disable our children by putting teachers in impossible situations. Putting boys in separate all-boy academies is one solution to creating order, but one that widens the communication gap between boys and girls and can exacerbate disturbing manifestations of masculinity. Are we really at the stage where we want to be pessimistic about the possibility of teaching boys and girls together?

Diminishing gaps between boys and girls and opening up more channels for open communication might help to disrupt negative patterns of sexism and homophobia that hurt all of our communities and make life unendurable for many males who fail to fit the requirements for normative masculinity. And, even more importantly, it may contribute to the development of the characteristics that enhance the academic success and moral character of all students. In short, we need to reinvestigate what we think is best for boys. Nurturing boys as youth, rather than as men in the making, might serve society and boys themselves better, by encouraging the development of the qualities that we seek to inspire in all of our children.

Admittedly, writing this book took far too long. I wrote this book on the back porch in the summer when the kids were at day camp, while my father slept in his hospital room, and in between teaching, raising two daughters, and becoming an administrator at James Madison College. Thus, I have much gratitude for those who have supported me through this long process.

My biggest intellectual supporter has been historian of education Barbara Beatty. She commented on nearly every chapter of the book and has been cheering me on for many years. Intellectual partner and intimate friend, our collaborations, both personal and professional, have been immensely enriching.

There are numerous colleagues who have read either large or small portions of the book, and their commentary has improved my work, I hope, although I cannot pretend to have incorporated all of their suggestions. Jonathan Zimmerman read the entire manuscript and has both boosted my spirits and pushed me in new directions. Stephen Lassonde, whose own work has inspired me, has been a big support and influenced my own scholarship. Paula Fass has spurred me to broaden my angle of vision in thinking about the history of childhood. Steven Schlossman has been involved with this project for many years now and has always been willing to critique and inspire me in my scholarly efforts, for which I am deeply grateful. Other scholarly colleagues who read and offered useful feedback on different portions of the book include Barry Franklin, Tamara Myers, Jeff Mirel, Maris Vinovskis, E. Wayne Carp, and Priscilla Ferguson. My many colleagues in the Society for the History of Children and Adolescents, including Steven Mintz, have been sources of inspiration and have constituted a most collegial group of scholars.

I have been blessed at James Madison College with an extremely supportive dean, Sherman Garnett, who has been my ally and believed in my ability to finish this manuscript during its long genesis. When I took a new job as associate dean, he supported me in prioritizing the completion of this manuscript. I am deeply grateful for his belief in my ability to produce the manuscript while taking on new responsibilities. My home college, James Madison, and Michigan State University have both provided funding for research and time off that were essential to my writing of the book.

Susan Stein-Roggenbuck and Mark Largent at James Madison both took time out of their busy schedules to read and comment on portions of the manuscript. Lisa Fine, of the Center on Gender in Global Context, provided a platform for me to share my work with the professional community at Michigan State University and offered insights into the book. My colleagues Andaluna Borcila, Gene Burns, and Andrea Freidus have buoyed my spirits on numerous occasions. Another professional colleague, Jasmine Lee, has inspired me with her dedication to youth and has collaborated with me on our advocacy for students in K–12 education—work that furthered my thinking on this book.

I have also been the beneficiary of three incredible undergraduate assistants: Mitch Goldsmith, Justin Drwencke, and Elaine Cao. Each of these students provided research support and helped me with the nitty-gritty details of footnotes and indexing.

My editor at Johns Hopkins, Greg Britton, has helped to hasten this book along by holding me accountable and sending upbeat e-mails, reminding me that the book was worthy of an audience. I am grateful for his faith in me and his patience.

The personal support I have received from my friends and family has made what has been unthinkable thinkable. My dear friend and colleague Linda Racioppi and her daughter Anna Miller have been indispensable on both personal and professional fronts. Sieg Snapp and Vicki Morrone and their children Laly and Tori have been a major component of our East Lansing family for many years and have always lent a willing ear about my latest findings. After all these years, I continue to relish the personal and professional conversations I have with the friend of my youth, Lisa Davis.

During the last big push toward the completion of this manuscript, I have had the unwavering support of my immediate family. Their faith in me was unwavering, and they accepted that in order to finish the book I had to spend some weekends at the office. Like many women, I have had difficulties balancing the demands of being a good partner, a good parent, a dedicated teacher, and a scholar. I am blessed to have had the support of my partner Nancy and two beloved daughters Mia and Regina through the process of writing this book. My life would be incomplete without all of them.

My parents, Mary Louise and Bill (who is now deceased), have always believed in me and enjoyed hearing about the stories of my "bad boys." I only wish that Dad were here to see the final product. My many siblings—Kate, Sheila, Mary Ellen, Henry, Meg, and Elizabeth—have always been there for me, and I consider myself fortunate indeed to have such a loving and supportive family. My brother Bill died in his early thirties, but his own story has inspired me to probe more deeply into conceptions of masculinity and boyhood.

My good fortune extends beyond my own family of origin. My brother-in-law and sister-in-law, Jack and Beth Gardner, have treated our children as their own and have generously shared their time and home with us. My mother-in-law Lorraine Sullivan has made a big contribution to this effort, by timing her visits so that she could provide extra help during times when I was swamped with work, and has heaped love and attention on our family.

One more word about my partner Nancy. I have counted on her enduring support, faith in my abilities, and loving care of me and our children for twenty-five years. Maybe one of these days we'll get to tie the knot.

NOTES

Introduction

1. Christina Hoff Sommers, *The War against Boys: How Misguided Feminism Is Harming Our Young Men*, 1st Touchstone ed. (New York: Simon & Schuster, 2001).

2. Victor M. Rios, *Punished: Policing the Lives of Black and Latino Boys*, New Perspectives in Crime, Deviance, and Law Series (New York: New York University Press, 2011).

3. Anthony L. Brown, "'Same Old Stories': The Black Male in Social Science and Educational Literature, 1930s to the Present," *Teachers College Record* 113 (2011): 2064.

4. Michelle Alexander, *The New Jim Crow: Mass Incarceration in the Age of Colorblindness* (New York: New Press, 2010).

5. Stanley Cohen, *Folk Devils and Moral Panics: The Creation of the Mods and Rockers*, 3rd ed. (New York: Routledge, 2002).

6. David B. Tyack and Larry Cuban, *Tinkering toward Utopia: A Century of Public School Reform* (Cambridge, MA: Harvard University Press, 1995). Tyack and Cuban have noted the lack of attention paid to progress in public education's expansion to greater portions of the population.

7. Emma Smith, "Failing Boys and Moral Panics: Perspectives on the Underachievement Debate," *British Journal of Educational Studies* 51 (September 2003): 282–95.

8. Alexander, *New Jim Crow*.

9. Gilberto Q. Conchas and James Diego Vigil, *Streetsmart Schoolsmart: Urban Poverty and the Education of Adolescent Boys* (New York: Teachers College Press, 2012), 5.

10. Institute on Education Sciences, "Youth Indicators 2011, America's Youth: Transitions to Adulthood," http://nces.ed.gov/pubs2012/2012026/tables/table_14.asp.

11. Catherine Y. Kim, Daniel J. Losen, and Damon T. Hewitt, *The School-to-Prison Pipeline: Structuring Legal Reform* (New York: New York University Press, 2012), 35.

12. Data is from the National Association for Single Sex Education, www.singlesexschools.org/schools-schools.htm, accessed January 17, 2013.

13. Catherine Gewertz, "Black Boys' Educational Plight Spurs Single-Gender Schools," *Education Week* 26 (June 20, 2007), 3.

14. American Civil Liberties Union, Prepared for U.S. Department of Education, Office of Civil Rights, *Preliminary Findings of ACLU "Teach Kids, Not Stereotypes" Campaign* (New York: American Civil Liberties Union, 2012), 4, www.aclu.org/files/assets/doe_ocr_report2_0.pdf.

15. Pedro Noguera, *The Trouble with Black Boys: And Other Reflections on Race, Equity, and the Future of Public Education,* 1st ed. (San Francisco: Jossey-Bass, 2008); Gewertz, "Black Boys' Educational Plight," 5.

16. Michael Gurian, *Boys and Girls Learn Differently! A Guide for Teachers and Parents,* rev. 10th anniversary ed. (San Francisco: John Wiley & Sons, 2010).

17. For an overview of this research see Joan C. Chrisler and Donald R. McCreary, *Handbook of Gender Research in Psychology* (New York: Springer, 2010).

18. To be fair, there are currently many researchers who are questioning the antifeminist assumptions at the root of this work. See, for instance, Marcus Weaver-Hightower, "Dare the School Build a New Education for Boys?" *Teachers College Record,* February 14, 2005, www.tcrecord.org/content.asp?contentid=11743; and Smith, "Failing Boys and Moral Panics."

19. American Civil Liberties Union, *"Teach Kids, Not Stereotypes" Campaign.*

20. David Tyack and Elisabeth Hansot, *Learning Together: A History of Coeducation in American Public Schools* (New York: Russell Sage Foundation, 1992).

21. For some recent data, see National Information Center for Children and Youth with Disabilities, *Who Are the Children in Special Education? NICHCY Research Brief,* July 2003, 6, which finds that boys make up two-thirds of the children in special education. In 1999, Oswald, Coutinho, Best, and Singh found that blacks were 2.4 times more likely to be identified as educable mentally retarded and 1.5 times more likely to be identified as seriously emotionally disturbed. See Donald P. Oswald, Martha J. Coutinho, Al M. Best, and Nirbhay N. Singh, "Ethnic Representation in Special Education: The Influence of School-Related Economic and Demographic Variables," *Journal of Special Education* 32 (1999): 194. The historical statistics have been garnered from my perusal of the statistical reports of the various school districts of Detroit, Chicago, Cleveland, Philadelphia, Boston, and New York.

22. Joseph L. Tropea describes the informal rules that have governed boys' dispositions in an important essay on special education, "Bureaucratic Order and Special Children: Urban Schools, 1890–1940s," *History of Education Quarterly* 27 (Spring 1987): 29–53.

23. Jeffrey Mirel, *The Rise and Fall of an Urban School System, Detroit, 1907–1981* (Ann Arbor: University of Michigan, 1993).

24. Ira Katznelson, *When Affirmative Action Was White: An Untold History of Racial Inequality in Twentieth-Century America,* Reprint (New York: W. W. Norton, 2006).

25. Emily Cahan, "Toward a Socially Relevant Science: Notes on the History of Child Development Research," in *When Science Encounters the Child: Perspectives on Education, Child Welfare, and Parenting,* ed. Barbara Beatty, Emily Cahan, and Julia Grant (New York: Teachers College Press, 2008), 16–34.

Chapter 1 · Schooling the "Dangerous Classes"

1. A.P., "The Street-Arabs of New York," *Appleton's Journal* 9 (January 4, 1873), 47.

2. Edward Crapsey, *The Nether Side of New York; or, The Vice, Crime, and Poverty of the Great Metropolis* (New York: Sheldon, 1872), 119.

3. Edward Everett Hale, "The State's Care of Its Children," in Board of Managers of the House of Refuge, Philadelphia, *Prize Essays in Juvenile Delinquency* (Philadelphia: Edward and John Biddle, 1855), 17.

4. U.S. Census Bureau, "Population of the 100 Largest Cities and Other Urban Places in the United States: 1790–1990," Population Division Working Paper no. 27 (Washington, D.C.: U.S. Census Bureau, 1988), accessed September 20, 2007, www.census.gov/popula tion/www/documentation/twps0027/twps0027.html.

5. U.S. Bureau of the Census, "Historical Census Statistics on the Foreign-Born Population of the United States: 1850–1990," Population Division Working Paper no. 29 (Washington, D.C.: U.S. Bureau of the Census, 1999), table 19, accessed September 20, 2007, www.census.gov/population/www/documentation/twps0029/twps0029.html.

6. E. Wayne Carp, *Family Matters: Secrecy and Disclosure in the History of Adoption* (Cambridge, MA: Harvard University Press, 1998), 6–8; Lori Askeland, "Informal Adoption, Apprentices, and Indentured Children in the Colonial Era and the New Republic, 1605–1850," in *Children and Youth in Adoption, Orphanages, and Foster Care*, ed. Lori Askeland (Westport, CN: Greenwood Press, 2006), 8–9.

7. Steven Mintz, *Huck's Raft: A History of American Childhood* (Cambridge, MA: Harvard University Press, 2004), 137–38.

8. Brian Gratton and Jon Moen, "Immigration, Culture, and Child Labor in the United States, 1880–1920," *Journal of Interdisciplinary History* 34 (2003): 355–91.

9. Timothy J. Gilfoyle, *A Pickpocket's Tale: The Underworld of Nineteenth-Century New York* (New York: W. W. Norton, 2006); Christine Stansell, *City of Women: Sex and Class in New York, 1789–1860* (New York: Knopf, 1996); Mintz, *Huck's Raft*.

10. Stansell, *City of Women*.

11. Gilfoyle, *Pickpocket's Tale*; Timothy J. Gilfoyle, "'Street-Rats' and 'Gutter-Snipes': Child Pickpockets and Street Culture in New York City, 1850–1900," *Journal of Social History* 37 (Summer 2004): 853–82; David B. Wolcott, *Cops and Kids: Policing Juvenile Delinquency in Urban America, 1890–1940* (Columbus: Ohio State University Press, 2005).

12. "Boys as Leaders of the Mob in the New York Draft Riots, July 1863," *Harper's Weekly* (July 25, 1863): 466; reprinted in Robert H. Bremner, *Children and Youth in America 1933–1973: A Documentary History* (Cambridge, MA: Harvard University Press, 1970), 1:756–57; Mintz, *Huck's Raft*, 139.

13. Peter C. Holloran, *Boston's Wayward Children: Social Services for Homeless Children, 1830–1930* (Boston: Northeastern University Press, 1994), 105.

14. David J. Rothman, *Conscience and Convenience: The Asylum and Its Alternatives in Progressive America* (Boston: Little, Brown, 1980).

15. Robert M. Mennel, *Thorns and Thistles: Juvenile Delinquents in the United States, 1825–1940* (Hanover, NH: University Press of New England, 1973), xxv.

16. Hale, "State's Care of Its Children," 22.

17. Robert S. Pickett, *House of Refuge: Origins of Juvenile Reform in New York State, 1815–1857* (New York: Syracuse University Press, 1969), 49.

18. Michael B Katz, *The Irony of Early School Reform: Educational Innovation in Mid-Nineteenth Century Massachusetts* (Cambridge, MA: Harvard University Press, 1968), 164.

19. Priscilla Ferguson Clement, *Welfare and the Poor in the Nineteenth-Century City* (Madison, NJ: Fairleigh Dickinson University Press, 1985), 123.

20. Quoted in Joseph M. Hawes, *Children in Urban Society: Juvenile Delinquency in Nineteenth-Century America* (New York: Oxford University Press, 1971), 38.

21. Hawes, *Children in Urban Society*, 52.

22. Carl F. Kaestle, *The Evolution of an Urban School System: New York City, 1750–1850*

(Cambridge, MA: Harvard University Press, 1973), 137; David Tyack and Michael Berkowitz, "The Man Nobody Liked: Toward a Social History of the Truant Officer, 1840–1940," *American Quarterly* 29 (Spring 1977): 38.

23. Steven L. Schlossman, "Delinquent Children: The Juvenile Reform School," in *The Oxford History of the Prison: The Practice of Punishment in Western Society*, ed. Norval Morris and David J. Rothman (New York: Oxford University Press, 1995), 383.

24. *11th Annual Report of the Managers of the Society for the Reformation of Juvenile Delinquents* (New York, 1836), 28.

25. Nathaniel C. Hart, *Documents Relative to the House of Refuge Instituted by the Society for the Reformation of Juvenile Delinquents, in 1824* (New York: Mahlon Day, 1832), 23.

26. Enoch Cobb Wines and Theodore William Dwight, *Report on the Prisons and Reformatories of the United States and Canada: Made to the Legislature of New York, January, 1867* (Albany, 1867); reprinted in Bremner, *Children and Youth in America*, 723.

27. Hawes, *Children in Urban Society*, 41.

28. Barbara M. Brenzel, *Daughters of the State: A Social Portrait of the First Reform School for Girls in North America, 1856–1905* (Cambridge, MA: MIT Press, 1983); Mary Odem, *Delinquent Daughters: Protecting and Policing Adolescent Female Sexuality in the United States, 1885–1920* (Chapel Hill: University of North Carolina, 1995).

29. Mennel, *Thorns and Thistles*, 22–23.

30. Bradford Kinney Peirce, *A Half Century with Juvenile Delinquents; or, The New York Hour of Refuge and Its Times* (New York: D. Appleton, 1869), 95.

31. Hart, *Documents Relative to the House of Refuge*, 29.

32. Suffolk County (Mass.) Inspectors of Prisons, *Report of Inspectors of Prisons for the County of Suffolk, on the Condition of the Jail, Boston Lunatic Hospital, and Houses of Industry, Reformation, and Correction, July 1863* (J. E. Farwell, Printers to the City, 1863), 36, 42.

33. Holloran, *Boston's Wayward Children*, 30.

34. Brenzel, *Daughters of the State*. See also Alexandra W. Pisciotta, "Race, Sex, and Rehabilitation: A Study of Differentials in the Juvenile Reformatory, 1825–1900," *Crime & Delinquency* 29 (1983): 254–69.

35. Brenzel, *Daughters of the State*, 38.

36. Steven L. Schlossman, *Transforming Juvenile Justice: Reform Ideals and Institutional Realities, 1825–1920* (DeKalb: Northern Illinois University Press, 2005), 40–41.

37. Hart, *Documents Relative to the House of Refuge*, 277.

38. Brenzel, *Daughters of the State*, 46.

39. Timothy A. Hacsi, *Second Home: Orphan Asylums and Poor Families in America*, 1st ed. (Cambridge, MA: Harvard University Press, 1998).

40. Rothman, *Conscience and Convenience*, 268.

41. Michael B. Katz, *The Irony of Early School Reform: Educational Innovation in Mid-Nineteenth Century Massachusetts* (Cambridge, MA: Harvard University Press, 1968); Holloran, *Boston's Wayward Children*.

42. Elijah Devoe, *The Refuge System; Or, Prison Discipline Applied to Juvenile Delinquents* (New York: J. B. M'Gown, 1848), 48.

43. Hawes, *Children in Urban Society*, 28.

44. Eric C. Schneider, *In the Web of Class: Delinquents and Reformers in Boston, 1810s–1930s* (New York: New York University Press, 1992), 49.

45. Schlossman, *Transforming Juvenile Justice*, 105.

46. "Reform School Homicide," *Chicago Tribune* (January 6, 1870).

47. Charles Loring Brace, *The Best Method of Disposing of Our Pauper and Vagrant Children* (New York: Wynkoop, Hallenbeck & Thomas, 1859), 3.

48. Gilfoyle, *Pickpocket's Tale*, 31.

49. "1880 Federal Census, New York Juvenile Asylum," transcribed by Verna Drake for the Illinois State Genealogy Association, www.rootsweb.com/~ilsgs/1880ny84.html, accessed August 2, 2007.

50. Boston Children's Friends Society, *Twenty-Ninth Annual Report* (Boston, 1862), reprinted in Bremner, *Children and Youth in America*, 668.

51. Boston Children's Aid Society, *First Report of the Executive Committee* (Boston, 1865), reprinted in Bremner, *Children and Youth in America*, 734.

52. Charles Loring Brace, *The Dangerous Classes of New York, and Twenty Years' Work among Them* (New York: Wynkoop & Hallenbeck, 1880), 253.

53. Quote is from *Annual Report*, 1865, 1, cont. 35, Hillcrest Collection, Library of Congress, cited in Julie Berebitsky, *Like Our Very Own: Adoption and the Changing Culture of Motherhood* (Lawrence: University Press of Kansas, 2000), 19.

54. *First Annual Report, Massachusetts Society for the Prevention of Cruelty to Children* (Boston: Wright and Potter, 1882), 12.

55. Marilyn Irvin Holt, *The Orphan Trains: Placing Out in America* (Lincoln: University of Nebraska, 1994), 144.

56. Stephen O'Connor, *Orphan Trains: The Story of Charles Loring Brace and the Children He Saved and Failed* (Boston: Houghton Mifflin, 2001), xvii.

57. Brace, *Dangerous Classes of New York*, 28.

58. O'Connor, *Orphan Trains*, 167. Quote is from a circular by Charles Loring Brace, entitled *A Statement to the Public of a Portion of the Work of the Children's Aid Society*, 1863, 1–2.

59. On Brace's ambivalent attitude toward street boys, see also Lori Askeland, "'The Means of Draining the Streets of These Children': Domesticity and Romantic Individualism in Charles Loring Brace's Emigration Plan, 1853–1861," *American Transcendental Quarterly* 12 (June 1998): 145–62.

60. O'Connor, *Orphan Trains*, 218.

61. Brace, *Dangerous Classes*, 340.

62. Ibid., 79, 97–99.

63. Clay Gish, "Rescuing the 'Waifs and Strays' of the City: The Western Emigration Program of the Children's Aid Society," *Journal of Social History* 33 (Fall 1999), 124.

64. Holloran, *Boston's Wayward Children*, 45–46.

65. "Circular to Farmers and Mechanics, and Manufacturers in the Country, from the Children's Aid Society," in *Frederick Douglass' Paper* 50, December 1, 1854, col. G, 19th Century U.S. Newspapers, http://infotrac.galegroup.com.proxy1.cl.msu.edu/itw/info mark/761/477/6676525w16/purl=rc1_NCNP_0_GT3004989870&dyn=11!xrn_1_0_ GT3004989870&hst_1?sw_aep=msu_main.

66. "Children's Aid Society—To Farmers and Mechanics in the Country," in *Daily Cleveland Herald* 138, June 11, 1855, col. B, 19th Century U.S. Newspapers, http://info trac.galegroup.com.proxy1.cl.msu.edu/itw/infomark/761/477/6676525w16/purl=rc1_ NCNP_0_GT3004989870&dyn=11!xrn_1_0_GT3004989870&hst_1?sw_aep=msu_main.

67. Holt, *Orphan Trains*, 44–45.

68. Linda Gordon, *The Great Arizona Orphan Abduction* (Cambridge, MA: Harvard University Press, 2001).

69. Brace, *Dangerous Classes*, 112–13.

70. Holt, *Orphan Trains*, 125–26.

71. Gordon, *Great Arizona Orphan Abduction*.

72. Joan Jacobs Brumberg, *Kansas Charley: The Boy Murderer* (New York: Penguin, 2004).

73. Gordon's *Great Arizona Orphan Abduction* makes clear the emotive dimensions of this type of family formation in her account of a 1905 orphan train.

74. Viviana A. Zelizer, *Pricing the Priceless Child: The Changing Social Value of Children* (Princeton, NJ: Princeton University Press, 1994).

75. Gilfoyle, *Pickpocket's Tale*, 31.

76. "Lost Boys at the Industrial School," *Daily Cleveland Herald*, Sept 23, 1863, issue 224, col. B, 19th Century U.S. Newspapers, http://infotrac.galegroup.com.proxy1.cl.msu.edu/itw/infomark/758/253/6673732w16/purl=rc1_NCNP_0_GT3012934736&dyn=28!xrn_1_0_GT3012934736&hst_1?sw_aep=msu_main.

77. See annual reports of the Cleveland Children's Aid Society, Western Reserve Historical Society, Cleveland.

78. See Gilfoyle, *Pickpocket's Tale*, on the New York City ship schools. On Massachusetts, see Holloran, *Boston's Wayward Children*. See also B. K. Peirce, *A Half Century with Juvenile Delinquents*.

79. "The 'Gamins' at Sea," *Milwaukee Sentinel*, December 18, 1871, issue 297, col. B., excerpted from *New York World*, accessed in 19th Century U.S. Newspapers, http://callisto10.ggimg.com/imgsrv/FastPDF/NCNP/WrapPDF=contentSet=NCNP=recordID=5KUM-1871-DEC18-003-F.pdf.

80. New York Department of Public Charities and Correction and Henry Draper, *Cruise of School-Ship 'Mercury' in Tropical Atlantic Ocean, 1870–1871* (New York: New York Printing, 1871), 3.

81. Gilfoyle, *Pickpocket's Tale*, 37.

82. "Will a School-Ship Pay?" *Daily Evening Bulletin* (San Francisco), August 12, 1874, issue 108, col. E., 19th Century U.S. Newspapers. http://infotrac.galegroup.com.proxy1.cl.msu.edu/itw/infomark/758/253/6673732w16/purl=rc1_NCNP_0_GT3000282600&dyn=32!xrn_1_0_GT3000282600&hst_1?sw_aep=msu_main.

83. *Prison Reform in the United States: Proceedings of a Conference Held at Newport, Rhode Island, August 1 and 2, 1877* (New York: National Printing, 1877), 8, 11.

84. See, for instance, George Leib Harrison, *Chapters on Social Science as Connected with the Administration of State Charities* (Philadelphia: Allen, Lane & Scott, 1877).

85. Philadelphia Board of Public Education, *Thirty-Ninth Annual Report*, 1857, 10–12; Kaestle, *Evolution of an Urban School System*; Maris A. Vinovskis, *Education, Society, and Economic Opportunity: A Historical Perspective on Persistent Issues* (New Haven, CT: Yale University Press, 1995); David Tyack, *The One Best System: A History of American Urban Education* (Cambridge: Harvard University Press, 1974).

86. Baltimore School Commissioners, *Thirtieth Annual Report*, 1859, 42–43.

87. "Compulsory Education," *Milwaukee Sentinel*, April 23, 1867, issue 96, col. C., 19th Century U.S. Newspapers, http://infotrac.galegroup.com.proxy1.cl.msu.edu/itw/infomark/758/253/6673732w16/purl=rc1_NCNP_0_GT3012856428&dyn=35!xrn_3_0_GT3012856428&hst_1?sw_aep=msu_main.

88. "Education—Compulsory," *Frank Leslie's Illustrated Newspaper*, February 11, 1871, issue 802, col. A., pg. 358, 19th Century U.S. Newspapers, http://callisto10.ggimg.com/imgsrv/FastPDF/NCNP/WrapPDF=contentSet=NCNP=recordID=5FGL-1871-FEB11-002-F.pdf.

89. Harrison, *Chapters on Social Science*, 57.

90. Philadelphia Board of Public Education, *Fifty-Eighth Annual Report*, 1876, 22.

91. Kaestle, *Evolution of an Urban School System*.

92. William J. Reese, *America's Public Schools: From the Common School to "No Child Left Behind"* (Baltimore: Johns Hopkins University Press, 2005), 61; Robert Osgood, "Undermining the Common School Ideal: Intermediate Schools and Ungraded Classes in Boston, 1838–1900." *History of Education Quarterly* 37 (Winter 1997): 381–82; Tyack, *One Best System*, 69.

93. Lawrence Arthur Cremin, *The Transformation of the School; Progressivism in American Education, 1876–1957*, 1st ed. (New York: Knopf, 1961).

94. Joseph L. Tropea, "Bureaucratic Order and Special Children: Urban Schools, 1890–1940s," *History of Education Quarterly* 27 (Spring 1987): 31.

95. Jonathan Zimmerman, *Small Wonder: The Little Red Schoolhouse in History and Memory* (New Haven, CT: Yale University Press, 2009), 33–34.

96. "A Teacher Killed by a Pupil," *New York Times*, February 5, 1882, ProQuest Historical Newspapers: The New York Times (1851–2008), http://search.proquest.com.proxy1.cl.msu.edu/docview/94112784/13D98BA74B133B54E50/1?accountid=12598.

97. "Killed by His Teacher," *New York Times*, May 29, 1886, ProQuest Historical Newspapers: The New York Times, http://search.proquest.com.proxy1.cl.msu.edu/docview/94386678/13D98BADC502A1B13DE/2?accountid=12598.

98. Zimmerman, *Small Wonder*.

99. Detroit Board of Education, *28th Annual Report*, 1870; *34th Annual Report*, 1876.

100. New York Board of Education, *Reports on Corporal Punishment* (New York: Board of Education, 1877), 7, 16.

101. "Minority Report of Committee on Corporal Punishment," April 13, 1880, in Boston School Committee, *Annual Report of the Superintendent*, 1880, 145–50.

102. "Compulsory Education," *St. Louis Globe-Democrat*, February 27, 1878, p. 4, issue 277, col. B., 19th Century U.S. Newspapers, http://callisto10.ggimg.com/imgsrv/FastPDF/NCNP/WrapPDF=contentSet=NCNP=recordID=5AKD-1878-FEB27-004-F.pdf.

103. "Compulsory Education," *North American and United States Gazette* (Philadelphia) 13, January 6, 1872, col. F, 345, 19th Century U.S. Newspapers, http://infotrac.galegroup.com.proxy1.cl.msu.edu/itw/infomark/475/59/10604876w16/purl=rc1_NCNP_0_GT3009356442&dyn=8!xrn_2_0_GT3009356442&hst_1?sw_aep=msu_main.

104. David B. Tyack and Elisabeth Hansot, *Learning Together: A History of Coeducation in American Public Schools*, (New York: Russell Sage Foundation, 1992), 95.

105. Ibid., 78.

106. Cleveland Board of Education, *64th Annual Report of the Superintendent of Schools*, 1900; Report of the Superintendent of Schools to the Board of Education of the City of Cleveland, *The Special Schools and Curriculum Centers*, 1929–1930.

107. Detroit Board of Education, *One Hundred Years: The Story of the Detroit Public Schools, 1842–1942*, published as *Superintendent's Annual Report*, 1941–1942, 19; Grace E. Mitchell, "The Development of Compulsory Attendance in the Detroit Public Schools" (master's thesis, University of Michigan, 1940), 13, 17, 20.

108. Edith Abbott and Sophonisba Preston Breckinridge, *Truancy and Non-attendance in the Chicago Schools: A Study of the Social Aspects of the Compulsory Education and Child Labor Legislation of Illinois* (Chicago: University of Chicago Press, 1917), 61.

109. Boston School Committee, *Annual Report of the Superintendent*, 1892, 18–19.

Chapter 2 · The Nature of Boy Nature

1. Charles Dudley Warner, *Being a Boy* (New York: Houghton Mifflin, 1897), xi. See also Kenneth B. Kidd, "Farming for Boys: Boyology and the Professionalization of Boy Work," *Children's Literature Association Quarterly* 20 (1995): 149.

2. Crista DeLuzio, *Female Adolescence in American Scientific Thought, 1830–1930* (Baltimore: Johns Hopkins University Press, 2007).

3. Jean-Jacques Rousseau, *Émile: Or, Treatise on Education* (New York: D. Appleton, 1892).

4. Matthew Frye Jacobson, *Whiteness of a Different Color: European Immigrants and the Alchemy of Race*, 1st Harvard University Press ed. (Cambridge, MA: Harvard University Press, 1999); David R. Roediger, *The Wages of Whiteness: Race and the Making of the American Working Class*, rev. ed., Haymarket Series (London: Verso, 2007); Thomas A. Guglielmo, *White on Arrival: Italians, Race, Color, and Power in Chicago, 1890–1945* (New York: Oxford University Press, 2003); Ian Haney-López, *White by Law: The Legal Construction of Race*, rev. and updated, 10th anniversary ed., Critical America (New York: New York University Press, 2006).

5. "Editorial Comment," *Work with Boys: A Magazine of Methods* 6 (April 1916): 134.

6. Kidd, "Farming for Boys," 149.

7. Leonard Benedict and Amzi Clarence Dixon, *Waifs of the Slums and Their Way Out* (New York: Fleming H. Revell, 1907), 67.

8. Josiah Flynt, "Club Life among Outcasts," *Harper's Monthly Magazine* 90 (April 1895): 712.

9. Warner, *Being a Boy*, 150.

10. Lorinda Cohoon, "Necessary Badness: Reconstructing Post-bellum Boyhood Citizenships in *Our Young Folks* and *The Story of a Bad Boy*," *Children's Literature Association Quarterly* 29 (2004): 5–31.

11. Thomas Bailey Aldrich, *The Story of a Bad Boy* (London: George Routledge and Sons, 1877), 7.

12. Mark Twain, *Huckleberry Finn* (New York: Harper & Brothers, 1896).

13. Granville Stanley Hall, *Adolescence* (New York: D. Appleton, 1904).

14. A depiction of Mohawk Brave is included in George Walter Fiske, *Boy Life and Self-Government* (New York: Association Press, 1921), 16. On the modernist implications of playing Indian, see Philip J. Deloria, *Playing Indian* (New Haven, CT: Yale University Press, 1999).

15. Fiske, *Boy Life and Self-Government*, 15l.

16. David I. MacLeod, *Building Character in the American Boy: The Boy Scouts, YMCA, and Their Forerunners, 1870–1920* (Madison: University of Wisconsin, 1983), 68–69.

17. Henry A. Gibson, *Boyology; or, Boy Analysis* (New York: Association Press, 1922).

18. Joseph R. Kett, *Rites of Passage: Adolescence in America, 1790 to the Present* (New York: Basic Books, 1977), 199–200.

19. Clifford Putney, *Muscular Christianity: Manhood and Sports in Protestant America, 1880–1920* (Cambridge, MA: Harvard University Press, 2009).

20. Ibid., 119; William McCormick, *Fishers of Boys* (New York: Hodder and Stoughton, George H. Doran, 1915), 22.

21. On manly androgyny in the nineteenth century, see for instance Donald Yacovone, "'Surpassing the Love of Women': Victorian Manhood and the Language of Fraternal Love," in *A Shared Experience: Men, Women, and the History of Gender*, ed. Laura McCall and Donald Yacovone (New York: New York University Press, 1998).

22. Ann Douglas, *The Feminization of American Culture* (New York: Farrar, Straus and Giroux, 1998).

23. MacLeod, *Building Character in the American Boy*.

24. Kett, *Rites of Passage*, 227.

25. Howard Chudacoff, *Children at Play: An American History* (New York: New York University Press, 2008), 1.

26. Anthony M. Platt, *The Child Savers: The Invention of Delinquency* (Chicago: University of Chicago Press, 1977).

27. Howard S. Braucher, "Play and Social Progress," *Annals of the American Academy of Political and Social Science* 35 (1910): 111.

28. Brian Gratton and Jon Roger Moen, "Immigration, Culture, and Child Labor," *Journal of Interdisciplinary History* 34 (Winter 2004): 355–91.

29. Ernest Lynn Talbert, *Opportunities in School and Industry for Children of the Stockyards District* (Chicago: University of Chicago Press, 1912).

30. Giovanni Ermenegildo Schiavo, *The Italians in Chicago: A Study in Americanization* (New York: Arno Press, 1975), 67.

31. Miriam Umstadter Blaustein, *Memoirs of David Blaustein* (New York: McBride, Nast, 1913), 202.

32. Frank Tracy Carlton, *Education and Industrial Evolution* (New York: Macmillan, 1908), 243.

33. Pauline Goldmark, "Boyhood and Lawlessness," in *West Side Studies* (New York: Survey Associates, 1914), 11.

34. Philip Davis and Grace Kroll, *Street-Land: Its Little People and Big Problems* (Boston: S. J. Parkhill, 1915), 35.

35. David Nasaw, *Children of the City: At Work and at Play* (Garden City, NY: Anchor Press / Doubleday, 1985).

36. Cary Goodman, *Choosing Sides: Playground and Street Life on the Lower East Side*, 1st ed. (New York: Schocken Books, 1979), 17.

37. Ibid., 15.

38. Pauline Goldmark, "Boyhood and Lawlessness," in *West Side Studies* (New York: Survey Associates, 1914), 11.

39. E. Anthony Rotundo, *American Manhood: Transformations in Masculinity from the Revolution to the Modern Era* (New York: Basic Books, 1994).

40. Ibid., 35.

41. Woods Hutchinson, "Can the Child Survive Civilization?" in *Proceedings of the Annual Playground Congress and Yearbook* (New York: National Playground Association, 1908), 236.

42. Michael Gold, *Jews without Money: A Novel* (New York: Carroll & Graf, 2004), 46.

43. Braucher, "Play and Social Progress," 244.

44. Allen Burns, "Relation of Playgrounds to Juvenile Delinquency," *Second Annual Playground Congress, Yearbook* (New York: Playground Association of America, 1908): 175.

45. Jane Addams, *The Spirit of Youth and the City Streets* (New York: Macmillan, 1920).

46. Ibid., 53.

47. Ibid., 61.

48. "Killed by Play Policeman: One Lad Shoots Another at Flatbush Boys' Club," *New York Times (1857—Current file)*, May 3, 1905. www.proquest.com.proxy2.cl.msu.edu .proxy1.cl.msu.edu.proxy2.cl.msu.edu.proxy1.cl.msu.edu/.

49. Addams, *Spirit of Youth and the City Streets*, 63.

50. Ibid., 80.

51. Boys and Girls Clubs of America, "Our History," accessed October 2, 2009. www .bgca.org/whoweare/Pages/History.aspx.

52. William Byron Forbush, "A Sketch of the History of the Boys' Club Movement in America," *Work with Boys* 6 (January 1906): 17.

53. Charles S. Bernheimer and Jacob M. Cohen, *Boys' Clubs* (New York: Baker and Taylor, 1914), 82.

54. Peter C. Baldwin, " 'Nocturnal Habits and Dark Wisdom': The American Response to Children in the Streets at Night," *Journal of Social History* 35 (2002), 598. See also J'Nell L. Pate, *Hazel Vaughn Leigh and the Fort Worth Boys' Club* (Fort Worth: Texas Christian University Press, 2000).

55. Gail Bederman, *Manliness and Civilization: A Cultural History of Gender and Race in the United States, 1880-1917* (Chicago: University of Chicago Press, 1996).

56. Kett, *Rites of Passage*, 199.

57. "Military Drill for Boys' Clubs," *Charities Review* 4 (March 1895): 235–38.

58. Maury Klein, *The Life and Legends of E. H. Harriman* (Chapel Hill: University of North Carolina Press, 2001), 42.

59. "A Club for Street Boys," *New York Times*, January 3, 1885, 3, ProQuest Historical Newspapers, New York Times (1851–2006), http://search.proquest.com.proxy1.cl.msu .edu/docview/94279466/13C16DCA937350D4856/2?accountid=12598.

60. MacLeod, *Building Character in the American Boy*, 65.

61. Charles Stelzle, *Boys of the Street: How to Win Them* (New York: Fleming H. Revell, 1904), 54, 37.

62. Frank S. Mason, "Character Making in Street Boys' Clubs," *Religious Education* 2 (October 1907): 141.

63. Jansen, "Boys' Clubs."

64. Alvan F. Sanborn, "About Boys and Boys' Clubs," *North American Review* 167 (August 1898): 254–56.

65. Rotundo, *American Manhood*; and Michael Kimmel, *Manhood in America: A Cultural History*, 3rd ed. (New York: Oxford University Press, 2010).

66. Jansen, "Boys' Clubs," 742.

67. Chicago Boys' Club, "Membership in Chicago Boys' Club after Six Years," 1907, box 1, file 1, Chicago Boys' and Girls' Club Papers (CGBC), Chicago Historical Museum (CHM).

68. Benedict and Dixon, *Waifs of the Slums*, 32. On evangelism in urban reform see Paul S. Boyer, *Urban Masses and Moral Order in America, 1820-1920* (Cambridge, MA: Harvard University Press, 1992).

69. "Chicago Boys' Camp," newspaper clipping, *Tri-County Gazette*, 27, 1916, box 3, file 2, CGBC, CHM.

70. Putney, *Muscular Christianity*. See also Kett, *Rites of Passage*.

71. Chicago Boys Club, *The Boys Club Manual*, n.d., box 46, file 6, CGBC, CHM, 6.

72. Chicago Boys' Clubs, "For the Underprivileged Boys of the Crowded City," n.d., box 3, file 7, CGBC, CHM. See also Carter Julian Savage, "'In the Interest of the Colored Boys': Christopher J. Atkinson, William T. Coleman, and the Extension of Boys' Clubs Services to African-American Communities," *History of Education Quarterly* 51 (November 2011): 486–518.

73. Chicago Boys' Clubs, *Boys' Club Manual*, I.6.

74. Richard R. Valencia, *The Evolution of Deficit Thinking: Educational Thought and Practice* (New York: Routledge, 1997).

75. Anthony Sorrentino, "It's an Inside Job: An Italian-American Community Organization on Chicago's Near West Side and the Chicago Area Project, 1934–1974," 39, accessed September 23, 2009, http://tigger.uic.edu/depts/hist/hull-maxwell/vicinity/nws1/documents/ethnicity/italian/sorrentino/sorrentino1.htm.

76. Benedict and Dixon, *Waifs of the Slums*, 171.

77. Board of Directors Minutes, October 14, 1908, box 3, file 1, CGBC, CHM.

78. Ibid., June 11, 1913, box 3, file 2; January 11, 1921, box 3, file 6.

79. Chicago Boys' Club, "For the Underprivileged Boys of the Crowded City," n.d., box 3, file 7, CGBC, CHM.

80. George D. Chamberlain, "The Mass Boys' Club," from *Advancement*, a publication of the Boys' and Girls' Clubs of Philadelphia 2 (September 1913), in box 3, file 2, 2, CGBC, CHM.

81. Superintendent's Report to the Association of Commerce, 1928–29, box 3, file 7, CGBC, CHM.

82. "Building Strong Bodies," in *Chicago Boys' Club Two News* 5 (October 1930), n.p., box 48, file 2, CGBC.

83. Theodore Roosevelt, *The Strenuous Life: Essays and Addresses* (New York: Century, 1902).

84. On the social control approach, see for instance Paul Boyer, *Urban Masses and Moral Order in America, 1820–1920* (Cambridge, MA: Harvard University Press, 1978).

85. Dominick Cavallo, *Muscles and Morals: Organized Playgrounds and Urban Reform, 1880–1920* (Philadelphia: University of Pennsylvania Press, 1981).

86. Flynt, "Club Life among Outcasts," 713.

87. Ocean Howells, "Play Pays: Urban Land Politics and Playgrounds in the United States," *Journal of Urban History* 34 (September 2008): 966.

88. Steven A. Riess, *City Games: The Evolution of American Urban Society and the Rise of Sports* (Urbana: University of Illinois Press, 1991), 136.

89. Henry Stoddard Curtis, *The Practical Conduct of Play* (New York: Macmillan, 1915), 192.

90. On this point, in addition to Howells, "Play Pays," see Chudacoff, *Children at Play*.

91. Curtis, *Practical Conduct*, 264.

92. Ibid., 121.

93. Robin F. Bachin, *Building the South Side: Urban Space and Civic Culture in Chicago, 1890–1919* (Chicago: University Of Chicago Press, 2008), 56.

94. Charles Zueblin and Helen Bernice Sweeny, *American Municipal Progress* (New York: Macmillan, 1916), 267.

95. Benjamin McArthur, "The Chicago Playground Movement: A Neglected Feature of Social Justice," *Social Service Review* 49 (1975): 383.

96. Ibid.

97. "Growth of Recreation Idea: New York Leads All Cities in Recreation Centres," *New York Times*, August 12, 1905.

98. Riess, *City Games*.

99. Cavallo, *Muscles and Morals*.

100. Elliot J. Gorn and Warren Goldstein, *A Brief History of American Sports* (Urbana: University of Illinois, 1993), 174–75; Benjamin G. Rader, *American Sports: From the Age of Folk Sports to the Age of Televised Sports* (Upper Saddle River, NJ: Pearson-Prentice Hall), 106–7.

101. Luther Halsey Gulick, *A Philosophy of Play* (New York: C. Scribner's Sons, 1920).

102. George Ellsworth Johnson, *Education through Recreation* (Cleveland, OH: Survey Committee of the Cleveland Foundation, 1916).

103. G. Stanley Hall, preface to J. Adams Puffer, *The Boy and His Gang* (Boston: Houghton Mifflin, 1912), xi.

104. Gulick, *Philosophy of Play*, 92.

105. Ibid., 98.

106. Ibid., 84.

107. George E. Johnson, *Education through Recreation*, 18.

108. Elizabeth Burchenal, "Session on Athletics for Girls," in *Proceedings of the Third Annual Playground Congress and Yearbook* (New York: Playground Association of America, 1910), 370, http://books.google.com/books?id=wGQAAAAAYAAJ.

109. Susan K. Cahn, *Coming on Strong: Gender and Sexuality in Twentieth-Century Women's Sports* (Cambridge, MA: Harvard University Press, 1998).

110. Riess, *City Games*.

111. Braucher, "Play and Social Progress," 102.

112. Johnson, *Education through Recreation*, 37.

113. Riess, *City Games*, 146.

114. Jeff Wiltse, *Contested Waters: A Social History of Swimming Pools in America* (Chapel Hill: University of North Carolina Press, 2007), 65.

115. Frances Blascoer, Eleanor Hope Johnson, and Public Education Association of the City of New York, *Colored School Children in New York* (New York: Public Education Association of the City of New York, 1915), 25–26.

116. Ibid.

117. Chicago Commission on Race Relations, *The Negro in Chicago: A Study of Race Relations and a Race Riot* (Chicago: University of Chicago Press, 1922), 274.

118. William M. Tuttle, *Race Riot: Chicago in the Red Summer of 1919* (Urbana: University of Illinois Press, 1996).

119. Chicago Commission on Race Relations, *Negro in Chicago*, 288–89.

Chapter 3 · The Perils of Public Education

1. Charles Sherman Carney, *Truancy in the Tenement District of Chicago* (Ann Arbor: University of Michigan Sociological Society, 1905), Appendix, Parental School Cases, n.p.

In this case, and in all such cases where the full names of children are used, I have disguised the name as a privacy protection.

2. Herbert M. Kliebard, *The Struggle for the American Curriculum, 1893–1958* (New York: Routledge, 2004), 5.

3. Elisabeth Antoinette Irwin, *Truancy: A Study of the Mental, Physical and Social Factors of the Problem of Non-attendance at School* (New York: Public Education Association, City of New York, 1915), 43.

4. Ibid., 10; Stephen Lassonde, *Learning to Forget: Schooling and Family Life in New Haven's Working Class, 1870–1940* (New Haven, CT: Yale University Press, 2007), 31.

5. Carney, *Truancy in the Tenement District of Chicago*, n.p.

6. Michael R. Olnek, "American Public Schooling and European Immigrants in the Early Twentieth Century: A Post-revisionist Synthesis," in *Rethinking the History of American Education*, ed. William J. Reese and John L. Rury (New York: Macmillan, 2008), 108.

7. Leonard Porter Ayres, *Laggards in Our Schools: A Study of Retardation and Elimination in City School Systems* (New York: Russell Sage Foundation, Charities Publication Committee, 1913), 6–7.

8. David Tyack and Elisabeth Hansot, *Learning Together: A History of Coeducation in American Public Schools* (New York: Russell Sage Foundation, 1992); Edward L. Thorndike, *The Elimination of Pupils from School*, Issue 4 of Department of the Interior, Bureau of Education, Bulletin (Washington, D.C.: Government Printing Office, 1908), 10.

9. Ayres, *Laggards in Our Schools*, 4, 7; David B. Tyack, *The One Best System: A History of American Urban Education* (Cambridge: Harvard University Press, 1974), 200–201.

10. Victoria Bissell Brown, "The Fear of Feminization: Los Angeles High Schools in the Progressive Era," *Feminist Studies* 16 (Autumn, 1990): 496; Tyack and Hansot, *Learning Together*.

11. On racial and ethnic prejudice in the measurement of schoolchildren's intelligence, see, for example, Diane Ravitch, *Left Back: A Century of Battles over School Reform* (New York: Simon & Schuster, 2001); and Paul D. Chapman, *Schools as Sorters: Lewis M. Terman, Applied Psychology, and the Intelligence Testing Movement, 1890–1930* (New York: New York University Press, 1990).

12. Earl Barnes, "The Feminizing of Culture," *The Atlantic Monthly* 109 (1912): 175. See also Barbara Miller Solomon, *In the Company of Educated Women: A History of Women and Higher Education in America* (New Haven, CT: Yale University Press, 1986), 142.

13. Claudia Goldin, "America's Graduation from High School: The Evolution and Spread of Secondary Schooling in the Twentieth Century," *Journal of Economic History* 58 (June 1998): 347.

14. Brown, "Fear of Feminization," 503.

15. U.S. Immigration Commission (1907–1910), William Paul Dillingham, and William Stiles Bennet, *Abstracts of Reports of the Immigration Commission: with Conclusions and Recommendations and Views of the Minority (In two volumes)* (Washington, D.C.: Government Printing Office, 1911), 43.

16. Granville Stanley Hall, *Educational Problems* (New York: D. Appleton, 1911), 1:584.

17. See J. Adams Puffer, *The Boy and His Gang* (Boston: Houghton Mifflin, 1912); Paul Hanley Furfey, *The Gang Age: A Study of the Preadolescent Boy and His Recreational Needs* (New York: Macmillan, 1926); William Byron Forbush, *The Boy Problem* (Boston: Pilgrim Press, 1908); and Luther Gulick Halsey, *A Philosophy of Play* (New York: C. Scribner's Sons, 1920).

18. Paula S. Fass, *Outside In: Minorities and the Transformation of American Education* (New York: Oxford University Press, 1991).

19. Tyack and Hansot, *Learning Together*, 180.

20. Brown, "Fear of Feminization," 506.

21. F. E. De Yoe and C. H. Thurber, "Where Are the High School Boys?" *School Review* 8 (April 1900): 236; Thorndike, *Elimination of Pupils from School*; and G. Stanley Hall, "Feminization in School and Home," *World's Work* (May 1908): 10237–44. See also G. Stanley Hall, *Adolescence: Its Psychology and Its Relations to Physiology, Anthropology, Sociology, Sex, Crime, Religion, and Education* (New York: D. Appleton, 1915). On Hall, see Dorothy Ross, *G. Stanley Hall: The Psychologist as Prophet* (Washington, D.C.: Government Printing Office, 1908); and Tyack and Hansot, *Learning Together*.

22. Louise Montgomery, *The American Girl in the Stockyards* (Chicago: Ginn, 1915), 466–67.

23. Joel Perlmann, *Ethnic Differences: Schooling and Social Structure among the Irish, Italians, Jews, and Blacks in an American City, 1880–1935* (Cambridge: Cambridge University Press, 1988), 178. Data derived from U.S. Immigration Commission, *Reports*.

24. Goldin, "America's Graduation from High School," 347, 352.

25. Jacob Riis, *The Children of the Poor* (New York: C. Scribner's Sons, 1905), 118.

26. Herbert M. Kliebard, *The Struggle for the American Curriculum, 1893–1958*, 3rd ed. (New York: Routledge, 2004), 7.

27. Reports on the U.S. Immigration Commission, *Children of Immigrants in Schools* (Washington, D.C.: Government Printing Office, 1911), 30:543.

28. Ibid.

29. Ibid., 30:357. For Cleveland and Detroit, 31:5.

30. Ayres, *Laggards in Our Schools*, 3.

31. Reports on the U.S. Immigration Commission, *Children of Immigrants in Schools*, 31, 10.

32. Helen Todd, "Why Children Work: The Children's Answer," in *Selected Articles on Child Labor*, ed. Edna D. Bullock (Minneapolis: H. W. Wilson, 1915), 208.

33. James L. Flannery, *The Glass House Boys of Pittsburgh: Law, Technology, and Child Labor* (Pittsburgh, PA: University of Pittsburgh Press, 2009), xiii.

34. David Nasaw, *Children of the City: At Work and at Play* (Oxford: Oxford University Press, 1986).

35. Stephen Provasnik, "Judicial Activism and the Origins of Parental Choice: The Court's Role in the Institutionalization of Compulsory Education in the United States," *History of Education Quarterly* 46 (2006): 311–47. Provasnik makes the point that it was not so much the legislation itself that compelled enforcement but the court's role in upholding these laws.

36. "Playing Hookey," *St. Louis Globe Democrat*, May 25, 1885, issue 2, col C, 10.

37. David Tyack and Michael Berkowitz, "The Man Nobody Liked: Toward a Social History of the Truant Officer, 1840–1940," *American Quarterly* 29 (Spring 1977): 33.

38. Carney, *Truancy in the Tenement Districts of Chicago*, 3.

39. Ibid., 25.

40. See Edith Abbot and Sophonisba Breckinridge, *The Delinquent Child and the Home* (New York: Arno, 1970, first published in 1912), 131.

41. Edith Abbott and Sophonisba Preston Breckinridge, *Truancy and Non-attendance*

in the Chicago Schools (Chicago: University of Chicago, 1917), 98, 92. See also John G. Richardson's analysis of these figures in *Common, Delinquent, and Special: The Institutional Shape of Special Education (Studies in the History of Education)* (New York: Routledge, 1999), 51.

42. Philadelphia Board of Education, *Annual Report*, 1925, 445.

43. In addition to Clifford R. Shaw, *Delinquency Areas: A Study of the Geographic Distribution of School Truants, Juvenile Delinquents, and Adult Offenders in Chicago* (Chicago, 1929), see, for instance, Clifford R. Shaw, *Juvenile Delinquency and Urban Areas*, rev. ed. (Chicago: University of Chicago Press, 1969); and Clifford R. Shaw in collaboration with Maurice E. Moore, *The Natural History of a Delinquency Career* (Chicago: University of Chicago Press, 1931).

44. Bryan Hogeveen, "'The Evils with Which We Are Called to Grapple': Élite Reformers, Eugenicists, Environmental Psychologists, and the Construction of Toronto's Working-Class Boy Problem, 1860–1930," *Labour / Le Travail*, no. 55 (Spring 2005): 42–43.

45. Kathleen Jones, *Taming the Troublesome Child: American Families, Child Guidance, and the Limits of Psychiatric Authority* (Cambridge, MA: Harvard University Press, 1999), 162.

46. "Chicago Area Project Diaries—1934–35," West Side Community Committee, box 10, file 12, 13, Chicago Area Project Papers (CAP), Chicago Historical Museum (CHM).

47. Kathryn M. Neckerman, *Schools Betrayed: Roots of Failure in Inner-City Education* (Chicago: University of Chicago Press), 154.

48. Ibid., 69.

49. Lassonde, *Learning to Forget*.

50. Fass, *Outside In.*

51. Harpo Marx with Rowland Barber, *Harpo Speaks . . . about New York* (New York: New York Review of Books, 2001), 16, 19.

52. Quotes are from Anthony Sorrentino, "It's an Inside Job: An Italian-American Community Organization on Chicago's Near West Side and the Chicago Area Project, 1934–1974," 1–10, accessed December 19, 2009, http://tigger.uic.edu/depts/hist/hull-maxwell/vicinity/nws1/documents/ethnicity/italian/sorrentino/prologue.htm. This unpublished memoir formed the basis of Burton Bledstein's essay "Tony: Growing Up Italian-American in the Vicinity of Halsted and Taylor Street, the Boyhood of Anthony Sorrentino."

53. File 3315, Chicago Commons Case Files, CHM. Boxes are not numbered for these case files because of inconsistencies in numbering.

54. Richardson, *Common, Delinquent, and Special*, 41.

55. James S. Hiatt, *The Truant Problem and the Parental School* (Washington, D.C.: Government Printing Office, 1915), 18.

56. Richardson, *Common, Delinquent, and Special*, 41.

57. The suggestion that male instructors for parental school classes should be of the "he-man" type was made by Arch O. Heck, *The Education of Exceptional Children* (New York: McGraw-Hill, 1940), 32.

58. White House Conference on Child Health and Protection, *Special Education: The Handicapped and the Gifted* (New York: Century, 1931), 494.

59. Robert L. Osgood, *For "Children Who Vary from the Normal Type": Special Education in Boston, 1838–1930* (Washington, D.C.: Gallaudet University Press, 2002), 119–20.

60. Tyack and Berkowitz, "Man Nobody Liked," 38.

61. Forest Chester Ensign, *Compulsory School Attendance and Child Labor* (Iowa City: Athens Press, 1921), 62, 70.

62. Boston School Committee, *Annual Report*, 1892, 22–23.

63. Osgood, *For "Children Who Vary from the Normal Type,"* 123.

64. Joan Gittens, *Poor Relations: The Children of the State in Illinois, 1818–1990* (Urbana: University of Illinois Press, 1994), 116.

65. Stephen John Provasnik, "Compulsory Schooling, from Idea to Institution: A Case Study of the Development of Compulsory Attendance in Illinois, 1857–1907" (Ph.D. diss., University of Chicago, 1999); Illinois Parental School Law of 1899, approved April 24, 1899.

66. Abbott and Breckinridge, *Truancy and Non-attendance in the Chicago Schools*, 60–61.

67. Gittens, *Poor Relations*, 116.

68. On the difficulties that New York City school teachers had with discipline in the 1920s, see Kate Rousmaniere, "Losing Patience and Staying Professional: Women Teachers and the Problem of Classroom Discipline in New York C. Schools in the 1920s," *History of Education Quarterly* 34 (Spring 1994): 49–68.

69. Life Story, Illinois Institute of Juvenile Research Papers (IJR), circa 1930s, box 51, file 4, CHM. Pasquale's name has been changed to protect his privacy.

70. Carney, *Truancy in the Tenement District of Chicago*, appendix, "Chicago Parental School Cases," n.p. The full names of truants are given in this text, but I have chosen not to use them.

71. Ibid.

72. Cynthia Kay Barron, "History of the Chicago Parental School, 1902–1975" (master's thesis, Loyola University, 1993).

73. Life Story, circa 1930s, box 42, unmarked file, Illinois Institute for Juvenile Research Papers, (IJR), CHM.

74. Irwin, *Truancy*, 24.

75. Clifford Robe Shaw, *The Jack-Roller, a Delinquent Boy's Own Story* (Chicago: University of Chicago Press, 1930), 61.

76. Jane Addams, "Ten Years' Experience in Illinois," *Annals of the American Academy of Political and Social Science* 38 (July 1911): 144.

77. Quotes are from Aphrodite Flamboura, "The Chicago Parental School" (master's thesis, DePaul University, 1953), 17.

78. Carney, *Truancy in the Tenement District of Chicago*, 25.

79. Chicago Board of Education, *First Annual Report of the Chicago Parental School*, 1902, 8.

80. Ibid.

81. Barron, "History of the Chicago Parental School," 64.

82. Steven A. Gelb, " 'Not Simply Bad and Incorrigible': Science, Morality, and Intellectual Deficiency," *History of Education Quarterly* 29 (Autumn 1989): 369; Richardson, *Common, Delinquent, and Special*, 15.

83. Chicago Board of Education, *First Annual Report of the Chicago Parental School*, 1902, 51.

84. Chicago Board of Education, *Second Annual Report of the Chicago Parental School*, 1903, 59.

85. T. H. MacQueary, "The Relation of the Public Schools to the Parental School," in *Proceedings of the Seventh National Conference of the Education of Backward, Truant, and Delinquent Children*, 1910, 123. See also Richard Louis Dugdale, *The Jukes: A Study in Crime, Pauperism, Disease, and Heredity* (New York: G. P. Putnam's Sons, 1895).

86. Nelson W. McLain, "Elementary Instruction in Agriculture for Schools for Backward, Truant, and Delinquent Children," 6, and E. E. York, "Disciplinary Methods in Day and Boarding Schools," 35, both in *Proceedings of the Third National Conference of the Education of Backward, Truant, and Delinquent Children* (Plainfield: Printing Department Indiana Boys' School, 1906).

87. Leila Zenderland, *Measuring Minds: Henry Herbert Goddard and the Origins of American Intelligence Testing* (New York: Cambridge University Press, 2001); Jones, *Taming the Troublesome Child*, 44.

88. William Healy, *The Individual Delinquent: A Text-Book of Diagnosis and Prognosis for All Concerned in Understanding Offenders* (New York: Little, Brown, 1918), 4.

89. Chicago Board of Education, *First Annual Report of the Chicago Parental School*, 49.

90. Carney, *Truancy in the Tenement District of Chicago*, 7.

91. Shaw, *Jack-Roller*, 62–63. In a footnote, the author mentions that, as a result of an investigation of these brutal practices, superintendent MacQueary was replaced. See also Loraine Gelsthorpe, "The Jack-Roller: Telling a Story," *Theoretical Criminology* 11 (2007): 515–42.

92. Carl Husemoller Nightingale, *On the Edge: A History of Poor Black Children and Their American Dreams* (New York: Basic Books, 1995). Nightingale makes this argument for African American parents in the period from the 1950s to the present in Philadelphia.

93. New York Board of Education, *Reports on Corporal Punishment* (New York: Board of Education, 1877), 14.

94. York, "Disciplinary Methods," 41–42, 44, 51.

95. In retrospect, almost all of their practices would now be deemed abusive. However, I am trying to distinguish, with great difficulty, between those practices that were then perceived as legitimate and those that individuals at the time would characterize as abusive.

96. Carney, *Truancy in the Tenement District of Chicago*, CPS case #10, n.p.

97. Memo, January 30, 1929, "Chicago Parental School for Boys," box 71, file 2, Welfare Council of Metropolitan Chicago Papers, CHM.

98. "Orders Arrest in School Floggings Case: Boys Bare Brutality in School," *Chicago Defender*, September 1, 1923, National Edition (1921–1967), http://search.proquest.com.pro xy1.cl.msu.edu/docview/491989462/13C108D69473BDA4304/1?accountid=12598. See complaints and hearings about the parental school in the Welfare Council of Chicago papers, especially, "Chicago Parental School," August 1955, box 285, file 2, Welfare Council of Metropolitan Chicago Papers, CHM.

99. Chicago Board of Education, "Parental School Report," *Annual Report of Superintendent of Schools*, 1924, 33.

100. "Charges of Cruelty in Truant's School," *New York Times*, August 3, 1912, ProQuest Historical Newspapers, (1831–2005), 16, http://search.proquest.com.proxy1.cl.msu.edu/doc view/97358606/13C1091A565344FB999/1?accountid=12598.

101. Life Story, circa, 1930s, box 44, file 9, IJR, CHM.

Chapter 4 · Bad or Backward?

1. "The Cat," Autobiography, Institute for Juvenile Research Papers (IJR), box 45, file 4, Chicago History Museum (CHM).

2. This data was acquired by my perusal of the annual school board or superintendent reports of the cities of Chicago, Detroit, Cleveland, Philadelphia and more limited scrutiny of cities such as St. Louis and Baltimore.

3. For separate histories of children with disabilities, see, for instance, Elizabeth J. Safford and Philip L. Safford, *Children with Disabilities in America: A Historical Handbook And Guide* (Westport, CT: Greenwood, 2006); Robert L. Osgood, *For "Children Who Vary from the Normal Type": Special Education in Boston, 1838–1930* (Washington, D.C.: Gallaudet University Press, 2000); Robert L. Osgood, *The History of Special Education* (Westport, CT: Greenwood, 2008); Margret A. Winzer, *The History of Special Education: From Isolation to Integration*, 1st ed. (Washington, D.C.: Gallaudet University Press, 1993); Barry M. Franklin, *From "Backwardness" to "At-Risk": Childhood Learning Difficulties and the Contradictions of School Reform* (Albany: State University of New York Press, 1994). Judith Sealander has an intriguing chapter, "Public Education of Disabled Children," in Sealander, *The Failed Century of the Child: Governing America's Young in the Twentieth Century* (Cambridge: Cambridge University Press, 2003).

4. See David Wolcott and Steven Schlossman, "In the Voices of Delinquents: Social Science, the Chicago Area Project, and a Boys' Culture of Casual Crime and Violence in the 1930s," in *When Science Encounters the Child: Education, Parenting, Parenting, and Child Welfare in 20th-Century America*, ed. Barbara Beatty, Emily D. Cahan, and Julia Grant (New York: Teachers College Press, 2006), 116–35. See also Linda Gordon, *Heroes of Their Own Lives: The Politics and History of Family Violence—Boston, 1880–1960* (Urbana: University of Illinois Press, 2002).

5. Charles Scott Berry, *The Education of Handicapped Children in Michigan* (Lansing: Michigan Department of Public Instruction, 1926).

6. Joseph Tropea, "Bureaucratic Order and Special Children: Urban Schools, 1890–1940s," *History of Education Quarterly* 27 (Spring 1987): 34.

7. Ibid., 32.

8. James H. Van Sickle, Lightner Witmer, and Leonard P. Ayres, *Provision for Exceptional Children in Public Schools* (Washington, D.C.: Government Printing Office, 1911), 33.

9. Osgood, *History of Special Education*, 42.

10. Osgood, *For "Children Who Vary from the Normal Type."*

11. Franklin, *From "Backwardness" to "At-Risk"*; Tropea, "Bureaucratic Order," 32.

12. More talented middle-class boys were sent to all-boys schools such as Philadelphia's Central High and Boston's Boys Latin High School. See David F. Labaree, *The Making of an American High School: The Credentials Market and the Central High of Philadelphia, 1838–1939* (New Haven, CT: Yale University Press, 1988).

13. U.S. Office of Education, "Schools and Classes for Subnormals," *Bulletin no. 5* (Washington, D.C.: Government Printing Office, 1928), 92, 118–19.

14. Chicago Board of Education, *Report of the Director of Special Schools for the School Year, 1922–23*, in *66th Annual Report of the Chicago Board of Education*, 27.

15. In Rosalind Rosenberg's, *Beyond Separate Spheres: Intellectual Roots of Modern*

Feminism (New Haven, CT: Yale University Press, 1982), she shows how women scientists challenged prevailing views of female intelligence.

16. Ethel L. Cornell, "Why Are More Boys Than Girls Retarded in School? II", *Elementary School Journal* 29 (November 1928): 226.

17. Safford and Safford, *Children with Disabilities in America*, 94.

18. Patrick J. Ryan, "Unnatural Selection: Intelligence Testing, Eugenics, and American Political Cultures," *Journal of Social History* 30 (April 1997): 669–85.

19. Diane Ravitch, *Left Back: A Century of Failed School Reforms* (New York: Simon & Schuster, 2000).

20. Michael D'Antonio, *The State Boys' Rebellion* (New York: Simon & Schuster, 2004).

21. "Fit the Misfits," *New York Times (1923—Current file)*, December 1, 1927, ProQuest Historical Newspapers, (1851–2009), 26, http://search.proquest.com.proxy2.cl.msu.edu/docview/104019655/13CC4BE3E315BF90E76/1?accountid=12598.

22. Chicago Board of Education, *Ninth Annual Report of the Chicago Parental School*, 1910, 1.

23. Tropea, "Bureaucratic Order," 32.

24. Osgood, *History of Special Education*, 11.

25. Ibid., 42.

26. Arthur Bernard Moehlman, *Public Education in Detroit* (Bloomington, IN: Public School, 1925), 122, 163.

27. Leonard Porter Ayres, Cleveland Foundation, and Survey Committee, *The Cleveland School Survey: Summary Volume*, (New York: Arno Press, 1917), 213.

28. Department of Child Study and Pedagogic Investigation, *Report on Child-Study Investigation* (Chicago: Chicago Board of Education, 1899), 14.

29. Ibid., 44, 47. See also Franklin, *From "Backwardness" to "At-Risk,"* who also notes the early discussions of possible cognitive dysfunctions of backward children.

30. Kimberly Kode, *Elizabeth Farrell and the History of Special Education* (Arlington, VA: Council for Exceptional Children, 2002); Lightner Witmer, *The Special Class for Backward Children* (Philadelphia: Psychological Clinic Press, 1911).

31. Elizabeth E. Farrell, "Schools for Backward Children," *Proceedings of the National Education Association* (1906): 1054–55.

32. Kode, *Elizabeth Farrell*, 3.

33. Ibid., 23–24.

34. Ibid., 28.

35. Ibid., 53–55, 64.

36. Witmer, *Special Class for Backward Children*, 36.

37. Ibid., 42–45.

38. Ibid., 47, 49, 52.

39. Ibid., *Special Class for Backward Children*.

40. Ravitch, *Left Back*; and Jeffrey Mirel, *The Rise and Fall of an Urban School System* (Ann Arbor: University of Michigan Press, 1999).

41. Ada M. Fitts, "The Function of Special Classes for Mentally Defective Children in the Public Schools," *Ungraded* 2 (June 1917): 205.

42. Jane Bernard-Powers, *The "Girl Question" in Education: Vocational Training for Young Women in the Progressive Era* (New York: Routledge, 1992).

43. Case record #1166, Chicago Commons Case File Papers, CHM.

44. William J. Reese, *America's Public Schools: From the Common School to "No Child Left Behind"* (Baltimore: Johns Hopkins University Press, 2005).

45. Osgood, *For "Children Who Vary from the Normal Type."*

46. Joseph M. Hawes in *Children in Urban Society: Juvenile Delinquency in Nineteenth-Century America* (New York: Oxford University Press, 1971) details the origins of the concern over the influence of children's literature, such as dime novels, on juvenile delinquency. It is pure speculation on my part to presume an actual influence on behavior of literature.

47. E. W. Burgess, "The Study of the Delinquent as a Person," *American Journal of Sociology* 28 (May 1923): 664.

48. William Healy, the pioneering psychologist and criminologist, was one of the adherents of this view. See William Healy, *The Individual Delinquent: A Text-Book of Diagnosis and Prognosis for All Concerned in Understanding Offenders* (New York: Little, Brown, 1918).

49. "Rates of Delinquency in Which the Chicago Area Project Has Been Operating," Chicago Area Project (CAP), box 27, file 6, CHM.

50. Chicago Board of Education, "Report of Director of Special Schools," *Annual Report*, 1918, 53, 73.

51. "Rates of Delinquency in Which the Chicago Area Project Has Been Operating." See also Steven Schlossman and Michael Sedlak, *The Chicago Area Project Revisited* (Santa Monica, CA: Rand, 1983), 85. On Sorrentino, see David S. Tanenhaus, *Juvenile Justice in the Making* (Oxford: Oxford University Press, 2004), 148.

52. Augusta Bronner, *The Psychology of Special Abilities and Disabilities* (Boston: Little, Brown, 1921), 2, 112, 140–41, 104.

53. Robert Bruce Bain, "'Our Greatest Social Welfare Agency': Cleveland's Public School Policies for Educating Problem Boys, 1917–1938" (Ph.D. diss., Case Western Reserve University, 1990), 119.

54. George Whitman, "Why Do Pupils Go Wrong?" *School Topics* 3 (April 29, 1921), 3. Quote was cited in Bain, "'Our Greatest Social Welfare Agency,'" 154.

55. Board of Education of the City of Cleveland, *The Special Schools and Curriculum Centers*, 79.

56. Cleveland Board of Education, *Boys' School First Annual Report*, 1922, 29; Bain, "'Our Greatest Social Welfare Agency,'" 149.

57. Clayton R. Wise, "Thomas A. Edison School for Boys," *Journal of the NEA* 17 (December 1928): 277.

58. Ibid., 279.

59. Bain, "'Our Greatest Social Welfare Agency,'" 238–39.

60. Ibid., 236–39.

61. John T. Robinson, "Students and Faculty Work to Improve Life in School," *Journal of Educational Sociology* 21 (May 1948): 518.

62. Detroit Board of Education, *Eighty-First Annual Report*, 1924, 57.

63. Detroit Board of Education, *Eighty-Second Annual Report*, 1925, 13.

64. Detroit Board of Education, *Eighty-First Annual Report*.

65. Detroit Board of Education, *Education of the Handicapped in the Detroit Public Schools*, 1937, 71–72.

66. Henry Obel, principal, "Second Annual Report of Moore School for Boys, 1936," box 34, file 3, United Community Service Papers, Walter Reuther Library, Wayne State University, Detroit (WRL), 14.

67. "Grant Request for Handicapped Children to Rackham Fund, 1933," box 94, Detroit Board of Education Papers, WRL.

68. Detroit Board of Education, "Superintendent's Report," *Annual Report*, 1938–1939, 83.

69. Minutes, Western Area Project Notebook, December 8, 1941, box 8, file 5, Lewis Larkin Papers, WRL.

70. Notes, Western Area Project, January 10, 1940, box 6, file 7, Lewis Larkin Papers, WRL.

71. Detroit Board of Education Department of Special Education, *Annual Report*, 1942–1943 and 1943–1944, box 94, Detroit Board of Education Papers, WRL.

72. Area Workers Staff Meeting, Western Area Project, March 23, 1945, box 12, file 3, Lewis Larkin Papers, WRL.

73. David L. Angus and Jeffrey E. Mirel, *The Failed Promise of the American High School, 1890–1995* (New York: Teachers College Press, 1999).

74. See Edward H. Stullken, "Misconceptions about Juvenile Delinquency," *Journal of Criminal Law and Criminology* 26 (July 1935): 228–34, for some biographical information.

75. Edward H. Stullken, *Tenth Annual Report*, Montefiore School, 1938–1939.

76. Chicago Board of Education, *First Annual Report of Montefiore School*, 1929–1930. Submitted by Edward Stullken, principal, to Dr. Frank G. Bruner, director of Special Schools.

77. Ibid., 2.

78. Edward H. Stullken, "How the Montefiore School Prevents Crime," *Journal of Criminal Law and Criminology* 26 (July 1935): 228–34. Stullken claimed that approximately 10 percent of the Montefiore boys had "total reading disability" but not faulty intelligence (232).

79. Chicago Board of Education, *Seventh Annual Report of Montefiore School*, 1935–1936, 101.

80. Chicago Board of Education, *Eighth Annual Report of Montefiore School*, 1936–1937, 2, 28.

81. Chicago Board of Education, *Second Annual Report of Montefiore School*, 1930–1931, 28.

82. My data on this point is derived from the autobiographies of delinquents taken from the Illinois Institute of Juvenile Research files at the Chicago Historical Museum; the Chicago Commons Case Files, also taken from the Chicago Historical Museum; and files from the Chicago Area Project, which are in both the Chicago Historical Museum and Special Collections at the University of Illinois at Chicago.

83. Chicago Board of Education, *Second Annual Report of Montefiore School*, 19.

84. Isabella Dolton, "The Montefiore School: An Experiment in Adjustment," *Journal of Educational Sociology* 6 (April 1933): 483–84.

85. Chicago Board of Education, *Eighth Annual Report*, 24.

86. Case History, box 49, file 1, circa 1940s, IJR, CHM.

87. "Dice Players Draw Pistols When Teacher Interferes," *Chicago Daily Tribune*, November 15, 1935, 10, ProQuest Historical Newspapers (1849–1989), http://search.proquest.com.proxy1.cl.msu.edu/hnpchicagotribune/docview/181710414/13D7F4D96FC546AB8D1/1?accountid=12598.

88. "Head of School Refuses to Act in Bus Disorder," *Chicago Daily Tribune*, December 18, 1965, sec. 1, 3, ProQuest Historical Newspapers (1849–1989). http://search.proquest .com.proxy1.cl.msu.edu/docview/178833317/13C16BADBC7585B7E27/1?accountid=12598.

89. "Rob, Assault Woman on Bus: 18 Pupils Tear Clothes of Victim Pupils Assault Woman in Bus," *Chicago Daily Tribune*, January 22, 1957, sec. Part 1, 1, ProQuest Historical Newspapers (1849–1989), http://search.proquest.com.proxy1.cl.msu.edu/docview/180053 639/13C16BD86721B9EFEE7/1?accountid=12598.

90. "Montefiore School Principal Urges More Sympathy," *Chicago Daily Tribune*, February 5, 1959, Part 2, A5, ProQuest Historical Newspapers (1849–1989), http://search .proquest.com.proxy1.cl.msu.edu/docview/182244189/13C16BE6A1345AD6043/1?account id=12598.

91. "Montefiore: Chicago Public School," accessed April 10, 2013, www.montefiore.cps .k12.il.us/.

Chapter 5 · "The Boys' Own Story"

1. Life Story, box 44, Illinois Institute for Juvenile Research Papers (IJR), Chicago Historical Museum, Chicago (CHM). Some files are unmarked in these archives, while others are numbered.

2. Gail Bederman, *Manliness and Civilization: A Cultural History of Gender and Race in the United States, 1880–1917* (Chicago: University of Chicago Press, 1996).

3. There are many accounts of the juvenile court movement. See Anthony Platt, *The Child Savers: The Invention of Delinquency*, exp. ed. (Chicago: University of Chicago, 1969); Robert M. Mennel, *Thorns and Thistles: Juvenile Delinquents in the United States, 1825–1940* (Hanover, NH: University Press of New England, 1973); Victoria Getis, *The Juvenile Court and Progressives* (Urbana: University of Illinois Press, 2000); Kathleen W. Jones, *Taming the Troublesome Child: American Families, Child Guidance, and the Limits of Psychiatric Authority* (Cambridge, MA: Harvard University Press, 2002); and Joseph M. Hawes, *Children in Urban Society: Juvenile Delinquency in Nineteenth-Century America*, 1st ed. (New York: Oxford University Press, 1971).

4. Hawes, *Children in Urban Society*, 246.

5. David B. Wolcott, *Cops and Kids: Policing Juvenile Delinquency in Urban America, 1890–1940* (Columbus: Ohio State University Press, 2005), 133.

6. Getis, *Juvenile Court and Progressives*, 189.

7. Barry C. Feld, *Bad Kids: Race and the Transformation of the Juvenile Court* (New York: Oxford University Press, 1999), 6.

8. Timothy D. Hurley, "Origin of the Illinois Juvenile Court Law," in *The Child, the Clinic and the Court*, ed. Jane Addams (New York: Johnson Reprint, 1971), 321.

9. David S. Tanenhaus, *Juvenile Justice in the Making* (New York: Oxford University Press, 2005), 8.

10. Julia Lathrop, "The Background of the Juvenile Court in Illinois," in *The Child, the Clinic and the Court*, ed. Jane Addams (New York: Johnson Reprint, 1971), 291.

11. Miriam VanWaters, "The Juvenile Court from the Child's Viewpoint," in *The Child, the Clinic and the Court*, ed. Jane Addams (New York: Johnson Reprint, 1971), 218.

12. Mennel, *Thorns and Thistles*, 135.

13. Feld, *Bad Kids*, 67.

14. Getis, *Juvenile Court and Progressives*, 46.

15. "Bringing Up Father," Annual Report, 1930, Big Brothers Association, box 1, Big Brothers Association Papers, Temple Urban Archive, Temple University, Philadelphia.

16. *West Side Studies, Carried on under the Direction of Pauline Goldmark* (New York: Survey Associates, 1914), 16–17.

17. Wolcott, *Cops and Kids*, 84.

18. Henry Winfred Thurston, *Delinquency and Spare Time* (New York: Survey Committee of the Cleveland Foundation, 1918), 3.

19. Helen Cody Baker, Memo of afternoon spent in courtroom of Judge Bicek, circa 1933, for Welfare Council of Chicago, box 71, file 3, Welfare Council Papers, CHM.

20. Robert H. Bremner, "Other People's Children," *Journal of Social History* 16 (April 1983): 83–103; Feld, *Bad Kids*, 73.

21. Mabel Carter Rhoades, *The Case Study of Delinquent Boys in the Juvenile Court of Chicago* (Chicago: University of Chicago Press, 1907), 59–60.

22. Steven L. Schlossman, *Love and the American Delinquent: The Theory and Practice of "Progressive" Juvenile Justice, 1825–1920*, 1st ed. (Chicago: University of Chicago Press, 1977), 59.

23. Ibid., 58.

24. Ibid., 148.

25. *West Side Studies, Carried on under the Direction of Pauline Goldmark*, 125.

26. Ibid., 91–93.

27. Welfare Council of Metropolitan Chicago, "Excerpts from the Reports of Some of Our Visitors Regarding Their Contact with the Juvenile Court in Recent Weeks," circa 1933, box 71, file 3, Welfare Council Papers, CHM.

28. Schlossman, *Love and the American Delinquent*, 164.

29. John R. Sutton, *Stubborn Children: Controlling Delinquency in the United States, 1640–1981* (Berkeley: University of California Press, 1993).

30. Kriste Lindenmeyer, *A Right to Childhood: The U.S. Children's Bureau and Child Welfare, 1912–46* (Urbana: University of Illinois Press, 1997).

31. Wolcott, *Cops and Kids*, 77; and Peter C. Holloran, *Boston's Wayward Youth: Social Services for Homeless Children, 1830–1930* (Boston: Northeastern University Press, 1994), 208–9.

32. Mrs. Joseph T. Bowen, "The Early Days of the Juvenile Court," in *The Child, the Clinic and the Court*, ed. Jane Addams (New York: Johnson Reprint Corp., 1971).

33. Among many others on this topic, see Steven Schlossman and Stephanie Wallach, "Crime of Precocious Sexuality—Female Juvenile Delinquency in the Progressive Era," *Harvard Educational Review* 48, no.1 (February 1978): 30; Mary E. Odem, *Delinquent Daughters: Protecting and Policing Adolescent Female Sexuality in the United States, 1885–1920* (Chapel Hill: University of North Carolina Press, 1995); Ruth M. Alexander, *The "Girl Problem": Female Sexual Delinquency in New York, 1900–1930* (Ithaca, NY: Cornell University Press, 1998); Anne Meis Knupfer, *Reform and Resistance: Gender, Delinquency, and America's First Juvenile Court*, 1st ed. (New York: Routledge, 2001); and Tamara Myers, *Caught: Montreal's Modern Girls and the Law, 1869–1945* (Toronto: University of Toronto Press, 2006).

34. See, for instance, Kathy Peiss "Charity Girls and City Pleasures: Notes on Working-Class Sexuality, 1880–1920," in *Powers of Desire: The Politics of Sexuality*, ed. Ann Barr

Snitow, Christine Stansell, and Sharon Thompson, 5th ed. (New York: Monthly Review Press, 1983).

35. Odem, *Delinquent Daughters*, 103; Jane Addams, *The Spirit of Youth and the City Streets* (New York: Macmillan, 1920).

36. Odem, *Delinquent Daughters*, 115.

37. Elizabeth Lunbeck, *The Psychiatric Persuasion: Knowledge, Gender, and Power in Modern America* (Princeton, NJ: Princeton University Press, 1995); Tamara Myer, "Embodying Delinquency: Boys' Bodies, Sexuality, and Juvenile Justice History in Twentieth-Century Quebec," *Journal of the History of Sexuality* 14 (October 2006): 383–414.

38. Howard P. Chudacoff, *How Old Are You? Age Consciousness in American Culture* (Princeton, NJ: Princeton University Press, 1992); Stephen Lassonde, *Learning to Forget* (New Haven, CT: Yale University Press, 2007).

39. Lassonde, *Learning to Forget*.

40. Eric C. Schneider, *Vampires, Dragons, and Egyptian Kings: Youth Gangs in Postwar New York* (Princeton, NJ: Princeton University Press, 2001), 53.

41. Frederic Milton Thrasher, *The Gang: A Study of 1,313 Gangs in Chicago* (Peotone, IL: New Chicago School Press, 2000), ix.

42. Ibid., 3–4.

43. Ibid., 26.

44. Andrew J. Diamond, *Mean Streets: Chicago Youth and the Everyday Struggle for Multiracial Empowerment, 1908–1969* (Berkeley: University of California Press, 2009), 32–33. Diamond is also skeptical of viewing working-class male culture as "unproblematic" (35).

45. James W. Messerschmidt, *Masculinities and Crime: Critique and Reconceptualization of Theory* (New York: Rowman & Littlefield, 1993), 84.

46. Richard Majors and Janet Mancini Billson, *Cool Pose: The Dilemmas of Black Manhood in America* (New York: Touchstone, 1993), 1–6.

47. Bryan Hogeveen discusses a similar phenomenon in Toronto in his essay "'The Evils with Which We Are Called to Grapple': Élite Reformers, Eugenicists, Environmental Psychologists, and the Construction of Toronto's Working-Class Boy Problem, 1860–1930," *Labour/Le Travail* 55 (Spring 2005): 37–68.

48. William Healy, *Mental Conflicts and Misconduct* (Boston: Little, Brown, 1917).

49. Getis, *Juvenile Court and Progressives*, 70.

50. William Healy, *The Individual Delinquent: A Text-Book of Diagnosis and Prognosis for All Concerned in Understanding Offenders* (New York: Little, Brown, 1918); and Jones, *Taming the Troublesome Child*.

51. Steven Schlossman and Michael Sedlak, "The Chicago Area Project Revisited," *Crime & Delinquency* 29 (1983): 393.

52. Solomon Kobrin, "The Chicago Area Project—A 25-Year Assessment," *Annals of the American Academy of Political and Social Science* 322 (March 1959): 19–29.

53. Clifford Robe Shaw, *The Jack-Roller, a Delinquent Boy's Own Story* (Chicago: University of Chicago Press, 1930), 3. Shaw also acknowledged his debt to W. I. Thomas, who pioneered the use of these types of "personal" documents in his own research. He cites W. I. Thomas and Dorothy Swaine Thomas, *The Child in America* (New York: Alfred A. Knopf, 1928) in his explanation of his methodology.

54. Clifford Robe Shaw, *Delinquency Areas* (Chicago: University of Chicago Press,

1929). See also Clifford Robe Shaw and Henry D. McKay, *Juvenile Delinquency and Urban Areas: A Study of Rates of Delinquency in Relation to Differential Characteristics of Local Communities in American Cities* (Chicago: University of Chicago Press, 1972); and Clifford R. Shaw and Henry D. McKay, *Social Factors in Juvenile Delinquency: A Study of the Community, the Family, and the Gang in Relation to Delinquent Behavior for the National Commission on Law Observance and Enforcement* (Washington, D.C.: Government Printing Office, 1931), 31.

55. Shaw, *Delinquency Areas*, 87.

56. "North Side Civic Committee," circa early 1940s, box 93, file 6, Chicago Area Project Papers (CAP), CHM.

57. Anthony Sorrentino, "The Chicago Area Project after 25 Years," *Federal Probation* 23 (1959): 41.

58. Noel A. Cazenave, "Chicago Influences on the War on Poverty," in *Urban Public Policy*, ed. Martin A. Melosi (University Park: Penn State University Press, 2004), 54.

59. "Proposal for Combination of Chicago Area Project and Program of Parole Supervision," box 8, file 6, CAP, CHM.

60. Solomon Kobrin, "Legal and Ethical Problems of Street Gang Work," *Crime & Delinquency* 10 (April 1964): 154.

61. Schlossman and Sedlak, "The Chicago Area Project Revisited," 402.

62. "Russell Square Community Committee," n.d., box 11, file 85, Stephen Bubacz Papers, University of Illinois, Chicago, Special Collections.

63. Schlossman and Sedlak, "The Chicago Area Project Revisited," 441; "Meeting of the Truant Officers," December 1, 1939, box 27, file 6, CAP, CHM.

64. "Report on the Investigation of the Area Project," circa 1939, box 27, file 4, CAP, CHM.

65. Cases, Illinois Youth Commission, box 11, file 89, Stephen Bubacz Papers, University of Illinois, Chicago, Special Collections.

66. "Reaching the Gang: A Report of Work with a Boy's Gang in the Near North Side," 1945, box 11, file 147, Stephen Bubacz Papers.

67. William Julius Wilson, *When Work Disappears: The World of the New Urban Poor* (New York: Vintage, 1997).

68. "The Chicago Area Project: An Experimental Program for the Treatment and Prevention of Delinquency," 1930, file 16, Stephen Bubacz Papers.

69. Walter Reckless, *Six Boys in Trouble: A Sociological Case Book* (Ann Arbor, MI: Edwards Brothers, 1929), 35.

70. Clifford Robe Shaw, *The Natural History of a Delinquent Career* (Chicago: University of Chicago Press, 1931).

71. Ibid., 15.

72. Ibid., 19.

73. Ibid., 22–23.

74. Thrasher, *Gang*, 26.

75. Lowell Juliard Carr, *Organizing to Reduce Juvenile Delinquency: The Michigan Plan for Better Citizenship* (Ann Arbor: Michigan Delinquency Information Service, 1936), 43.

76. Life Story, box 50, file 8, IJR, CHM.

77. I first found these quotes in the manuscript "Chicago Area Project" in the Stephen Bubacz Papers. I subsequently found very similar quotes in Shaw's *Jack-Roller*, although these quotes are not attributed to the jack-roller himself.

78. Life Story, box 41, file 4, IJR, CHM.

79. "Meeting with Youth from the Vicinity of Jefferson Intermediate School," July 15, 1939, Lewis B. Larkin Papers, Walter Reuther Library, Wayne State University, Detroit (WRL).

80. "Memorandum to the Board of Directors of the Chicago Area Project," January 10, 1944, box 1, file 22, Lewis Larkin Papers, WRL.

81. "Near Northwest Side Survey," Diary of the Area Project Representative, 1938, box 108, file 8, CAP, CHM.

82. Dominic A. Pacyga, *Polish Immigrants and Industrial Chicago: Workers on the South Side, 1880–1922* (Columbus, Ohio State University Press, 1991), 68–69.

83. Linda Gordon, *Pitied but Not Entitled: Single Mothers and the History of Welfare, 1890–1935*, Harvard University Press paperback ed. (Cambridge, MA: Harvard University Press, 1995).

84. David Wolcott and Steven Schlossman, "In the Voices of Delinquents: Social Science, the Chicago Area Project, and a Boys' Culture of Casual Violence in the 1930s," in *When Science Encounters the Child: Education, Child Welfare, and Parenting in 20th Century America*, ed. Barbara Beatty, Emily Cahan, and Julia Grant (New York: Teachers College Press, 2006), 122.

85. Linda Gordon, *Heroes of Their Own Lives: The Politics and History of Family Violence—Boston, 1880–1960* (New York: Viking, 1988).

86. Sarah Chinn, *Inventing Modern Adolescence: The Children of Immigrants in Turn-of-the-Century America* (Piscataway, NJ: Rutgers University Press, 2008), 5.

87. Gordon, *Heroes of Their Own Lives.*

88. Paula S. Fass, *The Damned and the Beautiful: American Youth in the 1920s* (New York: Oxford University Press, 1979).

89. Shaw, *Jack-Roller*, 84.

90. C. J. Pascoe, *Dude, You're a Fag: Masculinity and Sexuality in High School* (Berkeley: University of California Press, 2007), 17.

91. Shaw and McKay, *Social Factors in Juvenile Delinquency*, 4–5.

92. Ibid., 4–11.

93. Shaw, *Delinquency Areas*, 40.

94. Field Notes, John L. Brown, July 7, 1937, box 47, file 3, Chicago Area Project Papers, CHM.

95. This aspect of the family lives of Chicago's delinquents is well documented in Wolcott, *Cops and Kids.*

96. Life Story, box 44, file 8, IJR, CHM.

97. I am aware of the research that demonstrates that corporal punishment, appropriately administered, is not intrinsically harmful, especially to young children. See Diana Baumrind, "The Discipline Controversy Revisited," *Family Relations* 45 (October 1996): 405–14. However, the type of punishment that is described in the records does not fit the rubric that Baumrind identifies. Carl Husemoller Nightingale also describes the impact of physical discipline on African American youth in Chicago. See Carl Husemoller Nightingale, *On the Edge: A History of Poor Black Children and Their American Dreams* (New York: Basic Books, 1995).

98. Brown Field Notes, January 1, 1937, file 152, Stephen Bubacz Papers.

99. Life Story, box 46, file 5, IJR, CHM.

100. Life Story, box 45, file 4, IJR, CHM.

101. See for instance, Stephen M. Whitehead and Frank J. Barrett, eds., *The Masculinities Reader* (Malden, MA: Blackwell, 2001).

102. Letter from M. C. Krug to Angelo Patri, March 1, 1935, box 2, Angelo Patri Papers, Library of Congress.

103. Julia Grant, "A 'Real Boy' and Not a Sissy: Gender, Childhood, and Masculinity, 1890–1940," *Journal of Social History* 37 (2004): 829–51.

104. Elizabeth Lunbeck, *The Psychiatric Persuasion: Knowledge, Gender, and Power in Modern America* (Princeton, NJ: Princeton University Press, 1994).

105. Thrasher, *The Gang*, 222.

106. Life Story, box 50, file 8, IJR, CHM.

107. Don Romesburg, "The Tightrope of Normalcy: Developmental Citizenship, and American Adolescence, 1890–1940," *Journal of Historical Sociology* 21 (December 2008): 428.

108. Life Story, box 50, file 8, IJR, CHM.

109. "Chicago Area Project Diaries—1934–35," box 10, file 1, Red Wings, 64, and Burley Lions, 29, CAP, CHM.

110. "Forest Tigers—Central Community Center," October 10, 1938–February 2, 1939, Lewis B. Larkin Papers, WRL.

111. Thrasher, *Gang*, 316.

112. Clifford Shaw, *The Jack-Roller: A Delinquent Boys' Own Story* (Chicago: University of Chicago Press), 85.

113. "Diary of a Community Worker in the Russell Square South Chicago Community," John L. Brown, field worker, box 47, file 3, IJR, CHM.

114. Thrasher, *Gang*, 317.

115. Life Story, box 44, file 10, IJR, CHM.

116. Life Story, box 55, IJR, CHM.

117. Stephen Robertson, "*Crimes against Children: Sexual Violence and Legal Culture in New York City, 1880–1960*," Studies in Legal History (Chapel Hill: University of North Carolina Press, 2005), 61.

118. Don Romesburg, "'Wouldn't a Boy Do?' Placing Early Twentieth-Century Male Sex Work into Histories of Sexuality," *Journal of the History of Sexuality* 18 (September 2009): 367.

119. Life Story, box 46, file 5, IJR, CHM.

120. Marjorie Bell, "The School and the Juvenile Court Work Together," *Journal of Educational Sociology* 6 (April 1933): 471–72.

121. "Walk with Ed Smith—Sixth and Stimson Gang," October 1, 1939, box 10, file 11, Lewis B. Larkin Papers, WRL.

122. Chicago Area Project Diaries, 1934–35, box 10, file 12, CAP, CHM.

123. Elijah Anderson, *Code of the Street: Decency, Violence, and the Moral Life of the Inner City*, 1st ed. (New York: W. W. Norton, 1999).

Chapter 6 · Black Boys and Native Sons

1. Richard Wright, *Black Boy* (New York: Harper Collins, 2008), Kindle edition.

2. Ibid.

3. Martin Summers, *Manliness and Its Discontents: The Black Middle Class and the Transformation of Masculinity, 1900–1930* (Chapel Hill: University of North Carolina Press, 2004), 3.

4. Ralph Ellison, *Invisible Man*, Vintage international ed. (New York: Vintage Books, 1990; Claude Brown, *Manchild in the Promised Land* (New York: Macmillan, 1965).

5. Edward Franklin Frazier and American Council on Education, *Negro Youth at the Crossways, Their Personality Development in the Middle States*, Schocken Paperbacks (New York: Schocken Books, 1967); Allison Davis, John Dollard, and American Council on Education, American Youth Commission, *Children of Bondage: The Personality Development of Negro Youth in the Urban South* (American Council on Education, 1956); and Kenneth B. Clark, "Color, Class, Personality and Juvenile Delinquency," *Journal of Negro Education* 28 (July 1959): 240–51.

6. Catherine Y. Kim, Daniel J. Losen, and Damon T. Hewitt, *The School-to-Prison Pipeline: Structuring Legal Reform* (New York: New York University Press, 2012).

7. Campbell Gibson and Kay Jung, *Historical Census Statistics on the Foreign-Born Population of the United States: 1850–2000* (Washington, D.C.: U.S. Census Bureau, 2006), 50, 80.

8. Ray Stannard Baker, *Following the Color Line: American Negro Citizenship in the Progressive Era*, American Perspectives (New York: Harper & Row, 1964, first published 1908), 113.

9. Allan H. Spear, *Black Chicago: The Making of a Negro Ghetto, 1890–1920* (Chicago: University of Chicago Press, 1969), 11; and James R. Grossman, *Land of Hope: Chicago, Black Southerners and the Great Migration* (Chicago: University of Chicago Press, 1991).

10. Grossman, *Land of Hope.*

11. Kimberley L. Phillips, *AlabamaNorth: African-American Migrants, Community, and Working-Class Activism in Cleveland, 1915–1945* (Urbana: University of Illinois Press, 1999), 136, 139.

12. "Preliminary Report on 'Community Backgrounds of Negro Delinquency," submitted to the Committee on Findings and Recommendations for the Conference on Juvenile Delinquency in the Negro Community," May 24, 1932, Welfare Council Papers, box 145, file 3, CHM (Chicago History Museum).

13. "The Problem, n.d., circa 1942," 1, box 2, file 98, Chicago Area Project Papers (CAP), CHM.

14. Joint Committee on Negro Child Study in New York City, *A Study of Delinquent and Neglected Negro Children before the New York City Children's Court*, 1925, 6, 21, http://name.umdl.umich.edu/ABL6603.0001.001.

15. See Michelle Alexander, *The New Jim Crow: Mass Incarceration in the Age of Colorblindness* (New York: New Press, 2010) for a contemporary analysis of the issue.

16. Joint Committee on Negro Child Study in New York City, *Study of Delinquent and Neglected Negro Children*, 6, 12.

17. Kenneth L. Kusmer, *A Ghetto Takes Shape: Black Cleveland, 1870–1930* (Urbana: University of Illinois Press, 1978), 220.

18. Carol B. Stack, *All Our Kin: Strategies for Survival in a Black Community*, 1st ed. (New York: Harper & Row, 1974).

19. Joan Gittens, *Poor Relations: The Children of the State in Illinois, 1818–1990* (Urbana: University of Illinois Press, 1994), 44.

20. "Effect of the Depression in the Area 47th to 51st St., South Park, and New York Central Tracks Area," box 134, file 1, Ernest Burgess Papers, Special Collections, University of Chicago. See also Earl R. Moses, "Differentials in Crime Rates between Negroes and Whites Based on Comparisons of Four Socio-economically Equated Areas," *American Journal of Sociology* 12 (August 1947): 419–20.

21. Kusmer, *Ghetto Takes Shape*, 220.

22. Davarian L. Baldwin, *Chicago's New Negroes: Modernity, the Great Migration, & Black Urban Life* (Chapel Hill: University of North Carolina Press, 2007), 25.

23. I used a ProQuest Search, Michigan State University Libraries, to find newspaper articles that referenced immigrant and child in the title, which is how I came to this conclusion. Source accessed November 19, 2011, http://search.proquest.com.proxy2.cl.msu .edu/advanced?accountid=12598, search terms *immigrant* and *child*, years 1900–1930. Just to make sure that I was not missing something, I also substituted the words *Italian* and *Jewish* for *immigrant* and found similar results, except that Italians were accused of selling their children to "padrones" in one article.

24. The above search was complemented by one that used the terms *negro* and *child*, years 1900–1930. ProQuest Search, Michigan State University Libraries, accessed November 19, 2011, http://search.proquest.com.proxy2.cl.msu.edu/advanced?accountid=12598.

25. Robin Bernstein, *Racial Innocence: Performing American Childhood from Slavery to Civil Rights* (New York: New York University Press, 2011).

26. Cited in Elisabeth Lasch-Quinn, *Black Neighbors* (Chapel Hill: University of North Carolina Press, 1993), 18.

27. Abraham Epstein, *The Negro Migrant in Pittsburgh* (Pittsburgh: Kessinger, 2010), 47–49.

28. Grossman, *Land of Hope*, 141.

29. Nina Mjagkij, *Light in the Darkness: African Americans and the YMCA, 1852–1946* (Lexington: University Press of Kentucky, 2003).

30. Carter Julian Savage, "'In the Interest of the Colored Boys': Christopher J. Atkinson, William T. Coleman, and the Extension of Boys' Clubs Services to African American Communities, 1906–1931," *History of Education Quarterly* 51 (November 2011): 516, http:// search.proquest.com.proxy1.cl.msu.edu/docview/908043475/13D98E8965C7858AB63/1?a ccountid=12598.

31. Ibid.

32. Hazel Rowley, *Richard Wright: The Life and Times* (Chicago: University of Chicago Press, 2008), 91.

33. Louise de Koven Bowen, *The Colored People of Chicago: An Investigation Made for the Juvenile Protective Association, by A. P. Drucker, Sophia Boaz, A. L. Harris [and] Miriam Schaffner* (Chicago: Rogers & Hall, 1913), 1–2.

34. Baker, *Following the Color Line*, 132.

35. William Edward Burghardt Du Bois, Elijah Anderson, and Isabel Eaton, *The Philadelphia Negro: A Social Study* (Philadelphia: University of Pennsylvania Press, 1899), 5.

36. James D. Anderson, *The Education of Blacks in the South, 1860–1935* (Chapel Hill: University of North Carolina Press, 1988), 281.

37. "Truancy Program of the Chicago Area Project: October 1939–June 1940," box 54, file 4, CAP, CHM.

38. See, among others, Baker, *Following the Color Line*, 142.

39. Philip Albert Boyer, *The Adjustment of a School to Individual and Community Needs* (Philadelphia: University of Pennsylvania Press, 1920), 34.

40. Kathryn M. Neckerman, *Schools Betrayed: Roots of Failure in Inner-City Education* (Chicago: University of Chicago Press, 2007), 23–24.

41. Albert Sidney Beckham, "The Intelligence of a Negro High School Population in a Northern City," *Pedagogical Seminary and Journal of Genetic Psychology* 54 (1939): 336.

42. Ibid., 24.

43. Chicago Commission on Race Relations, *The Negro in Chicago: A Study of Race Relations and a Race Riot* (University of Chicago Press, 1922), 239.

44. Arthur S. Hill, Leonard M. Miller, and Hazel F. Gabbard, "Schools Face the Delinquency Problem," *NAASP Bulletin* 37 (1953): 198.

45. Frances Blascoer, Eleanor Hope Johnson, and Public Education Association of the City of New York, *Colored School Children in New York* (Public Education Association of the City of New York, 1915), 18–19, 114.

46. Boyer, *Adjustment of a School*, 27, 32.

47. Eric C. Schneider, *Vampires, Dragons, and Egyptian Kings: Youth Gangs in Postwar New York* (Princeton, NJ: Princeton University, 2001), 107.

48. Epstein, *Negro Migrant in Pittsburgh*, 72.

49. de Koven Bowen, *The Colored People of Chicago*, 2, 4.

50. Ibid., 4.

51. Ibid., 30.

52. Joint Committee on Negro Child Study in New York City, *Study of Delinquent and Neglected Negro Children*, 37.

53. Grossman, *Land of Hope*, 128.

54. Charity Organization Society of the City of New York, "Children of the Circle," *Survey* 15 (1905): 83.

55. Chicago Commission on Race Relations, *Negro in Chicago*, 253–54.

56. Ibid., 251.

57. Blascoer, Johnson, and Public Education Association of the City of New York, *Colored School Children in New York*, 13–14.

58. "White Teacher Says, 'I Love Negro Pupils,'" *Pittsburgh Courier*, ProQuest Historical Newspapers, 1.http://search.proquest.com.proxy1.cl.msu.edu/docview/201849073/13D7EDD0CC238C033B0/1?accountid=12598, accessed January 10, 2010.

59. Joint Committee on Negro Child Study in New York City, *Study of Delinquent and Neglected Negro Children*, 20.

60. For contemporary examples, see Anna C. McFadden, George E. Marsh, and Yunhan Hwang, "A Study of Race and Gender Bias in the Punishment of Handicapped School Children," *Urban Review* 24 (1992): 239–51.

61. "Complaints from Students and Their Parents, 1932–1961," Educational Equity League, box 8, file 1, Floyd Logan Papers, Temple Urban Archive, Philadelphia.

62. See, for instance, Richard W. Thomas, *Life for Us Is What We Make It: Building Black Community in Detroit, 1915–1945* (Bloomington: Indiana University Press, 1992).

63. Anthony Sorrentino, "The Chicago Area Project after 25 Years," *Federal Probation* 23 (1959): 44.

64. Ibid.

65. Thomas, *Life for Us Is What We Make It.*

66. Grossman, *Land of Hope.*

67. Baldwin, *Chicago's New Negroes.*

68. Southside Community Committee, Chicago, *Bright Shadows in Bronzetown; the Story of the Southside Community Committee* (Chicago: Southside Community Committee, 1949), 6, 8, 9.

69. Ira Katznelson, *When Affirmative Action Was White: An Untold History of Racial Inequality in Twentieth-Century America* (New York: W. W. Norton, 2005).

70. Blascoer, Johnson, and Public Education Association of the City of New York, *Colored School Children in New York*, 33.

71. "Big Brothers, Big Sisters, Southeastern Pennsylvania, History," accessed November 11, 2011, www.bbbssepa.org/atf/cf/%7B5094A2BA-319B-4E8B-9049-EB89383B1832%7D/BBBS%20SEPA%20History.pdf.

72. Big Brother case #2415, "Closing Summary," February 28, 1941, Big Brothers and Big Sisters Association of Southeastern Pennsylvania, Temple University Urban Archive, Philadelphia. To preserve the anonymity of the case, the name has been changed.

73. John H. Miller to Clifford Shaw, August 9, 1938, Ernest Burgess Papers, box 245, file 5, University of Chicago.

74. Earl R. Moses, "Community Factors in Negro Delinquency," *Journal of Negro Education* 5 (April 1, 1936): 225.

75. Lee Rainwater, William L. Yancey, and Daniel Patrick Moynihan, *The Moynihan Report and the Politics of Controversy: A Trans-action Social Science and Public Policy Report* (Cambridge, MA: MIT Press, 1967).

76. Edward Franklin Frazier, *The Negro Family in Chicago* (Chicago: University of Chicago Press, 1932), xi.

77. Ibid., 213–14.

78. Ibid., 217.

79. St. Clair Drake and Horace R. Cayton, *Black Metropolis: A Study of Negro Life in a Northern City*, 1st ed. (Chicago: University Of Chicago Press, 1993), 600.

80. Southside Community Committee, *Bright Shadows in Bronzetown*, 18–19.

81. Ibid., 21.

82. Ibid., 23.

83. "Effect of ADC on Colored Youth," circa 1940s, box 98, file 1, CAP, CHM.

84. "Application for Funds from Community Fund for 1944, Directed to Clifford Shaw, re: Victory Gardens," box 98, file 2, CAP, CHM.

85. Southside Community Committee, *Bright Shadows in Bronzetown*, 31–34.

86. Ibid., 117–18.

87. "Facts Show Double Shift and Crowded Schools No Longer Necessary—1960," Chicago Urban League Papers, School Committees, series 3, box 101, Special Collections, University of Illinois, Chicago.

88. Southside Community Committee, *Bright Shadows in Bronzetown*, 28.

89. William M. Tuttle, *Daddy's Gone to War: The Second World War in the Lives of America's Children* (New York: Oxford University Press, 1993), 177.

90. Ibid., 166.

91. Clifford Shaw, "Notes on Items Prior to December—1941," CAP, box 3, file 98, CHM.

92. "Five Year Highlights and Six Months Report of the Southside Community Committee, 1947," box 6, file 98, CAP, CHM.

93. "The Role and Function of an Area Youth Worker," circa 1940s, box 47, file 178, Wharton Centre Settlement House Papers, Temple Urban Archive, Temple University, Philadelphia.

94. Austin R. Johnson, "Nine Months Report on My Experience, Sources, and Evaluation in the Dunbar District," n.d., circa 1945, box 5, file 98, CAP, CHM.

95. Schneider, *Vampires, Dragons, and Egyptian Kings*, 196.

96. Ibid., 207.

97. V. P. Franklin, "The Wharton Centre and the Juvenile Gang Problem in Philadelphia, 1945–1958," in *W. E. B. DuBois, Race, and the City: The Philadelphia Negro and Its Legacy*, ed. Michael B. Katz and Thomas J. Sugrue (Philadelphia: University of Pennsylvania, 1998), 206; Kenneth Bancroft Clark, *Dark Ghetto: Dilemmas of Social Power*, 1st Wesleyan ed. (Middletown, CN: Wesleyan University Press, 1989), 100.

98. "Crime Prevention Units of Philadelphia—March 1946," box 53, file 4, Wharton Centre Papers, Temple Urban Archive.

99. Notes on Junior Stars, 14–18, "Recreation," May 3, 1954, box 49, file 210, Wharton Centre Temple Urban Archives.

100. "Group Progress Report," March 25, 1953, box 48, file 185, Wharton Centre Papers, Temple Urban Archive.

101. Howard G. Gibbs, "Values and Limitations of Decentralized Programs in Group Work," address, National Conference of Social Work, May 16, 1951, Wharton Centre Papers, box 48, file 189, Temple Urban Archive.

102. Clark, *Dark Ghetto*, 100.

103. William Julius Wilson, *When Work Disappears: The World of the New Urban Poor*, 1st ed. (New York: Alfred A. Knopf, 1996).

104. Daniel J. Losen and Gary Orfield, eds., *Racial Inequity in Special Education* (Cambridge, MA: Civil Rights Project, Harvard University, 2002); Beth Harry and Janette K. Klingner, *Why Are So Many Minority Students in Special Education? Understanding Race & Disability in Schools* (New York: Teachers College Press, 2005).

Epilogue

1. U.S. Department of Labor, Office of Policy Planning and Research, *The Negro Family: The Case for National Action* (Washington, D.C.: Government Printing Office, 1965).

2. Lee Rainwater, *The Moynihan Report and the Politics of Controversy: A Trans-action Social Science and Public Policy Report* (Cambridge, MA: MIT Press, 1967), 50.

3. Ibid., 52.

4. Ibid., 31–32, 34, 77.

5. Allison Davis, "The Socialization of the American Negro Child and Adolescent," *Journal of Negro Education* 8 (July 1939): 264.

6. U.S. Children's Bureau, *White House Conference on Children in a Democracy—Final Report* (Washington, D.C.: Government Printing Office, 1940).

7. Mid-Century White House Conference on Children and Youth, *A Healthy Personality for Every Child: A Digest of the Fact Finding Report to the Mid-Century White House Conference on Children and Youth* (Raleigh, NC: Health Publications Institute, 1951), 49.

8. Gordon W. Allport, *The Nature of Prejudice* (Cambridge, MA: Addison-Wesley, 1954).

9. James Samuel Coleman, *Equality and Achievement in Education*, Social Inequality Series (Boulder, CO: Westview Press, 1990).

10. Barbara Beatty, "Rethinking Compensatory Education: Historical Perspectives on Race, Class, Culture, Language, and the Discourse of the Disadvantaged Child," *Teachers College Record* 114 (November 2012): 1–11.

11. Sylvia L. M. Martinez and John Rury, "From Culturally Deprived to At Risk: The Politics of Popular Expression and Educational Inequality in the United States, 1960–1985," *Teachers College Record* 114 (November 2012): 1–31.

12. Frank Riessman, *The Culturally Deprived Child*, 1st ed. (New York: Harper, 1962), 12, 29, 34, 35.

13. Benjamin Samuel Bloom, Allison Davis, and Robert D. Hess, *Compensatory Education for Cultural Deprivation: A Report Based on Working Papers Contributed by Participants in the Research Conference on Education and Cultural Deprivation* (New York: Holt, Rinehart and Winston, 1965), 4, 35.

14. David J. Connor and Beth A. Ferri, "Integration and Inclusion: A Troubling Nexus; Race, Disability, and Special Education," *Journal of African American History* 90 (January 2005): 108. See also Rosalie S. Boone and Arlene King-Berry, "African American Students with Disabilities: Beneficiaries of the Legacy?" *Journal of Negro Education* 76 (July 2007): 334–45.

15. Joseph L. Tropea, "Bureaucratic Order and Special Children: Urban Schools, 1950–1960s," in *Urban Education in the United States: a Historical Reader*, ed. John Rury, 1st ed. (New York: Palgrave Macmillan, 2005), 244; Hobson v. Hansen, United States District Court for the District of Columbia, 1967.

16. Boone and King-Berry, "African American Students with Disabilities," 340.

17. Institute for the Study of Mental Retardation and Related Disabilities, Ann Arbor, "Segregation of Poor and Minority Children into Classes for the Mentally Retarded by the Use of IQ Tests," *Michigan Law Review* 71 (May 1973): 1212.

18. "Report of the Collaborative Study of Educational Programs for Handicapped Children," School District of Philadelphia, December 1968, Floyd Logan Papers, Temple Urban Archive, 7, 24.

19. Beth Harry and Janette K. Klingner, *Why Are So Many Minority Students in Special Education? Understanding Race & Disability in Schools* (New York: Teacher College Press, 2005).

20. Tropea, "Bureaucratic Order," 243.

21. Judith Sealander has an excellent chapter on special education in her book *The Failed Century of the Child: Governing America's Young in the Twentieth Century* (Cambridge: Cambridge University Press, 2003). See also Colin Ong-Dean, *Distinguishing Disability Parents, Privilege, and Special Education* (Chicago: University of Chicago Press, 2009).

22. D. Kim Reid and Michelle G. Knight, "Disability Justifies Exclusion of Minority Students: A Critical History Grounded in Disability Studies," *Educational Researcher* 35 (August 2006): 18–23.

23. Lennard J. Davis, "Constructing Normalcy: The Bell Curve, the Novel, and the Invention of the Disabled Body in the Nineteenth Century," in *The Disability Studies Reader*, ed. Davis (New York: Routledge, 1996), 3–16.

24. I borrowed this idea from Alice Domurat Dreger, *One of Us: Conjoined Twins and*

the Future of Normal (Cambridge, MA: Harvard University Press, 2004), where she argues this principle on behalf of conjoined twins.

25. Juvenile Arrests, 2008, Juvenile Justice Bulletin, 2009, U.S. Department of Justice, Office of Justice Programs, December 2009.

26. Ann Arnett Ferguson, *Bad Boys: Public Schools in the Making of Black Masculinity*, Law, Meaning, and Violence (Ann Arbor: University of Michigan Press, 2000), 1.

27. David B. Tyack makes the point that, the more progress we make in expanding educational opportunities, the more discontented we are with the progress we have made in *Tinkering toward Utopia: A Century of Public School Reform* (Cambridge, MA: Harvard University Press, 1995).

28. Michelle Alexander, *The New Jim Crow: Mass Incarceration in the Age of Color-blindness* (New York: New Press, 2010). Pedro Noguera, *The Trouble with Black Boys: And Other Reflections on Race, Equity, and the Future of Public Education*, 1st ed. (San Francisco: Jossey-Bass, 2008).

INDEX

Addams, Jane, 47–49, 58, 81, 84
adolescents/adolescence: characteristics of male, 128; gender segregation in special education, 95–96, 104–105; in Hall's *Adolescence*, 41–42; labor of, 73–74; male culture of, 65–66; masculinity and, 142, 151; mastery of public space and, 65–66; sexual activity and, 127, 146; youth culture and, 139
adoption, 23–24, 27, 28
African Americans: ability testing among youth, 159; academies and classes for boys, 3; boys clubs for, 40, 156; delinquency and, 152–153, 169–176, 182; discrimination in school, 161–162; family structure among, 168–170, 172, 177–178; gangs and, 172–175; Great Migration and, 149–157; hard-to-reach youth, 172–176; masculinity and, 3, 129, 150; race riots and, 64–66, 161–162, 172; racial conflict, 62–66, 153, 172; recreation for youth, 62–66, 156, 172; school achievement of, 178; school attendance of, 71, 73, 160; school segregation, 159; school violence, 90, 162–163; Southern migrants, 157–158, 161, 165; special education, 110–114, 171, 180–182, 184; suspensions and discipline, 3, 183–184; vocational schools, 160. *See also* Great Migration; Southside Community Committee
age grading, 33–34, 72–73, 98, 127–128
Aldrich, Thomas Bailey, 41
Alger, Horatio, 17, 25
Allport, Gordon, 179
Americanization, 58
apprenticeship, 15, 19, 29, 160
athletics for boys: baseball, 45–47, 58, 123–124, 139–140, 174–175; basketball, 55–57, 60, 62–63, 65, 139–140; boys' clubs and, 50, 56–57; gangs and, 61, 133; gymnasiums and facilities for, 56–57, 60; in high school, 59, 70; instinctual basis of,

43, 60, 61; masculinity and, 58; organized sports as solution to boy problem, 39, 59; resistance to competitive athletics, 53; racial and ethnic conflict and, 63–64. *See also* recreation
athletics for girls, 61–62
attention deficit disorder, 103
autism, 103

backwardness, 93–94, 100–105, 111
Baker, Helen Cody, 124
Baker, Ray Stannard, 157
Barnes, Earl, 69
Birth of a Nation (film), 155
Black Belt, 150–156, 165, 170–171
Black Boy (Wright), 149–150
Boston Boys' club, 52
Boston Children's Aid Society, 23, 26
Boston Children's Friends' Home, 23
Boston House of Reformation, 18–21
Boston Parental School, 80–81
Boston Public Schools: corporal punishment in, 35; disciplinary day school, 81; high school and, 71; intermediate schools and, 32–33; parental school, 80–81; ungraded classes and, 36, 99–100
Bowen, Louise DeKoven, 126–127
boy culture: adolescence and, 139–140; delinquency and, 145; masculinity as component of, 142; mastery of public space as characteristic of, 66; oppositional street culture of, 76–77, 129; role of sexuality in, 147–148
Boyer, Philip Albert, 158–159
boy nature: concept of, 5; Hall's theory of, 70; nostalgia and, 38; recapitulation thesis and, 41–42; redemption of boys by catering to, 37, 39; Rousseau's conception of, in *Emile*, 39; science and, 40–43; schools and, 70; truancy and, 75–76
boyology, 10, 42

About the Author

Julia Grant is an associate dean and professor at James Madison College, Michigan State University. Her published work includes *Raising Baby by the Book: The Education of American Mothers* (Yale, 1998) and *When Science Encounters the Child: Perspectives on Education, Child Welfare, and Parenting* (Teachers College, 2001), in addition to essays on the history of childhood, motherhood, the family, and the intersections between history and public policy.